Discovering Therapeutic Efficacy

Discovering Therapeutic Efficacy brings together selected papers and book chapters by Howard Bacal, spanning 40 years as a psychoanalyst, psychiatrist, and psychotherapist.

The book includes several key pieces of writing influenced by psychoanalytic figures Bacal had the rare opportunity to study under including Michael Balint, Wilfred Bion, Heinz Kohut, Marion Milner, J.D. Sutherland, and Donald Winnicott. The chapters variously describe how the concept of optimal responsiveness is pivotal to the uniqueness of therapeutic need and how each psychoanalytic dyad discovers its unique capacity to implement it. Bacal describes how this led him to develop specificity theory, a process theory of therapeutic possibility.

Discovering Therapeutic Efficacy is replete with illustrative clinical examples. It will be of great interest and of practical usefulness not only to psychoanalysts, but to every practitioner of dynamic psychotherapy as they strive to be as optimally responsive as they can to their patients and students.

Howard Bacal is a psychiatrist based in Los Angeles, USA. He has a private practice in psychoanalysis and psychotherapy and has more than 60 years' experience in the field.

World Library of Mental Health

The *World Library of Mental Health* celebrates the important contributions to mental health made by leading experts in their individual fields. Each author has compiled a career-long collection of what they consider to be their finest pieces: extracts from books, journals, articles, major theoretical and practical contributions, and salient research findings.

For the first time ever the work of each contributor is presented in a single volume so readers can follow the themes and progress of their work and identify the contributions made to, and the development of, the fields themselves.

Each book in the series features a specially written introduction by the contributor giving an overview of their career, contextualizing their selection within the development of the field, and showing how their own thinking developed over time.

Recent titles in this series:

On the Way to Collaborative Psychological Assessment: The Selected Works of Constance T. Fischer
By Constance T. Fischer

Passions, Persons, Psychotherapy, Politics: The Selected Works of Andrew Samuels
By Andrew Samuels

Beyond Language in Relational Psychotherapy: The Selected Works of Helena Hargaden
By Helena Hargaden

Quietly Subversive: The Selected Works of Dilys Daws
By Dilys Daws with Matthew Lumley

Culture, Consolation, and Continuing Bonds in Bereavement: The Selected Works of Dennis Klass
By Dennis Klass

Discovering Therapeutic Efficacy: Selected Works of Howard Bacal
By Howard Bacal

Discovering Therapeutic Efficacy

Selected Works of Howard Bacal

Howard Bacal

Routledge
Taylor & Francis Group
LONDON AND NEW YORK

Designed cover image: Howard Bacal

First published 2026
by Routledge
4 Park Square, Milton Park, Abingdon, Oxon OX14 4RN

and by Routledge
605 Third Avenue, New York, NY 10158

Routledge is an imprint of the Taylor & Francis Group, an informa business

British Library Cataloguing-in-Publication Data
A catalogue record for this book is available from the British Library

ISBN: 978-1-032-94448-7 (hbk)
ISBN: 978-1-032-94449-4 (pbk)
ISBN: 978-1-003-57080-6 (ebk)

DOI: 10.4324/9781003570806

Typeset in Sabon
by Taylor & Francis Books

This book is dedicated to my wife, Jacqueline, and to our children, Shana, Liane, and Ben.

Darling Jacqueline, I am so grateful for your consistent, loving support of my work throughout the years, which began in 1968, when we first met in London, the year I published my first paper.

I have also been significantly sustained during every hour of my work by the presence of my dear doggie friends Hamish, Toffy, Wheeler, and Brodie.

And a big thank you, too, to esteemed colleagues Midge Breslin, Melanie Burke, Lucyann Carlton, Bill Coburn, Jimmy Fisher, Jim Fosshage, Meryle Gellman, Bruce Herzog, Hazel Ipp, Frank Lachmann, William Laurie, Les Lenoff, Peter Maduro, Carol Munschauer, Gianni Nebbiosi, Ken Newman, Mel Segal, Bob Stolorow, Peter Thomson, and Jeff Trop for enriching my ideas and encouraging their development.

Contents

Acknowledgements

Chapter 1. "Credo: My psychoanalytic adventure—a quest to conceptualize therapeutic efficacy" by Howard Bacal, 2017. Psychoanalytic Dialogues, Volume 27, Issue 1, 2017. Reproduced by permission of Taylor & Francis Group.

Chapter 2. "Notes on some therapeutic challenges in the analysis of severely regressed patients" by Howard Bacal, Psychoanalytic Inquiry © Bornstein Journal LLC, Daniel Goldin 1981, reprinted by permission of Taylor & Francis Ltd, www.tandfonline.com on behalf of Bornstein Journal LLC, Daniel Goldin.

Chapter 3. "Optimal responsiveness and the therapeutic process" from *Progress in Self Psychology*, edited by A. Goldberg. Copyright © 1985 by Guilford Press. Reproduced by permission of Taylor & Francis Group.

Chapter 4. "British object-relations theorists and self psychology: Some critical reflections" by Howard Bacal, from *The International Journal of Psycho-Analysis*, Volume 68, Issue 1. Copyright © Institute of Psychoanalysis, reprinted by permission of Informa UK Limited, trading as Taylor & Francis Group, www.tandfonline.com, on behalf of Institute of Psychoanalysis.

Chapter 5. "The selfobject relationship in psychoanalytic treatment" from *A Decade of Progress: Progress in Self Psychology, Volume 10*, edited by A. Goldberg. Copyright © 1994 The Analytic Press. Reproduced by permission of Taylor & Francis Group.

Chapter 6. "The psychoanalyst's selfobject needs and the effect of their frustration on the treatment: A new view of countertransference" from *Basic Ideas Reconsidered: Progress in Self Psychology, Volume 12*, edited by A. Goldberg. Copyright © 1996 The Analytic Press. Reproduced by permission of Taylor & Francis Group.

Chapter 7. "Shame: The affect of discrepancy" from *The Widening Scope of Shame*, edited by M. Lansky & A. Morrison. Copyright © 1997 The Analytic Press.

Chapter 9. "The use of theory in psychoanalytic practice" was originally published as chapter 2 in *The Power of Specificity in Psychotherapy: When Therapy Works—And When It Doesn't*, by H. Bacal and L. Carlton, published by Jason Aronson, 2011. Reprinted here by permission of Rowman & Littlefield Publishing Group.

Chapter 10. "Specificity theory," copyright © 2011 The Johns Hopkins University Press. This article first appeared in *American Imago*, Volume 68, Issue 2, Summer 2011. Published with permission by Johns Hopkins University Press.

Chapter 11. "The Budapest School's concept of supervision: Michael Balint's legacy to the development of psychoanalytic specificity theory" from *The Budapest School of Psychoanalysis*, edited by A. Rachmann. Copyright © 2016 The Analytic Press. Reproduced by permission of Taylor & Francis Group.

Chapter 12. "Discovering optimal responsiveness within the salience of emergent process," by Howard Bacal, 2024. *Psychoanalytic Inquiry*. Reproduced by permission of Taylor & Francis Group.

Every effort has been made to contact copyright holders. Please advise the publisher of any errors or omissions, and these will be corrected in subsequent editions.

Introduction

The book focuses on how optimal therapeutic responsiveness emerges within the unique process of any particular analytic dyad. The author describes how this constitutes a theory of therapeutic specificity, within which psychoanalytic constructs may or may not play a role. The many clinical examples demonstrate what is perhaps obvious, but remarkably underestimated—that the capacity for therapeutic effect ultimately depends upon the fit of the particular psychoanalytic couple.

Discovering Therapeutic Efficacy reflects a major focus throughout my career. I have always been interested in what determines therapeutic effect in psychoanalytic practice. I am grateful to my patients and my students, as well as to my teachers, as they have taught me so much about how therapy happens, or does not. I also learned about the latter through new understanding of experiences that were not so therapeutic in my own personal analyses, which I also describe in the book.

The chapters constitute discrete articles, though may usefully be read in sequence. As I reviewed my published works to select the chapters for this book, I discovered that I had begun to discern quite early on that therapeutic effect was not dependent upon prescriptive application of psychoanalytic theory. It seemed that what centrally mattered was perhaps obvious, but remarkably underestimated—the fit of the particular therapeutic couple. The potential for therapeutic efficacy can be found within the emergent process of the unique analytic dyad, which may or may not be illuminated by any psychoanalytic construct. I have published several papers about this, some of which are included in this book. I address the topic in depth in *The Power of Specificity in Psychotherapy—When Therapy Works—And When It Doesn't* (Bacal, 2011).

My work has been profoundly influenced by studying with certain unusually gifted, original thinkers during and after my training at the Institute of Psychoanalysis in London. These experiences promoted a questioning attitude in me toward mainstream psychoanalytic concepts. They also inspired me to offer a few of my own, which I describe in the book.

I qualified in Medicine at McGill University in 1958. My residency in psychiatry at the University of Cincinnati whetted my appetite for learning about

DOI: 10.4324/9781003570806-1

psychotherapy in depth. Maurice Levine, the chairman of the Department, introduced us to the "corrective emotional experience," the core concept of his analyst/mentor, Franz Alexander. At that time (in 1960), this idea was highly controversial, but we could observe its power as we worked with our patients. It accounted for much that was salutary in practice that was not always illuminated by the theories we were being taught. Nonetheless, I decided to learn more about them; most of our teachers in Cincinnati were training analysts, whom we idealized, and we came to believe that to become a really effective psychotherapist you had to become a psychoanalyst. I enrolled as a student at the Institute of Psychoanalysis in London, where I qualified in adult psychoanalysis in 1965, and child psychoanalysis in 1967.

The decade of the 1960s in London was an impressive period in psychoanalysis, when certain remarkably creative analysts in the British Psycho-Analytical Society were producing some of their most significant work. During my ten years in London, I had the rare opportunity to train with several of them, including Michael Balint, Wilfred Bion, Marion Milner, and Donald Winnicott; and then with Heinz Kohut upon my return to North America. Their influence on my work and on my development as a psychoanalyst[1] pervades every chapter, especially Chapters 1, 10, and 11.

It remains largely unacknowledged by the current American relational movement that this emphasis in psychoanalytic understanding started decades earlier in Britain. It was ubiquitous within the "Independent," or "Middle," Group in the British Psycho-Analytical Society, with which I was affiliated. I also learned a great deal about this at the Tavistock Clinic from its brilliant director, J.D. Sutherland, whose outlook was significantly influenced by the relational perspectives of his mentor, W.R.D. Fairbairn, and his colleague, Harry Guntrip. Guntrip's remarkable, innovative ideas spoke deeply to many of us—even to some who espoused quite different theoretical perspectives—when we heard him talk about them in person at The Royal Psychological Society in London in 1961.

I trained with Michael Balint in psychoanalysis and in leading discussion groups for general practitioners. These groups, which came to be known as "Balint Groups," were designed to improve the skills of general practitioners in addressing the psychological aspects of their work. In effect, they constituted an application of the Budapest approach to psychoanalytic supervision, which I describe in the book in Chapter 11: "The Budapest School's concept of supervision—Michael Balint's legacy to the development of psychoanalytic specificity theory."

While on staff at the Tavistock Clinic, I participated in psychotherapy outcome research with David Malan (Malan, Bacal, Heath, and Balfour, 1968; Malan, Heath, Bacal, and Balfour, 1975). The methodology we employed in this research significantly informed my discovery of how important dyadic fit is in determining therapeutic experience. It suggested that therapeutic process that led to whatever outcome is less dependent upon application of any formal theory and more a function of the specificity of dyadic interaction (see Bacal, 2011, pp. 3–4).

Shortly after I returned to North America (in 1971), I became intrigued with the perspectives of self psychology, and studied for several years with Heinz Kohut and his colleagues in Chicago. During the 1980s I introduced self psychology to the psychoanalytic community in Toronto. My admiration for Kohut's ideas included critiques of some of his concepts, which I describe in several chapters of the book, beginning in Chapter 3, with my 1985 article, "Optimal responsiveness and the therapeutic process." I offered this concept not only to question Kohut's view of *optimal frustration* as pivotal to therapeutic effect, but also to offer *optimal responsiveness* as its replacement in psychoanalytic practice. This concept pre-eminently signifies responsiveness that is experienced as specific to therapeutic need.

Chapter 4, my 1987 article, "British object relations theorists and self psychology: Some critical reflections," was the first to describe unnoted yet so evident connections between relational theories and the psychology of the self. Other chapters in the book also discuss this topic. I address it at length in the book, *Theories of Object Relations: Bridges to Self Psychology*, which I co-authored with Kenneth Newman in 1990.

The last chapter in these selected works revisits the concept, *optimal responsiveness*, where I illustrate how it can be effectively identified within the salience of emergent dyadic process (Bacal, 2024) as well as through the application of empathic attunement.

Note

1 I also had the special opportunity to present my third analytic "control case" to Anna Freud over 24 continuous case seminars. Miss Freud's responses to my clinical material so clearly articulated her father's views.

References

Bacal, H.A. (2011). *The power of specificity in psychotherapy: When therapy works—And when it doesn't.* Lanham, MD: Jason Aronson.

Bacal, H.A. (2024). Discovering optimal responsiveness in the salience of emergent process. *Psychoanalytic Inquiry*, 44(5), 1–11.

Bacal, H.A., & Newman, K.M. (1990). *Theories of object relations: Bridges to self psychology.* New York, NY: Columbia University Press.

Malan, D., Bacal, H., Heath, S., & Balfour, F. (1968). A study of psychodynamic changes in untreated neurotic patients—I. *The British Journal of Psychiatry*, 114 (510), 525–551

Malan, D., Heath, S.H., Bacal, H.A., & Balfour, H.G. (1975). Psychodynamic changes in untreated neurotic patients—II. Apparently genuine improvements. *Archives of General Psychiatry*, 32, 110–126.

1 My Psychoanalytic Adventure

A Quest to Conceptualize Therapeutic Efficacy

Chapter 1 chronicles the author's professional, yet very personal, journey from aspiring composer and pianist to psychoanalyst. Realizing his capacities didn't align with his musical ambitions, he pursued Medicine as his father had done but found little interest or aptitude in it. Discovering a talent for understanding people, he went into psychiatry. He then qualified in adult and child psychoanalysis at the Institute of `Psychoanalysis in London. The 1960s was an impressive decade for psychoanalysis in Britain, when remarkably creative people were producing some of their most significant work. During his ten years in London, the author had the rare opportunity to train with several of them, including Michael Balint, Wilfred Bion, Anna Freud, Marion Milner, Jock Sutherland, and Donald Winnicott; and then with Heinz Kohut upon his return to North America. Valuing yet critiquing aspects of self psychology, he recognized it as a quintessentially relational theory, and he replaced Kohut's concept of optimal frustration with optimal responsiveness. This emphasized the uniqueness of each patient's needed therapeutic experience, which may transcend the application of known psychoanalytic constructs. It led to the author's developing specificity theory, which focuses on therapeutic possibility within the emergent process and capacity of the particular patient–therapist dyad.

"Dr. Bacal, if you are accepted for psychoanalytic training, which group would you choose to affiliate yourself with?" So began my first interview with Ilse Hellman at The Institute of Psychoanalysis in London in 1960. I was nonplussed. I had not heard about "groups" at The Institute—and I didn't know which group my interviewer belonged to. No one at the University of Cincinnati, where I was currently doing a psychiatric residency, would seem to have heard about "groups" there, either. The only advice anyone gave me about my plan to train in London was a warning from Paul Ornstein, who was a junior staff member at the time, that he would steer clear of a Kleinian analysis. Kleinians, he told me, regarded the vicissitudes of the first few months of life as crucial for psychological development and he wouldn't want to go back that far!

I did not know how to answer Miss Hellman's question. In fact, I was feeling quite stupid not to have done my homework; I was speechless with anxiety,

DOI: 10.4324/9781003570806-2

especially because she seemed to convey that I must surely have given a lot of thought to my decision about which group I wanted to belong to. Finally, she relented, and patiently explained to me that there were three groups in the British Psychoanalytical Society: The Kleinian Group, designated the A group; The Freudian Group, designated the B group; and the Middle Group, which later came to be known as the Independent Group—comprising those analysts who were disinclined to identify themselves firmly with either group. My interviewer then fell silent, again awaiting my, now *informed*, decision—on the spot. I was, now, *really* worried. I had no idea what she was talking about. After what felt like an eternity of agonizing ignorance, during which I was certain that my chances of being accepted for training were doomed, I somehow blurted out, "Middle Group".[1] I was not quite sure why I said this. Probably because it seemed like the safest course to take—somewhere in between the two others, which sounded vaguely religious, and I *did* know that I did *not* want to join that sort of thing.[2] In retrospect, it was my first act as an *Independent* analyst; for me, this meant that I could be free to remain open to different ideas.

At least two earlier experiences strongly concretized the background to my response to Miss Hellman's question. The one constituted the complex impact on me of the "knowingness" of my brilliant mother, about whom I shall say a little more in a moment. The other was Aldous Huxley's (1996) *Point Counter Point*. As I searched for a solution to my disturbing state of ambivalence about the acquisition of omniscience, I discovered Aldous Huxley's masterpiece in a literature course during my junior year in college. What especially struck me in Huxley's novel was his presentation of a vision of reality that emphasized diverse aspects of experience, where different points of view were like contrapuntal melodic lines that might—or might not—be harmonious or consensual. I found these ideas exciting, and hopeful.

It would, however, be several years before I would be able to put such perspectives into practice. At that time, I had no plans to study psychoanalysis. I had not yet put together my lifelong preoccupation with my own inner world with the legitimacy or enjoyment of studying that of others. I had become musical director of my university review and had written several songs for it. I was interested in a career as a pianist or composer. My parents anxiously predicted, however, that I would "end up living in an attic" were I to pursue such a career. I heeded their warning only when I recognized that my talent did not quite match my ambitions for professional success in either of these areas. I agreed to set aside my dream and go to medical school instead, as my father had done, although I knew he'd played a pretty good jazz fiddle during the depression years. At that time (in the early 1950s), to actually pursue a career in the entertainment field was viewed with some scorn in my middle-class Jewish culture. William Shatner's father would sometimes give me a lift to university when I thumbed a ride outside my house in the morning. He lamented the intention of his son, "Willie," to go into show business. How could he contemplate such a thing when he had a perfectly good dress business to go into with his father?!

While my father enjoyed being a doctor—he was a much loved and admired pediatrician—the gloominess that hung within me on my graduation from medical school attested to my accommodation to my parents' anxiety. I was not especially interested in medicine nor was I very good at it. I was, however, surprised to discover, during my psychiatric rotation in medical school, that I easily apprehended, and was fascinated by, the psychodynamic understanding proffered by my teachers who, at that time (in 1957), were mostly psychoanalysts. The father of my best friend, Jock Cleghorn, Robert A. Cleghorn, was Professor of Psychiatry at McGill University (in Montreal, my hometown) and was training to become a psychoanalyst; and I'd had a few years of psychotherapy with a good psychoanalytic therapist who enabled me both to leave home at age 19 and to merge with the calmness of his even demeanor and the reassuring aroma of his Havana cigars. I tentatively wondered whether I could do this, too. Well, I did become an inveterate cigar smoker and, after my internship, I enrolled in a psychiatric residency training program, along with my best friend, and learned to do psychotherapy—and continued to smoke cigars, for many years, until I learned from Heinz Kohut, a recovered cigar smoker, himself, that it was possible to stop! But I am now getting way ahead of myself!

This psychiatric residency, at the University of Cincinnati, constituted in large measure an introduction to psychoanalytic thinking and practice. Its senior staff were all psychoanalysts. It also offered a somewhat unusual psychoanalytic culture, although I did not realize it at the time. Largely through the influence of its innovative chairman, Maurice Levine, whose analyst and mentor had been Franz Alexander, none of us remained strangers to the therapeutic ethos of the "corrective emotional experience." The elemental sense of this view of how analysis cures never left me, despite its fashionable vilification—and distortion—by the preponderance of the psychoanalytic establishment (Bacal, 1990). Alexander essentially asserted, as had Ferenczi, that it was a particular emotional experience in the context of the relationship between patient and analyst that was principally therapeutic. Levine also strongly underscored the importance of individualizing therapeutic intervention in creative ways.[3] It was in this setting, in Cincinnati, that I first encountered Michael Balint, who was a visiting professor in the department, from London. I learned, later, that Balint trained with Sandor Ferenczi in Budapest and had already assumed a leading role in Hungarian psychoanalysis when he emigrated to England in 1939 with his wife, Alice, also a psychoanalyst (see Bacal, 2016). I was impressed with Balint's teaching and, in an informal meeting with him, I expressed an interest in psychoanalytic training. His response was very positive; in particular, he encouraged me to undertake the training in London. So, rather than face the notorious many-headed monster of assessors at the (much nearer) Chicago Institute, or train at the fledgling Canadian Institute of Psychoanalysis in my native country, in a spirit of adventure I applied to the Institute of Psychoanalysis in London, England.

Somehow, I managed to survive the interviewing process, but not without Miss Hellman's sagaciously interpreting that one of my motivations for undertaking psychoanalytic training was to become equipped to cure my mother! I had been found out, but they accepted me. One of the major life experiences that undoubtedly contributed both to my interest in psychoanalysis and to my later way of viewing the treatment process was my struggle with the knowingness of my mother's complex and psychologically oriented mind. My mother was, without doubt, my first unofficial "analyst" (though she was not actually an analyst). My sense of her, when I was a child, was that she had cornered the market on validity. In particular, she believed that she knew me—especially my faults, and she had no difficulty articulating her subjectivity, often with ferocious intensity. No wonder I eventually found my way to self psychology!

Perhaps not surprisingly, I became captivated by the appeal of "understanding" and of being "understood." I seemed to be the only one who "understood" how I was feeling—I did a lot of that by myself—and I was, expectably, left looking for something a bit different. Psychoanalytic training seemed to promise the experience of both becoming properly understood and perhaps even coming to understand, like my mother did! The psychoanalysts seemed to know, even more than her!

It took me a long time not only to learn that could I not "know" anything, but more important to discover the pedestrian, yet astonishing, truth that was going to be most helpful to me and my patients—that there were many kinds of experiences of relatedness that led to a myriad of truths, depending upon who was relating to whom and in what ways.

When I was in London for the interviews, I asked Balint whom he would recommend as a training analyst. I showed him the list of training analysts that Maurice Levine had compiled for me. It comprised Anna Freud, Melanie Klein, Michael Balint, Willi Hoffer, Paula Heimann, and Marjorie Brierley. I now learned from Dr. Balint that no one in London would ever have put these people together on a list of recommended training analysts. They were from different "groups"! But we went over my list; and I learned, with some embarrassment, that Melanie Klein had died two weeks before I arrived, so she was out. Balint said that if I could engage Anna Freud as my analyst, every door would be open to me when I returned to North America. I didn't object, and then, magnanimously, I thought, he phoned Anna Freud right there and then and arranged an interview for me.

So, a few days after the Institute evaluations, I went along to 20 Maresfield Gardens—where Freud and his family lived when they came to London in 1938, where Anna Freud was now living, along with Dorothy Burlingham, and where the Freud Museum is now located—to meet with Miss Freud (everyone called her Miss Freud, just as they all called Melanie Klein Mrs. Klein), whose assessment was that I was too unmarked by life for her to analyze. She clearly hadn't got a good picture of my mother from our interview, or she wouldn't have come to that conclusion—wouldn't have rejected me out of hand. Marjorie Brierley was living in the country; that left Paula Heimann, Willi Hoffer, and Michael Balint. I did not get around to interviewing Heimann and Hoffer on that brief trip to London. In any case, I had begun to develop all sorts of transferences to Balint; and I decided to ask him to be my analyst. When I returned to London the following year to start analysis, I learned that he was a training analyst in the Middle, or Independent, Group. Which suited me. My experience over the next ten years with Michael Balint was, however, to be very mixed.

I was really looking forward to analysis, but soon after it began I discovered that I was back in the same boat—struggling with someone who really knew what was wrong with me. Although I protested his focus, because it made me feel so (familiarly) bad, of course it *had* to be right, because he *knew* me, and he, my analyst, must *know* what was right for me to know about myself.

Still, I did wonder, *was* he right, and how well did he know—*me*? At least, might there not be a better way for this activity called analysis to be carried out, at least with me? With some fervor, I suggested how it could be improved. In one session, when I was feeling especially hemmed in by my analyst's view of me, I implored him to consider a metaphor for a different way of relating. Rather than his hurling interpretations at me, could we be like two children sitting side by side, looking at something together and discussing what each of us saw in it? In retrospect, this was a passionate plea, not only to be "treated better";[4] it was also the anlage of a new perspective on therapeutic efficacy—the importance of attending to the uniqueness of the patient's psychological need and the recognition that therapeutic experience essentially depended upon the analyst's response to this. While analysts of the Independent Group offered a spectrum of relational perspectives not at all unlike that those of American relational analysts decades later, in practice the "true view" seemed to favor that of the analyst. It was to be some 12 years before I heard of Heinz Kohut's recommendation that the analyst stay with the patient's subjective experience, sometimes for prolonged periods, before offering his own view. It is perhaps not surprising that, when I learned about Kohut's ideas, I was drawn to them.

My analyst did not change his approach. And I could not anticipate a helpful response from anyone, an expectation generated by my experience of an uninvolved father who could never gainsay my mother's convictions. I resorted to writing down what I thought and felt. Toward the end of my first year of analytic training I drafted notes for a paper that I titled "Is analyzing necessary?" I assessed, probably wisely, though, that if I brought this stroke of inspiration to the light of day, I wouldn't get much further in my training school. I have in fact never written a paper with that title, but I went on to develop within *psychoanalytic specificity theory* the essence of a different way of practicing psychoanalysis. While therapeutic process pivots upon the vicissitudes of transference and countertransference—which, traditionally, could be regarded as determining the difficulties between me and Balint—it transcends this (see Bacal, 2015). The unfolding of a psychoanalytic treatment is apprehended more comprehensively by the idea of *the specificity of dyadic process* that emerges between that particular analyst and that particular analysand. The patient's optimal therapeutic experience will depend upon the capacity for specific reciprocal responsiveness between that therapist and that patient in the moment and over time. This capacity significantly depends upon dyadic fit, an aspect of therapeutic possibility whose importance we tacitly recognize but to which in practice we have tended to give lip service.

At the Institute of Psychoanalysis, I became interested in everything that my teachers in any of the "groups" had to offer. I attended the seminars of all three "groups"—Kleinian, Freudian, and Independent—during my training in adult and child psychoanalysis.[5] In my first class on the work of Melanie Klein, Elliott Jacques, a senior Kleinian analyst, told us that there were as many differences between how members of the Kleinian group worked with their patients as there were between the members of the Freudian and the Kleinian groups as a whole. At the time, I was somewhat skeptical about this assertion, as well as of Jacques's motives for sharing this news. I suspected that this was his way of pitching Klein to us—you know, it is not a rigid system, it is preeminently flexible in its usage; but I have since come to appreciate the deeper wisdom implied in his observation. We tend as analysts to believe that our theoretical orientations centrally determine how we work with our patients and how they experience our therapeutic efforts. My experience both as analyst and analysand leads me to question this. We bring so much more to the immediacy of our interaction with our patients than our formal psychoanalytic concepts. Our working model, however salient it is—whether classical, Kleinian, object-relational, Lacanian, interpersonal, relational, or self psychological—constitutes but one reflection of who we are with a particular patient in any particular context. Sometimes, the analysand experiences his analyst's work with him to be remarkably at variance with his theories. Perhaps the most famous example of this is Harry Guntrip's experience in analysis with Fairbairn. Fairbairn had developed a theoretical system that significantly challenged that of Freud, yet Guntrip's analysis with Fairbairn was strikingly classical. Guntrip, in effect, subsequently got from Winnicott in practice what Fairbairn espoused in theory (see Guntrip, 1975).

During my second year of training at the Institute, Anna Freud invited students in the Independent and Kleinian groups to attend her continuous case seminar. Two places were available. I enthusiastically applied, and I found myself back at 20 Maresfield Gardens once a week for 24 sessions presenting a continuous case to Anna Freud. Somewhere in my filing cabinet is a signed letter from Miss Freud thanking me for the flowers I sent her for her generosity in accepting me into her seminar; however, for whatever sum my great-grandchildren may be able to flog this letter at Sotheby's someday, they will likely profit more from it than I did from Miss Freud's seminar. Her comments on my case were delivered with her famous clarity and elegance, but they largely comprised recommendations to apply her father's theories. Presenting this particular case to Anna Freud at that time was especially problematic for me, since the case was being supervised individually by Wilfred Bion, who had a radically different take on psychoanalytic practice. Bion's views struck a responsive chord in me.

For Bion (1967), "the only point of importance in any session is the unknown ... in any session, evolution takes place. Out of the darkness and formlessness something evolves" (p. 272). Therapeutic effect, according to Bion, "[derives] from the emotional experience with a unique individual and not from generalized theories imperfectly 'remembered'" (p. 273). He wryly noted that if the analyst feels he has seen the patient before, he is treating the wrong patient. Bion was elaborating these ideas for his famous paper "On memory and desire" (Bion, 1967) during the period when he was supervising my third analytic control case. I could never quite emulate Bion's recommendation that the analyst expunge any prior conception or knowledge of the patient whom he is about to see. Bion's approach impressed upon me, however, the value of sustaining a not-knowing attitude of mind[6] and of privileging the unpredictable particularity of my patient as it emerged and affected me.

Some of the most powerful influences on my elaboration of a theory of therapeutic specificity entailed experiences with certain supervisors during my analytic training. I was fortunate to have had the opportunity to work with a few unusually creative and talented people. I have described the influence of Wilfred Bion. Others—in addition to Michael Balint who, despite my struggles with him in the analysis, was a superb teacher—included Donald Winnicott and Marion Milner. Winnicott and Milner both espoused a clinical approach that richly anticipated that of Kohut's self psychology. Of course, I could not know this at the time (around 1963–1967). The biggest impression they made on me was their implicit promotion of therapeutic work that was creative, that was specific to each patient, and that could transcend conventional psychoanalytic practice. Winnicott recognized (as had Ferenczi) that what is often important is not what the analyst interprets but how the analyst behaves. But there was no theory about this. Just clinical impressions that were not aired at psychoanalytic meetings, though they might be shared with students and close colleagues. I remember Winnicott telling me, sometime in 1967, how impressed he was with a young social worker that he watched treating a child when on a recent visit to New York. Had I heard of her? he asked. Her name was Virginia Axline, who wrote the remarkable book *Dibs, in Search of Self*. And Winnicott went on to extoll her remarkable therapeutic skill, "without making any interpretations at all!" (Actually, it seems that she did, but this is not what impressed Winnicott). Winnicott told a similar story about Melitta Schmideberg, the physician psychoanalyst daughter of Melanie Klein, who had taken a job working with psychotic children at a mental hospital north of London shortly after the Klein family emigrated to England in the late 1920s. "She knew not a stitch of English at the time," Winnicott told me, "yet her therapeutic effect on those children was amazing." I vividly recall the preliminary meeting I had with Winnicott when I was about to begin the analysis of a three-and-a-half-year-old girl five times a week under his supervision. The child's behavior had become chaotic and bizarre in the context of an impoverished Irish family in which she lived, in a meager one-room flat with her father, mother, and two-year-old sister. I asked Winnicott how to begin the treatment (as I had never worked with a child before and had not a clue what to do). Without hesitation, Winnicott answered, "If she holds out her hand, take it." I have never forgotten this. It became a metaphor not only for the responsivity that enabled me to be therapeutic for this little patient but for my work with adult patients as well. I had similar experiences with Marion Milner. During her supervision of one of my adult training cases, she understood my sensitive schizoid patient's retreat into the woods as an adolescent where he spent hours in holes he would dig as a way to find himself and to grow. She suggested that I understand this as his being like a delicate young plant that needs elemental tending as it begins to sprout new shoots.

This sort of supervision of my patients was also stirring a lot of conflict in me about how analysis cures, as my own experience of analysis was painfully different.

Yet, as a supervisor, Balint's emphasis on the uniqueness of both the individual and the dyad, between my patients and myself, very much appealed to me. In an early supervisory session, I was anxiously conveying to Balint that I was having trouble working with a particular patient, as she seemed to be uncomfortably like me in some respects. I was startled—but enormously helped—to hear him say, "Every patient is the same as every other, yet completely different." Some years later, I found myself writing, "And so is every therapist, and every therapist–patient couple; and who they are, uniquely together, ineluctably determine the shape and the outcome of therapy."

Balint supervised my first analytic control case for seven and a half years according to the Hungarian psychoanalytic training method, wherein the training analyst supervises the candidate's first case within the candidate's own analysis.[7] In the context of the supervision, there *was* a fit. We *shared* something that really interested both of us. I also became an associate of Michael and Enid Balint in one of their training groups, where we researched the effectiveness of general practitioner psychotherapy (Balint and Norell, 1973). These training groups were a form of applied psychoanalysis that centrally emphasized the task of understanding the particular doctor–patient relationship in depth, in an atmosphere of mutual learning. It is worthwhile quoting here Enid Balint's observations about the essence of Balint Group Training upon reviewing his work in 1993 with a research group of general practitioners:

> [Our aim was] to have a wider look at the … uncertainties which abound in working with patients; while at the same time not attempting to reduce them to neat patterns, leaving the perspectives as wide as possible in the realization that what one person sees from one angle cannot be seen from another's. … It seems that the unique relationship which occurs in the general practice setting informs us as to what the work is really about.
>
> (Balint, Balint, Courtenay, Elder, Hull, and Julian, 1993, pp. 98–99)

Working with Balint in these groups, and the psychoanalytic supervision during the analysis, enabled me to have a relationship with him that was specifically salutary for me—that is, one in which we shared ideas and opinions—which not only helped me to challenge a centrally deleterious organizing principle (that someone else really knew what was what) but also constituted an enlightening and vitalizing provision (see Lindon, 1994). The psychoanalytic supervisory work with Balint utilizing the Budapest method of supervision (Bacal, 2016) was remarkably valuable; it enabled me to appreciate, with striking immediacy, not only the impact on myself of the patient's transference and my associated responses to her but also how particular aspects of who I was affected my patient and the analysis.

I am sure that, to an appreciable extent, I picked up the importance of relational specificity from Balint, though he appeared to be more inclined to recognize this between me and my patients than between him and me. A curious situation. Perhaps this discrepancy was a psychoanalytic version of the familiar phenomenon of the heightened tolerance of the grandparent for his grandchildren (in this context, the grandchildren were the trainee–analysand's patients, i.e., my patients). My analytic grandfather, in this context, was Sandor Ferenczi. Balint regarded the clinical experiments of Ferenczi—his training analyst—with a mixture of admiration and skepticism. Balint endorsed experimentation in the analytic setting, but I sensed that he regarded Ferenczi's novel attempts to improve the effectiveness of psychoanalytic treatment as insufficiently disciplined. Perhaps this is why Balint rarely talked to me about Ferenczi's ideas, which I regret, as I believe it would have catalyzed the development of my own. I have wondered whether my analytic grandfather's innovative spirit may yet have reached me more powerfully, albeit indirectly.[8] When I eventually read Ferenczi's work, I knew that, in some respects, I had found a kindred spirit. Ferenczi intuitively understood that the variability of the patient's therapeutic needs required a certain flexibility of responsiveness on the part of the analyst and that there were ways in which the analyst normally functions therapeutically in addition to providing interpretation. He emphasized—as in fact did Balint—the importance of the analytic atmosphere, and he appreciated that it was influenced by the personality of the analyst and his style. Ferenczi was the first to note that the behavior of the analyst could affect the patient's transference, and he questioned whether it was always the patient's resistance that caused failures in treatment rather than the analyst's unwillingness to adapt his methodology to the special therapeutic needs of his patients. Ferenczi (1928) advised that we offer our understanding to the patient tentatively, for we may be wrong, and the patient may have a better theory about himself. He may even have a better suggestion as to how he should be treated (Ferenczi, 1931b).

Concurrent with my training at the Institute of Psychoanalysis, I was on staff at the Tavistock Clinic[9] where I learned from J.D. Sutherland about the innovative relational ideas of his analyst and mentor, W.R.D. Fairbairn, who was still practicing, in Edinburgh, and about the work of Fairbairn's foremost expositor, Harry Guntrip. Fairbairn's and Guntrip's ideas were regarded as too radical to be taught at the Institute of Psychoanalysis, but I was privileged to hear Guntrip deliver a stunning lecture at the British Psychological Society in

1963 that transcended much of what I was then being taught at the Institute. Both Fairbairn and Guntrip were seriously questioning the clinical relevance of classical Freudian theory. For Fairbairn, interpretation alone is therapeutically insufficient. Rather, Fairbairn wrote, "[It is] the actual relationship between the patient and the analyst [that] constitutes the decisive factor in psychoanalytical, no less than in any other form of psychotherapeutic cure" (Fairbairn, 1958, p. 385). By this "actual relationship," Fairbairn meant not only the transference relationship but also the total relationship between the patient and analyst as persons; in particular, "[a] ... relationship with a reliable and beneficent parental figure" (p. 377). In a paper I wrote some years later for a symposium in *Psychoanalytic Inquiry*, which had the task to reconsider Franz Alexander's concept of the corrective emotional experience (Bacal, 1990), I put this concept in the context of self psychology while underscoring Fairbairn's view of the centrality of relationship for therapeutic efficacy. I suggested that it was important and useful, clinically, to distinguish a corrective selfobject *relationship* from simply a selfobject *experience*. A selfobject relationship connotes the establishment of an expectation of reliability—in effect, a natural, or basic, sense of entitlement to be dependably listened to and understood and also an expectation that one's therapist will attempt to respond optimally to one's *particular selfobject relational* needs. In retrospect, I had taken a further step toward developing a theory of therapeutic specificity, as it applied to *relational self psychology*. I introduced this term in 1998 (Bacal, 1998b) but had already elaborated my view of self psychology as an essentially relational theory some years earlier (Bacal, 1994).

It was also at the Tavistock Clinic that I encountered a non-linear theory of therapeutic specificity during my participation in a formal psychotherapy research project. None of us who were involved in the research recognized this to be so at the time. Yet such theory was, in effect, embedded within the project's unique methodology to assess outcome, and it basically determined how we evaluated our results. The project, led by D.H. Malan, entailed the assessment of the psychological status of a series of formally untreated patients who had been seen at intake at the Clinic at least two years previously (see Malan, Bacal, Heath, and Balfour, 1968). The criterion for a person's inclusion in the study was never having seen a psychologist or a psychiatrist more than twice in his or her life. Our aim was to explore at a follow-up interview the extent to which improvement had occurred over time in particular ways without formal treatment.[10]

After reading the initial intake for each patient, each of us independently offered his view of what would constitute progress specific for that patient if he were to have undertaken a course of psychotherapy. In other words, we considered the attainment of true change on the basis of neither relief of symptoms nor the usual general categories of healthy social and psychological functioning but rather significant amelioration in specific aspects of the patient's life situation that appeared to reflect change in his or her susceptibility to experiences that stressed particular vulnerabilities.

While we rarely agreed when it came to formulating the patient's dynamics on the basis of traditional psychoanalytic concepts (even though our theoretical differences were minimal), we had little trouble reaching a consensus on what would constitute improvement for the particular patient. Further outcome research on our study itself (Malan, Heath, Bacal, and Balfour, 1975) also indicated the operation of an unpredictable process of specificity. It turned out that those who were most significantly changed on psychodynamic criteria either had experienced significant therapeutic effect from particular experience in their initial consultation or/and were subsequently able to "use" similar, specific "therapeutic" responsiveness from others. While this psychodynamic research illuminated the specificity of outcome for the particular individual, it also suggested that therapeutic process that led to whatever outcome is less dependent upon application of any particular formal theory and more a function of the specificity of dyadic interaction. In effect, the research findings implied that a different kind of theory would be needed in order to learn more about this—a theory that focuses upon and conceptualizes the very nature of a therapeutic process.

A process theory of dyadic specificity gives explicit substance to what Elliot Jacques asserted.[11] It can explain the efficacy of psychoanalysts who apply radically differing theoretical views; it offers a model that, in effect, integrates diverse psychoanalytic approaches.

Specificity theory builds upon Bion's view of psychoanalytic practice by proposing that we use psychoanalytic theories that do posit universal motives, stages of development, and curative interventions in a different way. It shifts our focus from a *designated response* based on structured concepts as the *sine qua non* of psychoanalytic cure to a *process* that seeks to *discover* within each dyad that which might be healing. Formal, and informal, structured psychoanalytic theories are variously necessary and all may emerge within process. No psychoanalytic theory that purports ubiquitous application can apply to psychoanalysis when viewed *as process*. An analyst who privileges the dyadic specificity of process will be simultaneously receptive to the emergence of structured concepts of any analytic tradition that may relevantly illuminate understanding of, and optimal responsiveness to, that patient's particular therapeutic needs. It is advisable not only that we not "know" in advance who the patient is, as Bion recommends, but also that we do not know how we may optimally be with him or her therapeutically from moment to moment until we may discover this through the unfolding specificity of our dyadic process.

I was excited to discover that Gerald Edelman's research on the development and function of the brain offered a remarkably accordant neurobiological substrate to this perspective on psychoanalytic treatment. Edelman has shown that the human mind is continuously formed and transformed through ongoing selective, specific interactions with itself and its environment. Closely related to this is the need for a theory of therapy that promotes the efforts of our brain to forestall closure prematurely. Edelman (2004) demonstrated that when the brain is confronted with novel stimuli, the neuronal connections are actively at work to organize and make sense of the stimuli until a familiar pattern is forged or attained. Our brain is not trying to form a scientifically accurate picture of the world, per se, but one that is familiar and meaningful to the perceiver. With this innate biological pull toward closure, curiosity and attention to the novel and unique is blunted. Specificity theory helps us keep our minds open—literally as well as figuratively—to counter this inherent tendency—that *can* be reinforced by the untimely application of structured concepts—and to reengage our curiosity to search out other elements that *may* transcend their relevance for the patient. My favorite metaphor, apropos, is that what we may discover beyond what formal theory tells us is therapeutic within each analytic dyad is analogous to the "dark matter" of the cosmos that may comprise much more of space/time than the stars themselves. Like the dark matter of space/time, "unformulated theory" does not easily lend itself to identification or description, yet to ignore it may be to disregard much of what is central within a psychoanalytic treatment.

I also discovered the work of certain infant researchers that strongly links specificity to development (see Lyons-Ruth, 2000; Sander, 2002; Tronick, 2003). This work also suggests that a process of specificity-fittedness lies at the heart of therapeutic action. Sander regards the earliest model of the micro-processing through which two unacquainted individuals come to know each other's mind as comprising "the negotiation between parent and child of increasingly complex forms of specifically fitted activity ... [which constitutes] the essential process through which development takes place" (Sander, 2002, p. 88).

Tronick's (2003) work has led him to recognize that "co-creative processes produce unique forms of being together, not only in the mother–infant relationship, but in all relationships" (p. 276).

> Relationships ... do not become increasingly de-contextualized (i.e., depersonified), they become increasingly personified, tied to an individual; they do not become more schematized, they become increasingly specific, and they do not become more universally applicable, they become less and less transferable.
>
> (pp. 476–477)

Specificity theory regards the effectiveness of psychoanalytic treatment as fundamentally determined by therapeutic possibility that becomes available to a particular dyad in the moment and over time. Therapeutic efficacy is ultimately determined by the capacities and limitations of the particular participants interacting within a particular system.[12] From this point of view, specificity theory can enhance our understanding of what may constitute therapeutic effectiveness, and therapeutic malfunction.

Balint's understanding continued to feel frequently inaccurate and often hurtful. I was a patient, though, and continued with the analysis, with the hope that my experience of it might improve. But after about nine and a half years, it seemed even to me that we should think about stopping, and we agreed to give it about eight more months to accomplish certain goals. However, this was not to be, as Balint soon developed serious cardiac problems and died about three months later. I sought a consultation with Donald Winnicott the following week, in which he corroborated my experience of Balint's capacity for obduracy, which was helpful. Sadly, Winnicott, who had been ill for some time, died about a month after I saw him for that single visit. It was to take me a further 15 years to apprehend my experience in analysis with Michael Balint not in terms of who was "at fault" but rather what constituted our specific limitations as an analytic couple. Why Balint and I were not a very good match in the analysis while I found him so remarkably accessible and beneficial in the context of supervisory work remains somewhat unclear to me. Perhaps it was as simple as the effect of my protesting his views of me personally in the former, whereas in the latter I not only didn't oppose them but was keen to learn from a wise father. I continued to regard Balint's innovative theories about early relatedness as especially illuminating (Balint, 1937, 1968). Perhaps, like Fairbairn with Guntrip (see Guntrip, 1975), he somehow could not take them into account with me.

I returned to North America, as planned, the following summer. It was 1971, and I had been in London for ten years. Three years later, a colleague suggested that I read a book by Heinz Kohut, which had just gone into its second printing. The recommendation that I read *The Analysis of the Self* came from Hans Aufreiter, one of the founders of the Canadian Psychoanalytic Society, who turned out to be an analytic sibling of Kohut; their first analyst was August Aichorn.

When I read *The Analysis of the Self* (Kohut, 1971), I felt that I had finally stumbled upon someone who would be able to understand some of what had eluded my previous analysts—both the unofficial one and the official one—and to respond more usefully. I saw Kohut over a period of six and a half years; I commuted to Chicago every other week, from London (Ontario) and from Toronto. My experience with Kohut comprised a valuable mixture of analytic work, consultation around my patients, and learning about this new theory he was calling "self psychology." Initially, Kohut's way of conveying interpretations that conveyed respect for my perspectives felt varnishing. I was unused to an empathically framed validation of my subjective experience. I also soon began to realize what I had only begun to sense from reading Kohut's book—that he had added a crucial ingredient to the relational perspective that I was then steeped in: the concept of a variably cohesive/variably vulnerable self, and its relation to its selfobjects.

Kohut had introduced the concept of the *self* as a central construct in psychoanalysis as well as postulating the need for the responsiveness of others that affected its cohesion and vitality—what he termed its *selfobjects*, phase-appropriately throughout the life cycle (Kohut, 1977). From the time I first learned about the selfobject concept from Kohut, I viewed it as quintessentially relational (see Bacal and Newman, 1990).[13] It made no sense to me apart from its contextualization within a relationship (Bacal, 1994, 1998a; Bacal and Newman, 1990). Kohut in fact did come to use the concept in a relational way, coining the term "self-selfobject relationship" (Kohut, 1984, pp. 49–52), but his emphasis was on intrapsychic experience; he apparently feared that if he did not do this, self psychology might degrade into a social psychology.

What also became progressively evident to me was that Kohut's (1984) conceptualization of analytic cure as entailing the transmuting internalization of the analyst's functions into self structure via "optimal frustration" was a holdover from classical psychoanalytic theory that was both incongruous with the practice of self psychology and with the way that Kohut actually worked.

My initial paper about this, which received a varied reception from self psychologists, was titled, "Optimal responsiveness and the therapeutic process" (Bacal, 1985), which comprises the second chapter in this book. In essence, I advanced the idea that when patients experienced their analysts as therapeutic, it happened not via a process of transmuting so-called optimal micro-frustrations, but rather through experiencing responsiveness that is therapeutically useable for that particular patient—responsiveness that regularly and legitimately draws upon a rich palette of possible therapeutic intervention, only one mode of which constitutes verbal interpretation, or explanation.

Kohut had advocated a two-step approach[14] to therapeutic action in psychoanalysis that comprised (1) Prolonged empathic immersion in the patient's subjectivity; (2) Explanation (interpretation) of what has been thus apprehended. I have always regarded this first step as essential. We gather relevant psychological data mainly through prolonged empathic attentiveness to the complexity of the patient's emotional and mental states—in effect, exploring, or investigating, the patient's subjectivity. But it seemed to me that confining the second step to explaining, or interpreting what the analyst has apprehended empathically, was to significantly delimit what the patient could experience therapeutically. I offered the concept of *optimal responsiveness*, which reflects *a way of working* that both expresses and legitimizes a wide range of modes and kinds of responsivity that patients variously experience as therapeutically useful.

The concept became integral to my elaboration of a *theory* of the dyadic specificity of therapeutic effect insofar as it also referred to the *particularity* of experience that is therapeutic for that patient. The analyst's responses that may be centrally therapeutic for a particular analysand—though possibly even anathema for another—may entail the offer of the analyst's empathically acquired information, that is, conveying to the analysand that she understands—if you like, empathizes or resonates with—the patient's experience; or offering a response in other modes, for example, as a discrete other, who may disagree with, or share in various ways and degrees, her subjectivity with the analysand. The latter, as I have suggested (Bacal, 2011, chapter 8), is irrelevantly termed "self-disclosure,"[15] as this is only one of the many ways that a patient may, or may not, experience the analyst as optimally responsive.

With the development of a theory of the specificity of process, that is, that *therapeutic effect is specific to the particular analyst–patient pair as it might emerge—or not—in their process*—we now propose that the two steps, understanding and response, not only overlap; they are inextricably linked, one with the other. We must now acknowledge that the measure of a therapy as psychoanalysis is neither "empathy" nor "response" but rather constitutes the fullness and complexity of both steps. In other words, the *sine qua non* of psychoanalytic therapy is not empathy culminated by verbal interpretation as the response in the second step but the entire process that includes understanding the complex mental/emotional states of another, and discerning responses that may be therapeutic for that patient, and possible for that analyst, in the uniqueness of their unfolding process (Bacal and Carlton, 2010).

My experience of Kohut was that he skillfully followed the first step in his sequence for therapeutic action but that, in practice, he did not adhere rigidly to his second step of confining himself to explanations; rather, he attempted to be optimally responsive—in effect, in consonance with specificity theory—to offer whatever *he* could that might be healing for *me*. As everyone knows, Kohut was inclined to write in quite long sentences, and one can sometimes lose the thread of what he is trying to say. He tended to deliver interpretations in the same way. But it did not matter, because he was on the whole empathically attuned to my psychological struggles and, for me, the optimal response from Kohut was not in his words—it was, as Elliott Markson (personal communication, 1978) so aptly put it, in the "music." Markson was referring to the quality of the therapeutic affect that the analyst's verbal communications may embody, which may transcend the meaning of the words themselves. Kohut would usually listen quietly and receptively and respectfully, sometimes for a long time, before he spoke. What he actually said—and he offered many carefully considered observations and explanations—was usually of secondary importance to me. I can barely recall any of it. But the melody that went along with what he spoke about harmonized with what *I* needed at the time: acceptance and optimism, delivered with warmth and kindness.

Much of the responsiveness that transcends the verbal implies the notion of a procedurally mediated responsivity. Responses that are therapeutic may be processed by the brain in ways that are experientially registered as such without "understanding" or "insight," that is, responses in addition to, or in lieu of, those which convey verbal understanding may be therapeutically decisive. An example of this, for instance, can be an action that conveys, "I sense your feeling and my response will convey this and what I think you need." I especially recall a particular instance of Kohut's responsiveness that felt like this. It occurred at the end of a weekend during which I had had three analytic sessions and was about to return home, not to see him again for another fortnight. Just as I was dejectedly leaving his office, he put an arm around my shoulder and gave me an encouraging hug. Kohut's empathy (Step 1) told him what my emotional state was at the time. His response was to *provide* what he sensed would be optimally therapeutic, rather than to offer an interpretation of what he sensed I needed (which would have been prescribed by his Step 2). He happened to be right. This was the provision of a response that—as John Lindon (1994) described—met a developmental need at that moment, and significantly promoted the progress of my treatment—and my life. Neither of us articulated its deeper meaning at the time, nor was I consciously aware of it then. I only felt that we connected in a way that made me feel that he deeply appreciated my emotional state at the moment. I was only able to articulate much later that his response had particular, profound meaning for me. What I needed was encouragement from a shielding fatherly presence to tide me over the next two weeks without him.

The question in these instances that is often raised is whether the analyst should have interpreted the analysand's need for an encouraging hug rather than provide it. I can only answer for myself. I do not think interpreting my need for it would have been nearly as therapeutic for *me*; indeed, I suspect it might have been felt as depriving—a frustration that was far from "optimal." As Fosshage (1998) put it,

> While communication of understanding is central to the analytic process and therapeutic action, it falls short … in capturing the full range of what patients seek and developmentally need and the complexity of the interaction that occurs within the psychoanalytic arena.
>
> (pp. 128–129)

What my analyst sensed was that I could use a response that was specific to *my* therapeutic need[16] at the time and that *he* was able to offer. During one session, Kohut—quite remarkably—told me, "Ferenczi had the right idea" (Kohut, personal communication, 1978).

A not-unrelated theme is how the specificity of dyadic process relates to spontaneity and improvisation. Any interaction, regardless of whether it is intentional, might have therapeutic potential. This supposition allows for the efficacy of surprise, spontaneity, and improvisation in the analytic encounter, as well as for those responses that may be more or less carefully thought through beforehand. The analyst's spontaneous activity may lead to what the Boston Change Process Study Group has called a "moment of meeting" (Stern, Sander, Nahum, Harrison, Lyons-Ruth, Morgan, and Tronick, 1998), that may "allow patients to overcome salient maladaptive expectancies and to participate in and develop new and salutary relational patterns" (Frank, as cited in Bacal and Herzog, 2003, p. 645).

In contrast to the view of the Boston Change Process Study Group, I do not consider "now moments" and "moments of meeting" (Stern, Sander, Nahum, Harrison, Lyons-Ruth, Morgan, and Tronick, 1998, pp. 913–915) to be either special or essential therapeutic encounters. If we consider that the spectrum of therapeutic responsivity is centrally determined by the capacity of the particular dyad for therapeutic interaction, a spontaneous engagement will be but one of the many ways that optimal therapeutic interaction may occur for *them*. Therapeutic efficacy is specific to the capacities and limitations of both participants as they are interactively evoked within the particular analytic dyad. The views of the Boston Change Process Study Group and my own are similar, though, insofar as we regard therapeutic interactions—including those that emerge "spontaneously"—as highly specific to the process of the particular dyad and that they entail a reciprocal process in which change occurs through "alterations in '[particular] ways of being with'" (Stern, Sander, Nahum, Harrison, Lyons-Ruth, Morgan, and Tronick, 1998, p. 918).

I try to be careful when using the term "enactment." I have found it useful in understanding the phenomenon of mutual dissociation as elaborated by Donnel Stern (2004; Bacal, 2015). However, like the term "parameter," it may privilege a particular way of working that can limit the nature of the analyst's therapeutic responsiveness. The term "parameter" was introduced by Eissler (1953) to refer to non-interpretive intervention that was, regrettably, sometimes necessary for some patients for a while who could not seem to utilize the "standard technique," but the sooner one could return to doing "proper analysis" the better. The term "enactment" can have the same connotation: The analyst and/or patient are doing something as a substitute for proper analysis. Specificity theory asserts a different perspective. Optimal responsiveness can be conveyed in a host of ways, some of which may be non-verbal, and which should optimally remain at that level. The creation of a facilitating environment (Winnicott, 1965), ambience (Wolf, 1976), or atmosphere (Balint, 1968; Ferenczi, 1931a) may be as important for a particular patient as articulated emotional or cognitive understanding. Specificity theory allows that it is not only legitimate but imperative that we respond to the particular therapeutic needs of our patients in whatever ways they can effectively use, providing this does not violate the patient's personal boundaries or the analyst's professional constraints and ethics.

In my own psychoanalytic practice, I have come to appreciate that one of the major determinants of therapeutic efficacy is how mutuality of need is regulated. In two papers that Peter Thomson and I collaborated on (Bacal and Thomson, 1996, 1998), we suggested that the patient–therapist relationship is much more reciprocal in nature than psychoanalysts have been willing to acknowledge. It is not only the patient who brings conscious and unconscious expectations to his therapist. The analyst normally has a variety of conscious and unconscious expectations of the patient, many of which comprise relational needs that are ordinarily responded to by the patient during the course of therapy. Some of these expectations are ubiquitous, and many more are specific to the particular analyst–patient pair. Many of them are embedded within the procedures and formalities of the treatment situation, with which the patient is, for the most part, usually willing to comply; the analyst as well as the patient may experience varying degrees of disruption in their relationship when their respective expectations are not met. The term "relatedness reaction" captures the nature of these disruptions more accurately than the term "countertransference reaction" (Bacal, 1998a; Bacal and Thomson, 1998). *Recognition of the specificity of reciprocal relatedness and the importance of its mutual regulation in any particular dyad can be pivotal to the therapeutic effect of that dyad.*

Kohut and I got on well, and my evident interest in his ideas seemed to bring us closer. However, when I suggested to Kohut with the exuberance of discovery that a certain concept developed by a particular British relational theorist corresponded closely to one of his tenets, a relatedness reaction occurred between us. His emphatic response was that if I wanted to find antecedents to his ideas, I should look to the work of Heinz Hartmann. Kohut's response did not feel good. Apart from its content—Kohut was referring to Hartmann's notion of the average expectable environment, which hardly constituted substantial backdrop to his ideas—Kohut's response to me did not reflect awareness of my psychological/emotional need. I was making a bid for an affectively vital sharing relatedness (see Herzog, 1998)—in retrospect, not entirely dissimilar to what I was looking for from Balint when I suggested a new model for our interaction. Attuning to such a need may have been difficult for Kohut to pick up in this context. He was not inclined to acknowledge that others may have anticipated his views, except seemingly an icon of classical psychoanalysis who had given a nod to the significance of the environment. He was not ready to consider that his psychology of the self and certain theories of "object relations" could be usefully synergistic, as I had implied.

Kohut's expectation for my recognition of the distinctiveness of his authorship—likely a specific selfobject need of his own—was obstructed by my suggestion, and his response did not meet my selfobject need for him to respond to it with enthusiasm. I was experiencing a *relatedness reaction*, and I suspect he was, too.

The frustration of my invitation to Kohut to join me in exploring the commonalities between self psychology and relational theory was not optimal but, fortunately, not disruptive of our therapeutic relationship. I did, however, hold to my view that self psychology and some relational theories not only had a good deal in common but also had much to offer each other. In the way that had become characteristic of my working through such impediments, I wrote about it—bringing together relational and self psychological concepts in group therapy (Bacal, 1985), then comparing British object-relations theories and self psychology (Bacal, 1987; Bacal and Newman, 1990).

My quest to conceptualize therapeutic efficacy has, more recently, led me to look at the psychoanalytic supervisory process through the lens of specificity theory (Bacal, 2011, 2016). Supervision is a curious kind of hybrid that variously comprises teaching, training and, in some ways, treatment (Bacal, 2011; Bromberg, 2013). Personal analysis may enable the student to come to know himself better, help him to "change," and potentially increase his effectiveness as a clinician. He or she will, however, still encounter specific challenges when engaging with the particular patient in ways that may not be addressed—indeed, which may not arise—in that setting. Neither personal analysis nor traditional supervisory work reliably offers this view. The Budapest approach to psychoanalytic supervision that was offered under the aegis of Sandor Ferenczi and in which I participated with Michael Balint embraced this challenge. This method of supervision entails the discussion of the student analyst's first case with his training analyst within the context of his analysis (see Bacal, 2016). I discuss this more fully in Chapter 11.

The Budapest analysts emphasized the advantage of this method over the traditional supervision session, as it provides a unique opportunity to study the student's countertransference in depth, in the here and now, with his analyst, in relation to this particular patient (Kovacs, 1936). No psychoanalytic institute now officially offers this kind of supervision (see Bacal, 2011, 2016). My impression, though, is that training analysts today are inclined to respond to their analysands' request for help with their "control cases" rather than suggest they take their questions back to their supervisor.

I have illustrated how an adaptation of the Budapest Institute's method of supervising can be effectively engaged by the student and her supervisor if there is a propitious fit between them (see Bacal, 2011, chapter 10). From the perspective of the specificity of dyadic process, the responses that a supervisor may offer to his supervisee will be helpful, if they are useable by that student and workable between her and her particular patient (see Kantrowitz, 2002). The application of specificity theory to supervision underscores the *uniqueness of each supervisory dyad and the emergent specificity of its process.* [17]

Specificity theory recognizes that the particularity of dyadic process may include but also may transcend the application of any formal theory or technique, with regard to either treatment or training. Both therapeutic and pedagogic potential will be determined by how each participant *specifically* affects the other and how each can respond to the other in their process. In consonance with my theory, I recognize that it reflects the particularity of *my* experience as analyst and analysand, supervisor, and supervisee. I enthusiastically invite you to consider its usefulness within your own practice.

Notes

1 Melanie Klein came to London in 1928, and her ideas had a major influence on the development of psychoanalysis in Britain ten years before Anna Freud arrived, with her father, effectively promoting his theories. Hence, the Kleinian Group was designated "A" and the Freudian Group "B."
2 I later found out that Ilse Hellman was a senior training analyst in the B Group.
3 One of Levine's notorious views was that the offering of an unexpected gift to a masochistic patient could be therapeutic.
4 Much later, I came across Ferenczi's view that not only might the analyst be wrong, and the patient right, but also the patient may have a better idea of how he might be treated (Ferenczi, 1928). Kohut (1984) was to put forward a similar view: "If there is one lesson that I have learned during my life as an analyst, it is the lesson that what my patients tell me is likely to be true—that many times when I believed that I was right and my patients were wrong, it turned out … that my rightness was superficial whereas their rightness was profound" (pp. 93–94).
5 Students of all groups attended the same classes during the first year at the Institute. Subsequently, they usually attended only those lectures and seminars that reflected their particular group affiliation.
6 Bion's attitude derived from Keats's concept of negative capability—the capacity to stay with uncertainty without reaching after fact or reason.
7 No separate session is set aside for this supervision. The student, whose analysis is five times a week, talks about his case as part of his associations during these sessions.

8 My explicit awareness of Ferenczi's distinctive ideas on the therapeutic process came much later. The papers in which they appeared were not on the curricula of analytic institutes at that time. Nonetheless, I had a growing sense that psychoanalysts were too often trying to put the square peg of their principles into the round hole of their patients' therapeutic needs.

9 The Tavistock Clinic is a treatment and training facility for psychoanalytic psychotherapy. During the 1960s, the Adult Department, where Bion's (1961) and Ezriel's (1973) group therapy methods were mainly taught and practiced (see Heath and Bacal, 1968), was headed by the Clinic's director, J.D. Sutherland. The Adolescent Department was run by Derek Miller, and the Department of Children and Parents was run by John Bowlby.

10 Our intent was to establish a baseline in order to challenge Eysenck's (1952) hypothesis that, in psychotherapy, one third of patients will improve, one third will get worse, and one third will remain the same. On the basis of our study of "untreated" patients, Eysenck turned out to be right on symptomatic criteria but not on psychodynamic criteria (see Malan, Bacal, Heath, and Balfour, 1968).

11 While I retain some uncertainty that specificity theory could in practice be utilized by Kleinian analysts, my supervisory experience with Wilfred Bion, a Kleinian icon, did very much demonstrate this. Despite Bion's apparent loyalty to Klein's theories, his clinical perspectives—and his own theory of therapy (see Bion, 1967)—were imbued with a radically open systems approach to his patients.

12 For those who are mathematically disposed, we could, with apologies to Albert, offer a descriptive equation to express this: E = SCR(PS), where E represents therapeutic efficacy, SCR the specific capacities for required reciprocal responsiveness of the participants, and PS the particular system, or systems, involved.

13 In this regard, Ernest Wolf, although a traditional self psychologist, defines the selfobject as "neither self nor object, but [rather] the subjective aspect of a self-sustaining function performed by a *relationship* [emphasis added] of self to objects who by their presence or activity evoke and maintain the self and the experience of selfhood" (Wolf, 1988, p. 184).

14 Kohut was not prescribing two discrete steps; he recognized that this was a way of working, within psychoanalytic process.

15 From the point of view of specificity theory the term "self disclosure" (see Bacal, 2011, pp. 107–114) is a misnomer, as it isolates a particular response of the therapist for consideration. Explicitly expressing aspects of oneself is only one of many responses by the analyst that may, or may not, be therapeutically usable by that patient or/and possible for that analyst in context.

16 This is no less true with regard to psychologic need than with respect to medical need. The medical community is coming to recognize the importance of developing the ability to specifically target certain foci of pathology without adversely affecting healthy tissue.

17 The Institute of Contemporary Psychoanalysis in Los Angeles offers workshops in psychoanalytic supervision to prepare graduates to supervise candidates' training cases. The format of the workshops is based upon Judy Kantrowitz's (2002) research on the supervisory process as a triadic match.

References

Bacal, H. (1985). Object-relations in the group from the perspective of self psychology. *International Journal of Group Psychotherapy*, 35 (4), 483–501.

Bacal, H. (1987). British object-relations theorists and self psychology: Some critical reflections. *International Journal of Psycho-Analysis*, 68, 81–98.

Bacal, H. (1990). The elements of a corrective selfobject experience. *Psychoanalytic Inquiry*, 10, 347–372. doi:10.1080/07351690.1990.10399611.

Bacal, H. (1994). The selfobject relationship in psychoanalytic treatment. In A. Goldberg (Ed.), *Progress in self psychology* (Vol. 10, pp. 21–30). Hillsdale, NJ: The Analytic Press.

Bacal, H. (1998a). Optimal responsiveness and the specificity of selfobject experience. In H. Bacal (Ed.), *How therapists heal their patients*. Northvale, NJ: Aronson.

Bacal, H. (1998b). Relational self psychology. Introduction to Vol. 14. In A. Goldberg (Ed.), *Progress in self psychology* (pp. xiii–xviii). Hillsdale, NJ: The Analytic Press.

Bacal, H. (2011). *The power of specificity in psychotherapy*. Lanham, MD: Aronson.

Bacal, H. (2015, October 17). *Beyond transference and countertransference: The dyadic specificity of psychoanalytic process*. Paper presented at the 38th Annual Conference on the Psychology of the Self, Los Angeles, CA.

Bacal, H. (2016). The Budapest School's concept of supervision: Michael Balint's legacy to the development of psychoanalytic specificity theory. In A. Rachman (Ed.), *The Budapest School of psychoanalysis* (pp. 140–163). New York, NY: Routledge.

Bacal, H., & Carlton, L. (2010). Kohut's last words on analytic cure and how we hear them now—A view from specificity theory. *International Journal of Psychoanalytic Self Psychology*, 5, 132–143. doi:10.1080/15551021003610059.

Bacal, H., & Herzog, B. (2003). Specificity theory and optimal responsiveness: An outline. *Psychoanalytic Psychology*, 20 (4), 635–648. doi:10.1037/0736-9735.20.4.635.

Bacal, H., & Newman, K. (1990). *Theories of object relations: Bridges to self psychology*. New York, NY: Columbia University Press.

Bacal, H., & Thomson, P. (1996). The psychoanalyst's selfobject needs and the effect of their frustration on the treatment: A new view of countertransference. In A. Goldberg (Ed.), *Basic ideas reconsidered: Progress in self psychology* (pp. 17–35). Hillsdale, NJ: The Analytic Press.

Bacal, H., & Thomson, P. (1998). Optimal responsiveness and the therapist's reaction to the patient's unresponsiveness. In H. Bacal (Ed.), *Optimal responsiveness: How therapists heal their patients* (pp. 117–140). Northvale, NJ: Aronson.

Balint, E., & Norell, J. (Eds.) (1973). *Six minutes for the patient*. London: Tavistock.

Balint, E., Balint, E., Courtenay, M., Elder, A., Hull, S., & Julian, P. (1993). *The doctor, the patient, and the group*. London: Routledge.

Balint, M. (1937). Early developmental states of the ego: Primary object-love. In *Primary love and psycho-analytic technique* (Vol. 1952, pp. 74–90). London: Tavistock.

Balint, M. (1968). *The basic fault*. London: Tavistock.

Bion, W. (1961). *Experiences in groups*. London: Tavistock.

Bion, W. (1967). Notes on memory and desire. *Psychoanalytic Forum's Journal*, 3, 271–280.

Bromberg, P. (2013). Hidden in plain sight: Thoughts on imagination and the lived unconscious. *Psychoanalytic Dialogues*, 23 (1), 1–14. doi:10.1080/10481885.2013.754275.

Edelman, G. (2004). *Wider than the sky*. New Haven, CT: Yale University Press.

Eissler, K. (1953). The effect of the structure of the ego on psychoanalytic technique. *Journal of the American Psychoanalytic Association*, 1, 104–143. doi:10.1177/000306515300100107.

Eysenck, H. (1952). The effects of psychotherapy: An evaluation. *Journal of Consulting and Clinical Psychology*, 16, 319–324. doi:10.1037/h0063633.

Ezriel, H. (1973). Psychoanalytic group therapy. In L. Wolberg & E. Schwartz (Eds.), *Group therapy 1973* (pp. 183–210). New York, NY: Intercontinental Medical Book Co.

Fairbairn, R.D. (1958). On the nature and aims of psychoanalytical treatment. *International Journal of Psychoanalysis*, 39, 147–167.

Ferenczi, S. (1928). The elasticity of psycho-analytic technique. In E. Jones (Ed.), *Final contributions to the theory and technique of psycho-analysis* (Vol. 1955, pp. 29–40). London: Hogarth Press.

Ferenczi, S. (1931a). Child-analysis in the analysis of adults. In *Final contributions to the theory and technique of psychoanalysis* (pp. 126–142). London: Hogarth Press. (Original work published 1955)

Ferenczi, S. (1931b). On the patient's initiative. In E. Jones (Ed.), *Final contributions to the theory and technique of psychoanalysis* (pp. 126–142). London: Hogarth Press. (Original work published 1955)

Fosshage, J. (1998). Optimal responsiveness and listening/experiencing perspectives. In H. Bacal (Ed.), *Optimal responsiveness: How therapists heal their patients.* Northvale, NJ: Aronson.

Guntrip, H. (1975). My experience of analysis with Fairbairn and Winnicott. *International Review of Psycho-Analysis*, 2, 145–156.

Heath, E., & Bacal, H. (1968). A method of group psychotherapy at the Tavistock Clinic. *International Journal of Group Psychotherapy*, 18, 21–30.

Herzog, B. (1998). Optimal responsiveness and the experience of sharing. In H. Bacal (Ed.), *Optimal responsiveness: How therapists heal their patients* (pp. 175–190). Northvale, NJ: Aronson.

Huxley, A. (1996). *Point counter point.* London: Dalkey Archive Press. (First published in 1928)

Kantrowitz, J. (2002). The triadic match: The interactive effect of supervisor, candidate, and patient. *Journal of the American Psychoanalytic Association*, 50, 939–996. doi:10.1177/00030651020500031201.

Kohut, H. (1971). *The analysis of the self.* New York, NY: International Universities Press.

Kohut, H. (1977). *The restoration of the self.* New York, NY: International Universities Press.

Kohut, H. (1984). The curative effect of psychoanalysis: The self psychological reassessment of the therapeutic process. In A. Goldberg & P. Stepansky (Eds.), *How does analysis cure?* (pp. 80–110). Chicago, IL: University of Chicago Press.

Kovacs, V. (1936). Training and control analysis. *International Journal of Psychoanalysis*, 17, 346–354.

Lindon, J. (1994). Gratification and provision in psychoanalysis. Should we get rid of "the rule of abstinence"? *Psychoanalytic Dialogues*, 4, 549–582. doi:10.1080/10481889409539038.

Lyons-Ruth, K. (2000). "I sense that you sense that I sense …": Sander's recognition process and the specificity of relational moves in the psychotherapeutic setting. *Infant Mental Health Journal*, 21 (1–2), 85–98. doi:10.1002/(SICI)1097-0355(200001/04)21:1/2-85:AID-IMHJ10-3.0.CO;2-F.

Malan, D., Bacal, H., Heath, S., & Balfour, F. (1968). A study of psychodynamic changes in untreated neurotic patients—I. *The British Journal of Psychiatry*, 114 (510), 525–551. doi:10.1192/bjp.114.510.525.

Malan, D.H., Heath, S.H., Bacal, H.A., & Balfour, H.G. (1975). Psychodynamic changes in untreated neurotic patients—II. Apparently genuine improvements. *Archives of General Psychiatry*, 32, 110–126. doi:10.1001/archpsyc.1975.01760190112013.

Sander, L. (2002). Thinking differently: Principles of process in living systems and the specificity of being known. *Psychoanalytic Dialogues*, 12 (1), 11–42. doi:10.1080/10481881209348652.

Stern, D. (2004). The eye sees itself: Dissociation, enactment and the achievement of conflict. *Contemporary Psychoanalysis*, 40, 197–237.

Stern, D., Sander, L., Nahum, J., Harrison, A., Lyons-Ruth, K., Morgan, A., & Tronick, E. (1998). Non-interpretive mechanisms in psychoanalytic therapy: The "Something More" than interpretation. *International Journal of Psycho-Analysis*, 79, 903–921.

Tronick, E. (2003). Of course all relationships are unique: How co-creative processes generate unique mother–infant and patient–therapist relationships and change other relationships. *Psychoanalytic Inquiry*, 23, 473–491. doi:10.1080/07351692309349044.

Winnicott, D. (1965). *The maturational processes and the facilitating environment*. London: Hogarth Press.

Wolf, E. (1976). Ambience and abstinence. In The Chicago Institute of Psychoanalysis (Ed.), *The annual of psychoanalysis* (Vol. 4, pp. 101–115). New York, NY: International Universities Press.

Wolf, E. (1988). *Treating the self*. New York, NY: Guilford Press.

2 Notes on Some Therapeutic Challenges in the Analysis of Severely Regressed Patients

This chapter explores some challenges psychoanalysts face when working with patients who regress deeply. This regression often brings forth primitive needs and expectations that complicate the therapeutic process. While this may disrupt the treatment, it may offer opportunities for therapeutic efficacy. The author discusses Michael Balint's theory of regression, particularly in terms of early object relations, emphasizing how regression not only serves as a form of resistance but may also represent an essential therapeutic need. Balint's concepts of "primary love" and "basic fault" are described, highlighting the patient's early relationships and the unconscious desire to repair past emotional wounds. This chapter suggests that understanding and responding to these dynamics can lead to a deeper therapeutic engagement with severely regressed patients, facilitating progress in the analytic process. The author describes how Kohut's self-selfobject relationship, along with the fantasy selfobject relationship, a concept introduced by the author, offer perspectives on early object relations and states of regression similar to Balint's. Each significantly advances our clinical understanding and ability to respond therapeutically to the severely regressed patient. The chapter includes an illustrative clinical example.

One of the major problems for the analyst in the treatment of patients who regress deeply is how to respond to unusual and sometimes primitive expectations or behavior in ways that will not disrupt the effectiveness of the analytic process; that will not further stimulate insatiable cravings; and that will not render the treatment non-psychoanalytic (although no "sin" is involved if this "needs" to happen for the therapeutic benefit of the patient). In addition, we need to consider the possibility that severely regressed states may be utilized by the psychoanalytic process to gain some elements of emotional health for the patient. In this paper, I propose to review these issues from the point of view of early object relations, as elaborated primarily by Michael Balint (1937). His work in this area has been insufficiently understood and utilized. Balint's view provides illuminating insights on the nature of regression and the problems involved in the treatment of regressed patients. I will then attempt to show that the concept of the self-selfobject relationship, a critical construct in Kohut's theoretical framework, offers a perspective on early

DOI: 10.4324/9781003570806-3

object relations and states of regression similar to Balint's. Each significantly advances our clinical understanding and ability to respond appropriately to the severely regressed patient.

What Is Regression and What Is Its Function?

There are many conceptualizations of the nature of regression. I will take as my starting point Balint's (1968) definition of regression, i.e., "primitive forms of behaving and experiencing which have emerged after more mature forms have established themselves." Balint culled from Freud's work the view that, clinically, regression may have four functions: (1) as a mechanism of defense; (2) as a factor in pathogenesis; (3) as a potent form of resistance; and (4) as an essential factor in analytic therapy (p. 127). In considering the complex field of regression, I will focus on the last two items, i.e., regression as a form of resistance and as an essential component in the analytic treatment. Since patients at times regress in ways that we would not have expected or wanted, we need to ask how and why these "problematic" regressions occur.

Ordinarily, we regard some regression in analysis as useful, and we sometimes speak of this as a "regression in the service of the ego" (Kris, 1936).[1] By this, we mean that the patient, under the influence of the analytic situation, begins to get in touch with previously warded-off, early libidinal, and/or aggressive wishes in relation to the analyst, and then deals with them either by employing mechanisms of defense and/or by acting out. Then, with the help of interpretation, he will come to articulate these wishes more openly. While these wishes may, at times, be passionately expressed, they do not clamor seriously and pervasively for gratification. The patient can accept or "make do" with, and use productively, our interpretative and reconstructive understanding. If, however, the regressive wish conveys by its intensity and pervasiveness that the patient requires another kind of response from the analyst, verbal interpretation alone will not do, and the analyst must decide how to regard this problematic regression, and how to respond to it. Whether the regression manifests itself by the patient insisting that he have more sessions or fewer sessions, that the analyst talk more or talk less, that he give more warmth by holding the patient or letting the patient hold the analyst, or whatever, an analyst working from a classical framework is inclined to view these as severe resistances. They will appear as invitations to act out that must somehow be converted into acceptable "analytic" behavior so that a proper analysis can continue. The patient must be enabled either to talk about what he "really" wants (for example, his wish for the analyst's exclusive attention, which may lie behind his clamor for an extra session, etc.) or, at least, to utilize a verbal defensive mechanism such as projection, e.g., "You hate me, as you obviously prefer your other patients, wife, etc." If, indeed, the patient's unusual demands constitute resistances of this sort, they should respond to more accurate, timely, and better formulated interpretative intervention than has been carried out up to that point, or even to rational encouragement that it is in the patient's "best interest" to verbalize—i.e., to be a "good" patient—rather than to carry on in this way. This is a time-honored approach, still recommended and carried out by many highly experienced analysts. However, if these responses to the patient's requests do not work, what are we to do? Should we conclude that this is evidence for our poor selection of the case for psychoanalysis, or poor management of the case once selected? Could it possibly be that this kind of regression is inevitable and necessary if the analytic process is to be effective for this patient? If the patient's request is not gratified, he may become noisy and disturbed, and we may indeed decide that he cannot bear the frustrations of the analytic procedure. However, we might do well to consider seriously that, if a patient needs to clamor so insistently for something other than "proper analysis," something might be wrong with the kind of proper analysis which the patient is getting.

In my experience, even with those patients whose regressive clamor constitutes primarily this type of resistance in the transference, responding in the way described will restore analytic propriety but at a price. The patient will have adjusted compliantly to the analyst's way of doing things, i.e., the patient will, by his compliance, have validated the analyst's "reason" and not his own, and will have responded to, or identified with, the analyst's authority. Worst of all, patient and analyst may have missed a significant opportunity for understanding important genetic roots of the patient's psychopathology.

One of Balint's (1937) signal contributions to our understanding of regression in analysis was his insistence that it needs to be apprehended not primarily as a one-person phenomenon, i.e., an intrapsychic process that can be described in terms of, let us say, libidinal or ego regression, but that regression during analysis aims mainly at establishing an object relationship of a specific sort between the patient and his analyst. This object relation has the characteristics of what he has called "primary love" (Balint, 1937). It is a relationship that the patient attempts to establish in the hope of correcting his "basic fault" (Balint, 1968). The object toward whom this attempt is directed is predominantly, although not exclusively, his analyst. Another related contribution of Balint (1968) is the notion that the nature and development of the regression is never determined solely by "the patient, his childhood, his character, the severity of his illness but [always as] the result of an interaction between the particular patient and his particular analyst" (p. 162). To some of us, this may sound self-evident, but it is a relatively new and not entirely established notion in psychoanalysis.

It should be noted that this view is different from the classical one, which would require that we ask whether the regressive manifestations constitute a demand primarily (or solely) for instinctual gratification, i.e., a return to a fixation point, or whether they constitute a defense, i.e., a transference resistance, the nature of which is as yet unclear. For Balint, the regression is always, above all, a manifestation of a wish for, and conditioned by, some sort of object relationship with the analyst.

"Primary Love" and the "Basic Fault": Early "Selfobject" Relationship and Early "Self Defect"

Balint's idea is that in normal development a primitive state of relatedness occurs between the infant and the mother, in which there is no distinction experienced by the infant between his needs and those of the mother.[2] Balint calls this primitive relationship "primary love" or "primary object love," and suggests that the inevitable disruptions in this harmonious experience or state lead to a "basic fault" (a geological metaphor) in the individual. In other words, something like a scar remains that becomes to all intents and purposes healed, but like a chronic tuberculous lesion is susceptible to breakdown under specific conditions. These are conditions which repeat or reflect the original disruption that caused the "fault" in the first place.

More recently, Kohut (1971) introduced the concepts of the selfobject and the self-selfobject relationship. The selfobject is experienced by the self and is, therefore, expected to function as if it were part of the self rather than as a separate entity. The inevitable shortcomings in the responsivity of the selfobject lead to a defect in the self that emerges in the individual's interpersonal relationships and, in particular, in the analytic situation in the form of a self-selfobject transference. This is a transference-like configuration in which the patient seeks to repair his self defect by attempting to elicit the phase-appropriate responsivity from the selfobject that was missing in his development (pp. 26–27). There are, however, important differences between the primary object relation described by Balint and the self-selfobject relationship of Kohut. While Balint's notion of "primary love" was referable to an ephemeral, ill-defined time/space in the relationship between the mother and the infant, Kohut's idea is that the need for the response by the selfobject is one that continues throughout life and is phase-appropriate to a whole series of developmental stages. In addition, while Balint regarded the relationship of primary love as a stepping stone to object love, Kohut (1966) regards the optimal self-selfobject relationship as the basis for the development and maturation of the self in all spheres of its functions and relationships.

Therefore, using Kohut's (1977) more systematic and comprehensive schema, we could conceive of Balint's relationship of primary love as a self-selfobject state akin to a very primitive or regressed merger state with the idealized maternal selfobject. The basic fault, then, should properly be regarded as basic only insofar as it is the result of a disruption or interference with this particular self-selfobject (merger) state, or relationship. It would, in this sense, be comparable to the defect in the self as understood by Kohut (1977, p. 2).

A further difference between Balint's and Kohut's perspectives is one that reflects a shift from what Kohut and Wolf (1978) have called a "maturation morality" in clinical work to an emphasis on the continuing phase-appropriate recognition of the nature of the patient's self-selfobject relations. In other words, clinical theoreticians prior to Kohut usually thought it necessary for the patient's progress to draw attention, at one point or another, to his being infantile. For example, the analyst whose work is in the classical tradition ultimately will offer his patient an interpretation that is determined by his conviction that the patient must modify, renounce, or sublimate his drives.

Similarly, an analyst, working within a "classical" object relations framework (to distinguish it from the self-selfobject object relations framework), will *understand* the regressive manifestations as indicative of the nature of the object relationship the patient wants to set up with the analyst and with others. He also will ultimately *convey* to the patient, in one way or another, that his regression is "primitive" and that he must finally accept reality, take responsibility for his life, and grow up. This, a kind of educative approach, would seem to have been the way Balint worked in his later years, having long before virtually given up attempting to weather the noisy manifestations of the regression without ultimate recourse to the exhortations of a "maturation morality." Thus, in my view, Balint also confused the tacitly agreed upon goals of analysis with the process of analysis.

In his earlier years, Balint seemed to be able to allow a different ambience to take hold (E. Balint, personal communication, 1971). In 1932, he had described a process that he called a "new beginning" (p. 151). In this process, the patient, having regressed to the experience of primary love in relation to his analyst, starts to discover for himself the real possibility of new and more mature object relationships.

As already implied, I believe that patients who are prone to precipitous regressions are those who have sustained early self-selfobject injury and who, therefore, have developed a basic fault, or defective self, at a relatively early level of object relationships. In using the word "early," I would like to make clear that this level of object relationships does not necessarily coincide, for example, with the oral stage of psychosexual development. The problem for these patients is a serious deprivation of basic parental responsivity, of caring and autonomy recognition. While this deprivation usually begins in early infancy, it also tends to continue during subsequent stages of development. Further, patients of this sort are not always those who present in a severely regressed state, but those who often look quite intact at the beginning of treatment. Indeed, they may look quite intact even immediately following hospitalization in the aftermath of a severe breakdown, e.g., a suicide attempt. Psychological testing and repeated psychiatric evaluations may show them to have no serious psychopathology, e.g., of the borderline type. Thus, although they may be clinically quite ill, they may present in different ways: as neurotic, with one or more stigmata of the various character or personality types with which we are familiar, or simply with a certain childlike quality, so that issues of trust, caring, and respect for autonomy arise early in the transference. These patients are "well" only because of a false self adaptation to their surroundings (Winnicott, 1960), including the new therapist from whom they are now seeking help. They may, however, come to look very ill indeed as the analytic process begins to touch them. Paradoxically, the severe regressions that occur in these patients result not only because the patient's surrounding environment (analyst or otherwise) inevitably repeats in some way the original traumatic injury in the area of the self-selfobject relationship, but also because a precondition for their occurrence is that the patient has built up a degree of trust and hope in the possibility of a new self-selfobject relationship. In other words, his hope for a "new beginning" corresponds to what he had always needed but what he had learned he must never dare look for in his childhood, because of the early, pervasive deprivation. The experience of emerging trust and hope, even in a subliminal or preconscious way, is reacted to by the patient as a danger signal of impending trauma, since it was precisely in this state that the repetitive let-down by the life-giving and hoped-for responsive selfobject was able repeatedly to traumatize the patient (Balint, 1968).

The Fantasy Selfobject Relationship

It is remarkable that these patients, who are rarely psychotic in the formal sense, maintain themselves as well as they do for long periods of time without therapy. My impression is that they have developed the capacity for a type of sustaining fantasy that they attach to potential selfobject figures. We could use the term *fantasy selfobject* for a selfobject that is *created* by the patient almost totally out of his own fantasy in a nuclear environment, when, in fact, such a real selfobject barely existed, if at all. It is a matter of degree, a degree crucially important for the evolution of a relatively stable, or relatively fragile, self.

Instead of wondering whether to regard these patients' regressive "demands" as resistances (either to regressing further or to growing up), we can greet them squarely, as inevitable manifestations of early selfobject needs that are now being expressed in these ways because of the opportunities the patient perceives in his relationship with the analyst.

Case Example

I would now like to describe in some detail a patient whose life situation and treatment illustrate what I have been discussing.

My first contact with Katherine was by telephone. She called and asked if I would take her in analysis. If I could not, she would go elsewhere (and she named two well-known psychiatric institutions in another country). All of this was said very much in the same breath, and I had the odd feeling of her being both eager for the possibility of an analysis with me and already resigned to going elsewhere if I did not tell her that I would accept her for treatment. She sounded like a frightened, appealing little girl, running away at the same time as she was trying to grab at something stable.

My impression of her at our first interview was of a highly intelligent, articulate, though rather rambling and confused, pretty, dark-haired young woman of 21, slightly overweight. She was somewhat childlike and bemused, evincing, in relation to me, a queer mixture of distancing and immediacy. I learned that she had just fled her husband of one year, a 47-year-old alcoholic psychopath, who had repeatedly beaten her in his episodic rage reactions. He had otherwise treated her, for the most part, and for the first time in her life, with affection, tenderness, and respect. There were no children.

She did not tell me until much later that she had attempted suicide on two occasions—once following an attack by her husband, after she had returned to him from two brief separations, and another time as a teenager, when she had given in to an urge to eat. It was unclear whether these attempts were serious.

Toward the end of our second assessment interview, Katherine expressed a preference for a woman analyst and for someone who was "older." I responded without interpretative inquiry by referring her to a colleague in the same city who filled the bill. In fact, I responded to her in a way that was unusual for me. In reply to her openly declared preference, I invited her to use my phone to call the woman analyst, which she did while I left the room. During her call, I came back to get some papers on my desk, but before reentering the room to get them, I knocked on the door.

Three days later, she phoned to ask if I would still be willing to have her as a patient. She had not seen the woman analyst but had decided she wanted me to undertake her analysis, although she fully intended to keep an appointment with that analyst, out of courtesy. In response to my question about her change of mind, she told me that when she sees something about a person that she likes, that means a lot to her. I said I was still puzzled, because it seemed to me that from what she had said, she did not like what she had seen. She told me she liked what I did in going along with her preference, allowing her to use my phone to call the woman analyst. She was especially impressed by what I did in the middle of her telephone conversation. Her perception was that when I came in to get my notes, I was a bit apologetic—as indeed I was—about intruding upon her. This meant that I was human and would treat her like another human being, and that I would take seriously what she said and what was important to her. I had begun, even then, to sense that she seemed to need to reject before she might accept, and that she needed me to tolerate this. But I did not have any idea then how much I was going to be asked to tolerate. Eventually, because of the problems that ensued, and the lack of an adequate supporting environment, I found it necessary to discontinue Katherine's analysis before it came to a satisfactory conclusion.

The following synopsis of Katherine's background is relevant to the themes in this paper. Katherine was born into a well-to-do middle-class family. According to Katherine's mother, she had to be force-fed as a baby, was a thumb sucker until age seven, and was a finicky eater. As a child, she was quiet, shy, and good (an accommodating child, she meant), although the mother thought Katherine was probably depressed because she cried a lot. Katherine described a family who did not play, parents who had no friends, and a house that was "empty." She had a few friends, but didn't bring them home because it was not too happy a place. She seemed to have grown up in a home in which a peculiar, cold climate prevailed, where little or no emotion was displayed between her parents or between them and the children. Her parents, she said, rarely talked to one another except to argue.

Katherine regarded her mother as "overemotional, extremely illogical, and close-minded." She described her as a hypochondriac who spent much of her day in bed, and who used Katherine as a kind of babysitter. In this sense, she was close to her mother. She felt important and needed by her for the purpose of providing a container into which mother poured her distress, worries, physical concerns, and complaints against the father, turning Katherine against him. Katherine had a sister, one year older, with whom she had a complex, problematic relationship.

Katherine described her father as an obese, self-indulgent, taciturn man, who treated her with a "laissez-faire attitude." She felt she did not have a relationship with him at all, except possibly when she was small, since he was "good with little children."

Thus, her experience of her mother was that of a highly narcissistic, immature figure, whom she herself had to mother and from whom she could get almost nothing for herself. She regarded her father as somewhat depressed, distant, and self-preoccupied, yet as someone to whom she would occasionally turn in the slim hope that she might get a different kind of response than the one she was always used to.

When she was nine, her maternal grandmother had a disfiguring stroke. Katherine seemed to be depressed at that time, but was devoted to her grandmother, visiting her frequently. She recovered from this depression and seemed to have been more or less normal emotionally until age 15. At that time, her anorexia nervosa began. She related this illness to the death of her grandmother, whom, on a few occasions (when she was ill), she had experienced as a caring figure. After Katherine left high school, she had a number of menial jobs including work in a dairy and as a clerk in a department store. She continued in this latter job well into her analysis, but often did not work at all.

Her sexual development was not remarkable except that she seemed to harbor a somewhat puritanical attitude toward her sexual desires. For her, pure sexual inclinations were morally reprehensible (an apparent legacy of her mother's attitude). At the same time, she was a person with passionate sexual needs. She had had one brief sexual affair with a boy her own age prior to what she described as a highly satisfying sexual relationship with her husband. She also had had an essentially cuddling relationship, without overt sexual involvement, with a girl her age a few months prior to her marriage.

As a teenager, she had been treated by a host of psychiatrists and internists for severe anorexia nervosa. She ultimately responded to the ministrations of a hypnotist who, for a few months, had also taken her into his home, ostensibly as part of the treatment. Prior to this, she had been admitted to two psychiatric institutions for depressive episodes associated with the vicissitudes of her anorexia nervosa. She fled from both after a few weeks. In the discharge note at one of these hospitals, it was observed that Katherine was offered individual psychotherapy three times a week, but that she refused to come to most of the sessions. When she did come, she often filled the hour with steady complaints. When it was pointed out to her by her psychotherapist that she was insisting on being seen more frequently but was refusing to come to the sessions when they were scheduled, she became defensive, irritable, and complained that she could not work with people who were so argumentative. She felt that she had to leave because she was being deprived of her "inalienable rights." At another institution, the discharge note mentioned that "her feelings and behaviors are superficial as a function of an expected duty, rather than what she really wants or feels." They had decided she was hysterical and manipulative, to which they reacted by attempting to set limits. She responded by discharging herself.

Although the diagnosis of borderline personality could be applied on the basis of her history, this diagnosis was never made by any of the psychiatrists and psychologists who interviewed and tested her extensively over the years. The general impression was that she had a neurotic personality disorder with recurrent depressions of moderate severity.

With respect to the woman analyst and myself, Katherine initially seemed to have rejected us both as unsuitable parent figures. She may well have bounced from the unsatisfactory father (myself) to the impossible, though more deeply desired, mother (woman analyst) and then back again. The early acting out could be regarded as illustrative of her use of the mechanism of primitive splitting. I think, though, that she came back to me because she imagined I could become a "new" object, corresponding to her fantasy selfobject, which she hoped to transfer to a "real" person.

In her initial analytic session, she announced that she was not ready to begin and still had a few questions to ask me. Foremost was, how would we know when to stop? Also, what would my role be in the analysis? She was worried that I would be too directive. She was suspicious of psychiatrists, feeling that they wanted "to get something out of the sessions." Her other main concern was that I might sit there passively, bored and uninterested, as she went on. These questions and concerns constituted two kinds of transference expectations. One was related to me as her father, and the other was a reflection of the relationship which prevailed throughout her life with her mother. If I showed any interest in her, she feared that I would become for her the mother who needed her for what she wanted to get out of her, who needed to pour into her what the patient had rebelled against in the feeding situation as an infant. Her mother used her then, and subsequently, as a selfobject for her own narcissistic outpourings, whether of food or of verbiage, throughout her life. At the same time, it gradually became evident that it was only in this mode of relating that she felt any sense of being worthwhile. She seemed to have developed a false self organization, wherein she felt she had a right to live only if she existed for someone else and could maintain a feeling that she was appreciated for this.

For some time, it was this latter transference that she brought to me. The atmosphere she created was a maddening one. It was my analysis. She was coming *for me*. In contrast to this, she also conveyed to me during the first weeks that she liked coming, describing the hospital in which my office was located as calmer than any she had ever been in. It is a place, she conveyed to me, that people really do not want to leave. When I contrasted this with her obvious relief at the end of each session, she was puzzled. This contradiction could be understood mechanistically as the way she dealt with intense ambivalence, i.e., by means of projective identification and primitive splitting of both the ego and the object, similar to her alternating rejection of me and the woman analyst. However, the dynamic and largely unconscious *determinants* of these maneuvers, i.e., her inclination to retreat at the end of the hour, were understandable as ways of attempting to preserve the fragile illusion of the fantasy self-selfobject relationship with me. In effect, I came to appreciate that I was dealing with a complex primitive situation in which her requirement that she exist for me (and others) was a defensive reversal against the "narcissistic" declaration of her own wish for someone else—especially me—to exist as a selfobject for her. This situation felt not only unjustifiably self-indulgent to her, but highly elusive and illusory. The deepest and most compelling need constituting her selfobject yearnings was that she be able to initiate, to give, and to have her childlike enthusiasm responded to. It also became apparent that when she was in or near these states of mind, she was most dangerously vulnerable, since they activated wishes that were never satisfied, i.e., wishes that were based almost wholly upon her own fantasies, and not experiential reality.

In the seventh month of her analysis, she conveyed to me, after missing several sessions, that she found it especially difficult to come sometimes and that this was when she felt particularly depressed. In connection with this, there were some things she could not tell me. She conveyed to me quite clearly that she anticipated that, from time to time, she would simply not be coming. She was adamant about this. My first reaction was a fairly strong countertransference one, since it was not my custom to automatically charge for missed sessions. We were both aware that she was enacting that same pattern with me that she had had with other therapists. We were also both aware that confrontation would prove useless. At first, I really felt that I could not go along with this, and said so. She made me realize, however, that she wanted to continue with me. While I did not as yet understand its meaning, I accepted her condition and agreed to charge her for missed sessions. That was the first shift that I made within myself, acceding to an unusual request or demand. In retrospect, I appreciate that she was asking me to tolerate the fact that all meaningful links between us would, from time to time, be rendered non-existent, a state of affairs that she had previously been exposed to in her relationships with her mother and father. It was a demand that I was eventually unable to accept for reasons which will become clear.

This liking to be with me, while apparently needing to run away, reflected (1) her wish to have more of the good kind of relationships she needed and less of the kind she did not; and (2) her need to preclude the development of too deep and meaningful a relationship with me, and to avoid the inevitable disappointment she knew she was not yet ready to handle. (Of course, both of these inevitably occurred. The question throughout this discussion is what are the conditions under which this kind of transference constellation can be effectively handled.) Not only did she sometimes not show up for sessions, but she insisted that their frequency sometimes be increased or decreased. Therefore, over a period of three years, the frequency of her sessions changed variously from one to five times per week. During these three years, she missed a total of 47 sessions.

Gradually, over the next year and a half, the transference resistance of her massively projecting her own wants onto me, and its manifestation as a defense in relation to her needs for other potential selfobjects, yielded to interpretation. She utilized it less insistently, and she became more aware of the existence of underlying needs for a totally harmonious fitting in of the environment with herself.

Put another way, rather than compulsively or automatically fitting into her environment by means of a false self compliance with presumed expectations, rather than functioning falsely as a selfobject for others, she began, under the influence of the analytic work, to become more healthy, in the sense that she became more internally sincere with herself. This, of course, I regarded as a therapeutic regression. As the resistances to becoming more aware of her early selfobject needs were cleared away, she began to make a series of demands that had a flavor different from those I have described earlier with respect to the acting out involved in the missing of sessions. For example, she wanted me to be less "remote," less formal, more like her "GP," with whom she seemed to have a friendly relationship. It took me a long while to realize that this was a necessary, basic atmosphere, or climate, for her (Wolf, 1976). Consonant with my personality, I was able to make the necessary shift over time.

She also came to insist, from time to time, that I be more definite and more responsive to her declarations of interest in pursuing this or that activity, rather than that I be caught up in anxiety about intruding narcissistically, like the mother. She needed me actually to correspond more closely to her fantasy selfobject than I did correspond (a fantasy selfobject based on her slim hopes vis-à-vis her father and grandmother who, at least, could be *imagined* as potentially responsive in the way she needed them to be).

My response to Katherine created quite a different ambience from what is classically regarded as analytic neutrality, and it did not come easily or all at once. I was helped by Kohut's (1977) idea that analytic neutrality means providing the normal human response that is appropriate to that particular patient (pp. 250–258). This response is to be distinguished from Alexander's (1952) "corrective emotional experience" in which the analyst adopts a specific role in relation to the patient (p. 30). With this patient, not to respond in the way that I did would not have been neutrality, but coldness. I would also agree with Ferenczi (1932), who maintained that this can only serve to *increase* the passionate quality of the patient's transference.

To give you a perspective of my analytic practice, I should point out that I am rarely faced with situations in which patients phone me, or ask for extra sessions, or request to see me after sessions, all of which this patient seemed to need and which I allowed. In other words, I felt that these responses were appropriate, normal human responses, *given the nature of her self organization.* I wish to stress that none of these responses to this patient produced the nightmare of interminably escalating intense demands and cravings—the so-called "malignant" regression (Balint, 1968, p. 146). In fact, Katherine's treatment, in my view, was progressing quite well at this point *because* she was regressing in this way. The deeper layer of the self that vitally needed appreciation and recognition for its aliveness and *real* need to give began to emerge. Along with this, she became increasingly vulnerable to any failure in responsiveness of the environment, especially of her parents and her sister and, equally so, of her analyst.

What is sometimes mistaken for a malignant regression are the manifestations of intense and catastrophic disappointment that the patient evinces when something goes wrong in the area of his specific self-selfobject vulnerability. Vulnerability to intense and catastrophic disappointment is most apt to occur when the patient is in or near the state of his pathognomonic regression[3]—in other words, when he attempts to trust again that his world might provide him with his basic selfobject requirements. Under the strain of this severe vulnerability, Katherine responded to the inevitable, often objectively microscopic, failures in her selfobject environment by intensified reactions similar to those she had shown earlier. She terminated her analysis no less than five times and attempted suicide three times in the third year of her analysis.

When such traumatic reactions occur in analysis, one's first thought is usually—and perhaps well should be—that either one's technique or perhaps even the total therapeutic endeavor was incorrect or ill-advised. The possibility must be raised that the patient was poorly selected for the treatment offered. Not a few analysts would stop right here. But I wish to consider an alternative possibility—that, as terrible as the traumatic reactions may be (and repeated serious attempts at suicide certainly are), they are not necessarily to be regarded as indications that our approach was wrong. Rather, in certain cases, some kind of catastrophic reaction is virtually inevitable, given the excessive degree of continuous early selfobject failure, together with the tacit invitation provided by the analytic situation to regress to very basic wishes for the human response of the selfobject—wishes that had almost never produced the needed responses in the past. True, this patient demonstrates a particularly severe instance of poor self-esteem regulation, having become, as a result of her experience, terribly vulnerable to selfobject failure. It is the severe example, however, that highlights the challenges one is often called upon to meet in less extreme instances.

Briefly, here are two examples which demonstrate Katherine's exquisite vulnerability and her devastating reaction to selfobject failure. Two and a half years after her analysis began, she responded catastrophically when she experienced my efforts to interpret a dream of intercourse with me as a comment on her possible psychopathology. (What I had done that offended her was to preface my interpretation of the dream by expressing puzzlement about an aspect of the manifest content of the dream that seemed "odd" to me.) She reacted by terminating her analysis and making her first suicide attempt since entering treatment. In her letter to me indicating that she was terminating, she wrote that the thought of further sessions was unbearable. "I seem to lack the necessary self-assurance (esteem or whatever) that would help me to tolerate them." She had experienced my interpretation as traumatic since, from her point of view, she was courageously bringing to me for the first time her need to be regarded as an acceptable, attractive, and lovable enough girl to justify having such dreams about her idealized analyst.

After she returned to treatment, it took us several weeks of hard work to understand the importance of the dream in terms of the self-selfobject relationship that she needed to establish with me. She did not need me to analyze the strangeness of the dream's content, except perhaps to acknowledge that *she* might regard it as strange and might be worried that I might regard it as strange that she would have a dream of intercourse with me.

Five months later, when she went to her father and told him that she wanted to be a nurse (this was the first attempt that she could recall to share her ambitions with him), she became so shocked by his characteristic, indifferent response (my response to the dream had been experienced as insulting) that she made another serious suicide attempt and was again admitted to the hospital.

Distinction Between Therapeutic Regression and Reaction to Selfobject Failure

These catastrophic reactions to failure of the selfobject, experienced by a patient as traumatic when in a state of profound regression, must be distinguished from the state of therapeutic regression in which the patient becomes more in touch with his primitive selfobject needs and demands more from the analyst. At this point, I was becoming aware that Katherine seemed particularly vulnerable whenever I was away. I responded after her first suicide attempt by setting up an arrangement with the hospital whereby she could come in on an ad hoc basis whenever I was out of town for the weekend. Initially, we did this on the basis of her feeling suicidal. After a while, however, I realized that she needed to come into the hospital for positive reasons, associated with her therapeutic regression. I began to appreciate this after an illuminating and somewhat alarming misunderstanding occurred in relation to one of her demands. This incident occurred some weeks after she had made her first suicide attempt.

One night, after I had been away for four days, she woke me up with a telephone call to tell me that she had called the ward earlier that evening and had expressed an ambivalent wish to be admitted to the hospital. She was living at her parents' home at the time, and felt she could stay there no longer. I experienced some irritation at being disturbed in my home so late at night and a feeling of being imposed upon in a way I did not want. I responded by attempting to assess, as a psychiatrist properly and realistically would, whether she was in a suicidal state. Satisfied that she was not, I confirmed with her that we would be meeting for her session in the morning. She did not show up for the session, and I learned only by evening that she had been looking for an apartment during the day (I actually spent the whole day trying to find her, thinking that this time she had truly done herself in).

When she came in for the following session, she told me that when she phoned me at night to speak to me about being admitted to the hospital, she was a bit annoyed that I did not take her wish to be hospitalized seriously. I had not understood that she felt a need to be on my "home turf." I conveyed to her that I understood that she must have felt rejected in terms of wanting to come "home" to me, and I came to understand her desperate need to find a home, the right kind of home, preferably with her analyst. This entailed, psychologically, that she *enter* me as someone who would provide her with a selfobject home/mother, that she needed me to envelop her with exactly the right ambience. For this patient, however, verbal understanding based on accurate empathy was sometimes insufficient. She needed, in some tangible way, to be on my "home turf" when I was not available, as well as my understanding of her need for this.

Gradually, she was able to come closer to an awareness that she missed me terribly when I was away, and that this was related to the threat of suicide. We agreed that there was something positive about this, and that it represented a real need for a concrete response, and so I arranged for her to be in the hospital on a regular basis when I was away.

When she was on the ward during these times, she did extremely well, looking to all intents and purposes like an extremely healthy youngster (it is hard to say of what age; perhaps variously between three and thirteen). She was enthusiastic and spontaneously helpful and engaging in relation to other patients. She emerged, therefore, in her regression, as a person coming to know that she needed and had never had a selfobject (1) who would regard her as a worthwhile female child with sexual drives to be respected and taken seriously; (2) who would not feed on her, and who, therefore, would be cognizant and appreciative of her generosity; (3) who would show a natural, fatherly protective interest; and (4) who would also be a selfobject responsive to her enthusiasms and ambitions. However, since the establishment of the good selfobject was for her largely a creation of her own—i.e., of her transference onto the analyst and others (including, at times, her nuclear figures) of a fantasied ideal self-selfobject relationship—she was exquisitely vulnerable to failure in her selfobject environment.

My responses to this patient undoubtedly contributed to the nature of her regression (as well as to her traumatic reactions). In addressing myself to her defenses against the experiencing of her selfobject needs, I gave her permission to be more honest with herself and with me about these selfobject needs and their frustration. Attempts to interpret her defenses as guarding against a bottom line of raw aggression that occasionally broke through in a devastating way—i.e., that she was full of rage—simply meant nothing to her. Although one could construe her terminating analysis as a kind of murder, and her suicidal attempts as primarily due to a destructive or aggressive drive directed outward or inward, I came rather to regard them as symptoms of her deep sense of futility, coupled paradoxically with the hope that she could still preserve the fantasy selfobject.

Everyone needs to be disillusioned, but early, massive, and continuing disillusionment in relation to basic selfobject needs for genuine caring and interest produces a deep wound that heals only with disfiguring and restrictive scar tissue. Some patients, like Katherine, are prepared to have this wound opened, since they know that only in this way is there a chance that it may ultimately heal properly. It can, of course, only be "opened" by the person who caused the wound in the first place, i.e., by the analyst, in the transference.

On Delusional Transference

From this point of view, the delusional transference that we sometimes see in these patients, in which the analyst is viewed as all bad (as I was viewed more than once by Katherine), is more meaningfully intelligible as a dissolution of this archaic, fantasied ideal selfobject relationship into its original negative (or bad) form. In other words, it is the *experience* of the bad selfobject rather than the use of splitting as a primitive defense against destructive drives that constitutes the delusional transference. Splitting of the object (and the ego) into good and bad is thus not the rock-bottom notion it is portrayed to be in the Kleinian view and its offshoots. Rather, splitting emerges only as a mechanism brought into operation in order to preserve the primitive, fantasied self-selfobject relationship that sustains the self. Put in another way, when the fantasied ideal transference breaks down due to selfobject failure, and the patient is flooded with the experience of the analyst as totally bad, not only has splitting failed as a defense but, more significantly, what the analyst then calls delusional transference is, for the patient, the real selfobject relationship with the unempathic parent. What the analyst calls "real" at that moment—his offering to the patient an interested, reliable relationship—is unreal to the patient who has never harbored this as anything but a fantasy. At a moment when a selfobject failure has occurred, this fantasy is obliterated. For this reason, Katherine was unable to regard me as a good object who would sustain her when her father let her down.[4] This occurred more directly, of course, when I let her down with respect to the interpretation of her dream.

With this orientation, if a diagnosis of resistance to regression is made, the patient's defenses should be considered as constituting protection against the dread of (a repetition of) the dissolution of the fantasied selfobject relationship that may exist in the transference. This has always been sensed, I believe, by analytic clinicians, but to my knowledge has never been put in these terms.

The Conditions of the Patient and the Tolerance of the Analyst

The demands on the analyst that the patient makes in his regressed state can perhaps best be described in terms of "conditions." From the beginning, one of Katherine's conditions was that I would have to tolerate her as a person who sometimes would not come to see me, or who would perhaps terminate her treatment with me. There were other conditions: that I would not react with rejection or ask her to exhibit more adult behavior when she tried to kill herself. Perhaps her most disturbing condition was one never verbalized, but which contained the most telling message by virtue of its effect on me—that during periods when she was deeply regressed, I would "carry" her with me much of the time. This is something I do not tend to do with my "ordinary" patients, except in some crises.

The challenge, then, for the analyst, is to determine clearly whether or not he can tolerate the special conditions under which the patient will accept him as a potentially therapeutic selfobject (Main, 1957). If the analyst cannot tolerate them, he must establish conditions under which he can proceed with the patient, or refer him elsewhere. A compromise sometimes is possible, but there should be no shame attached to the analyst's inability to accept the patient's conditions, nor censure of the patient for not accepting the compromise conditions.

We have all been warned about patients with whom we should not attempt "uncovering" therapy. They cannot take it, they will become psychotic, or become "impossible" in some other way. Our task, we were told, was to strengthen the defenses in these instances. In recent years, we have begun to have another crack at this challenge, originally tackled by Ferenczi. It may be possible to do something analytically for these very difficult patients, particularly if we listen seriously to their criticisms and even "technical propositions" (Ferenczi, 1931). It has always seemed to me that in the treatment of difficult patients we have seriously neglected an important aspect of the treatment situation: the nature of the difficulty produced by the interaction between the specific therapist and the particular patient who is giving him the difficulty. As simple and as self-evident as this may sound, discussions of difficult patients or of countertransference have tended to fall short of according sufficient consideration to the dyadic issue that, in my opinion, is usually crucial.

My countertransference response when Katherine first tried to kill herself was a clue for my later understanding of the existence of what I have called the fantasy selfobject transference: "How could she do this? I thought at last we had a relationship." The answer is evident, but not easy to accept. Katherine did *not* have an object relationship of substance with anyone, including the analyst. She was trying to *create* one with him. She needed him to provide for her an agreed semblance of approximate conditions that inactivated her "basic fault," making himself available in ways that would enable her to establish with him a fantasy self-selfobject transference. Only then could she build the internal psychic structure that she needed.[5] Since, however, this kind of situation is a fantasy transference, the main thrust of the process necessarily is the gradual disillusionment with, and the intrapsychic adjustment to, the failures of the analyst. It would be better if the analyst could entirely avoid *traumatically* disillusioning his patient. However, for reasons already elaborated, this is not entirely possible with a patient like Katherine. The situation in which I felt I could tolerate Katherine's "conditions," both her regressive expectations and her sometimes dangerous and deeply disturbing traumatic reactions to disillusionment, was one in which I had a *sustaining selfobject matrix* for both of us. This meant the availability of a professional surround in which colleagues understood and approved of what the patient and I were attempting to do, and a hospital setting that would provide a responsible, supportive, and protective milieu in addition to the analytic situation. The former, unfortunately, is as rare as the latter. Neither was available where Katherine was in treatment. The personnel in the hospital could barely accept as a suitable reason for her repeated admission to the psychiatric or medical wards that she needed to be on her analyst's turf while he was away and when she overdosed. The further elucidation of the dynamics of this requirement would be interesting and important, since it involves both transference and countertransference needs and limitations. For example, without this sustaining selfobject matrix, I was as prone to the difficulty in carrying on her analysis as she was prone to breaking it off, and for similar reasons. In effect, without it, neither of us could tolerate the strain. Virtually no one but her general practitioner continued to support her remaining in treatment after her first suicidal attempt. Without the presence of this GP, the therapy would have foundered much earlier than it did.

Following her third suicidal attempt, all external support for her continuing her analysis collapsed, and her GP was prevailed upon to commit her to a mental hospital from which she was released after a few months. Katherine has been in touch with me intermittently since her treatment was interrupted about one and a half years ago, and my continuing availability to be contacted by her appears to be an important sustaining factor. She remains grateful for our work together and has indicated her eagerness to resume her analysis, should the conditions that I refer to above become available. She has indicated that she understands these conditions must be met if we are to resume.

My patient would certainly be regarded as having had a "malignant regression" by many analysts. However, I believe that term to be an artifact—a kind of nasty label to cover up our inability to appreciate and to predict the inevitability that some patients will respond to our failures as selfobjects in disturbing and sometimes dangerous and deadly ways. As I hope I have shown, this situation can be predicted if we diagnose the situation correctly on the basis of the nature of the developing self-selfobject transference. My impression is that, as our understanding increases, so does our tolerance for the patient and, concomitantly, our clinical diagnoses tend to become less nasty. The reverse is also true. The limiting factor is not the inability of the patient to tolerate the rigors of the analytic process, but the lack of fit between the patient's selfobject needs and the analyst's capacity to accept these needs, as well as the patient's strong reactions to his failure to do so.

On the basis of the foregoing, the question of abstinence versus gratification with regressed patients is an incorrectly framed question. It is not whether, within an analytic procedure, we will gratify an impulse of the patient or insist on abstinence. It is rather a question of what is the understanding, appropriately responsive ambience for that patient (Wolf, 1976). Once this is recognized, the analyst will appreciate that this responsiveness is a necessary aspect of the analysis of his patient, and not a parameter or a seduction.

There are, indeed, instinctual cravings that we need to identify, but they do not belong to the area of the selfobject needs of the seriously regressed patient. Instinctual needs, whether oedipal or pre-oedipal, do not require responses other than in terms of our already well-established analytic language, if we are working with a patient who has an intact self. Regressed patients like Katherine, however, who have deeply cracked self structures (self defects, or basic faults), hold together just enough so that life is barely tolerable until they can establish the kind of self-selfobject relationship in which a self-consolidating analysis can take place. They may, at times, during the therapeutic process, temporarily fall apart. If we can understand that this may be necessary and inevitable, we may enable them to heal.

With regard to Katherine, one should have been prepared, on the basis of her history, for a difficult patient. Many, perhaps most, analysts would regard her as unsuitable for psychoanalytic therapy. I make no apology for accepting her. I did so because it seemed not only that virtually everything else had been tried, but that the alternative was no treatment at all (which some analysts would regard as the correct disposition). However, despite the enormous amount of trouble, anxiety, and time that she cost me, I would do it again, knowing even now what would lie in store for both of us. My gratitude to her is that she taught me a great deal about both the possible scope and the limitations of psychoanalysis. She showed me, in addition to Balint's view that analysis is not just the therapy of one person by another, that analysis is a process that is significantly affected by the therapist's capacity to respond appropriately to his patient's selfobject needs and, with a severely regressed patient, to his anguished reactions to the real limitations of the therapist's ability to help.

Notes

1 Kris originally expressed this idea in a quite different context.
2 This is similar to Winnicott's famous aphorism, "There is no such thing as a baby, [there is, rather] a nursing couple" (Winnicott, 1952, p. 99).
3 A regression to the state just prior to the occurrence of the "basic fault" (Balint, 1968).
4 Levine has emphasized the importance of the "sustaining object" for regressed patients (Levine, 1979).
5 Kohut (1977) has indicated that there are essentially two ways in which the analyst's responsivity can enable the patient to build intrapsychic structure with respect to self defects: where the analyst functions as an empathically understanding selfobject; and where he (inevitably) fails the patient in his responsivity as a selfobject, both in deed and in empathically communicating to his patient an understanding of his selfobject needs in *manageable doses*. "Optimal frustration" (p. 123) is the phrase which Kohut uses for the latter constellation, but "optimal gratification"—a notion which has not been properly studied—needs to take its place side by side as an equally respectable concept.

References

Alexander, F. (1952). Development of the fundamental concepts of psychoanalysis. In F. Alexander & H. Ross (Eds.), *The impact of Freudian psychiatry* (1961, p. 30). Chicago, IL: University of Chicago Press.

Balint, M. (1932). Character analysis and new beginning. In *Primary love and psychoanalytic technique* (new and enl. ed., 1965, pp. 151–164). London: Tavistock.

Balint, M. (1937). Early developmental states of the ego: Primary object-love. In *Primary Love and Psychoanalytic Technique* (1952, pp. 74–90). London: Tavistock.

Balint, M. (1968). *The Basic Fault*. London: Tavistock.

Ferenczi, S. (1931). On the patient's initiative. In *Final contributions to the problems and methods of psychoanalysis* (1955, p. 235). London: Hogarth Press.

Ferenczi, S. (1932). The analyst's attitude to his patients. In *Final contributions to the problems and methods of psychoanalysis* (1955, pp. 261–262). London: Hogarth Press.

Kohut, H. (1966). Forms and transformations of narcissism. *Journal of the American Psychoanalytic Association*, 14, 243–272.

Kohut, H. (1971). *The analysis of the self*. New York, NY: International Universities Press.

Kohut, H. (1977). *The restoration of the self*. New York, NY: International Universities Press.

Kohut, H., & Wolf, E. (1978). The disorders of the self and their treatment: An outline. *International Journal of Psychoanalysis*, 59, 413–425.

Kris, E. (1936). The psychology of caricature. *International Journal of Psychoanalysis*, 17, 285–303.

Levine, H. (1979). The sustaining object relationship. In *The annual of psychoanalysis*, 7 (pp. 261–262). New York, NY: International Universities Press.

Main, T.F. (1957). The ailment. *British Journal of Medical Psychology*, 30, 129–145.

Winnicott, D.W. (1952). Anxiety associated with insecurity. In *Collected papers* (1958, pp. 97–100). London: Tavistock.

Winnicott, D.W. (1960). Ego distortion in terms of true and false self. In *The maturational processes and the facilitating environment* (1965, pp. 140–152). London: Hogarth Press.

Wolf, E. (1976). Ambience and abstinence. In *The annual of psychoanalysis*, 4 (pp. 101–115). New York, NY: International Universities Press.

3 Optimal Responsiveness and the Therapeutic Process

The publication of Heinz Kohut's landmark work The Restoration of the Self *(1977) established optimal frustration as a central aspect of the curative process viewed from the perspective of self psychology. With one of his critics (his son), Kohut (personal communication, 1977) recognized the problematic nature of the question "What is optimal?" yet he never arrived at a satisfactory answer. Instead, Bacal argues that optimal responsiveness, defined as response tailored to each patient's unique needs, promotes therapeutic growth. Empathy, or vicarious introspection, is the process by which the therapist comes to understand the patient by attuning to his inner world. Optimal responsiveness refers to the therapist's acts of communicating his/her understanding to the patient that promotes specifically needed therapeutic experience. This approach, which is illustrated by a clinical example, can involve a variety of interventions beyond traditional verbal interpretation, reflecting the complexities of each therapeutic relationship.*

Although tacitly accepted as an important element in the therapeutic practice of psychoanalysis, the concept of *optimal frustration* has received little theoretical clarification. The publication of Heinz Kohut's (1977) landmark work *The Restoration of the Self* established optimal frustration as a central aspect of the curative process viewed from the perspective of self psychology. With one of his critics, Kohut (personal communication, 1977) recognized the problematic nature of the question "What is optimal?," yet he never arrived at a satisfactory answer.

I intend to reexamine this question in light of the related issue of "optimal gratification." My purpose is, in part, to demonstrate the significance of the latter, which has until recently been regarded with some suspicion as a form of countertransference acting-in, evoked perhaps by the patient's acting-in in the transference; as a manipulation of the transference itself by the analyst deliberately adopting a role (the so-called "corrective emotional experience" of Alexander, 1956); or, at most, as a useful but temporary parameter to be discarded at the first possible opportunity.

I will suggest that any discussion of the concepts of optimal frustration and optimal gratification becomes inevitably entangled in insurmountable theoretical difficulties and endless debate when separated from the more useful and

DOI: 10.4324/9781003570806-4

encompassing idea of *optimal responsiveness*, defined as the responsivity of the analyst that is therapeutically most relevant at any particular moment in the context of a particular patient and his illness. Empathy or vicarious introspection is the process by which the therapist comes to understand the patient by tuning in to his inner world. Optimal responsiveness, on the other hand, refers to the therapist's acts of communicating his understanding to his patient.

Optimal Frustration

The origin of the term "optimal frustration" is not clear. Although he credits Bernfeld (1928) with its first mention, Kohut (1972) appears to have first applied it to the psychoanalytic process. The idea of optimal frustration, however, has always been a cornerstone of psychoanalytic treatment. As early as 1946, Anna Freud wrote

> [As analysts,] we have to play a double game with the patient's instinctual impulses, on the one hand encouraging them to express themselves and, on the other, steadily refusing them gratification—a procedure which incidentally gives rise to one of the numerous difficulties in the handling of analytic technique.
>
> (p. 13)

> ... the ego [of the patient] is victorious when its defensive measures effect their purpose ... and so transform the instincts that, even in difficult circumstances, some measure of gratification is secured ...
>
> (p. 193)

However, the "measure of gratification" to which Miss Freud referred was not regarded as an aspect of the analytic process, but as one of its results.

While still working within the classical psychoanalytic perspective, Kohut and Seitz (1963) 61. Kotin sites 1963.defined optimal frustration as an experience that is intrinsically related to that of gratification in the therapeutic process:

> By contrast, optimal frustrations involve sufficient delay in satisfaction to induce tension-increase and disappointment in the attempt to obtain wish-fulfillment through fantasy; the real satisfaction occurs quickly enough, however, to prevent a despairing and disillusioned turning away from reality.
>
> (p. 356)

Kohut indicates that the infantile impulses that have encountered optimal frustration are transformed into neutralizing psychological structure by the internalization of innumerable experiences of optimal frustration, but that "[t]he barrier of defences, on the other hand, which walls off an unmodified residue of infantile strivings, is the result of the internalization of frustrating experiences and prohibitions of traumatic intensity" (Kohut & Seitz, 1963, p. 369).

In other words, *optimal* frustration of instinctual impulses promotes the development of internal structure comprised of transformed, or sublimated, instinctual drives; whereas *traumatic* frustration causes a protective barrier to be built up around these impulses, which are left unchanged. Gratification, or "real satisfaction," must be an inherent element of the therapeutic process at some point and in some measure, or else "optimal" frustration will be anything but optimal. Yet, Kohut and Seitz do not satisfactorily define what optimal frustration and its associated optimal gratification amount to in the psychoanalytic process. Nor, to my knowledge, has this theoretical lacuna been redressed elsewhere.

In *The Analysis of the Self*, Kohut (1971) reiterates his position, still within a classical framework, but focuses now upon the importance of optimal frustration for narcissistic equilibrium rather than for drive modulation:

> as continues to hold true for the analogous later milieu of the child, the most important aspect of the earliest mother–infant relationship is the principal of optimal frustration. Tolerable disappointments in the pre-existing (and externally sustained) primary narcissistic equilibrium lead to the establishment of internal structures which provide the ability for self-soothing and the acquisition of basic tension tolerance in the narcissistic realm.
>
> (p. 64)

> … The skillful analyst will assist the patient in keeping the patient's discomfort [vis-à-vis the necessary, i.e., therapeutic, frustration of the narcissistic transferences] within tolerable limits; i.e., he will conduct the analysis according to the principle of optimal frustration.
>
> (p. 199)[1]

Further, Kohut (1972) stated that omnipotent objects "become internalized every time the child discovers a flaw in them, providing the discovery is not of traumatic degree but optimally frustrating" (p. 869).

Kohut thus saw optimal frustration as central to the process of transmuting internalization, which he regarded as the essence of the process of analytic cure. As he wrote five years later,

> Little by little as a result of innumerable processes of microinternalization, the anxiety-assuaging, delay-tolerating, and other realistic aspects of the analyst's image become part of the analysand's psychological equipment, *pari-passu* with the *micro-frustration* [my italics] of the analysand's need for the analyst's permanent presence and perfect functioning in this respect. In brief, through the process of transmuting internalization [via optimal frustration] new psychological structure is built.
>
> (Kohut, 1977, p. 32)

Kohut (1977), however, also questions the validity of the view that some individuals with severe psychopathology have had caring mothers who, in attempting to gratify their children's wishes, have deprived them of the optimal frustration that would have enabled them to develop a mature ego. While acknowledging the possibility that these individuals might not have been sufficiently frustrated as children, he suggests that the determinants of their illness appeared to be more complex when viewed from the perspective of an analysis conducted on the basis of self psychology. By way of illustration, he cites his account of Mr. U whose

> mother and grandmother had ... apparently acted out an unconscious fantasy of their own [in] gratifying the child's drive wishes for their own purposes. Fully in tune with his every drive demand, they simultaneously disregarded the boy's maturing changing self, which cried out for a maternal (and later also paternal) confirming-admiring responses and approval [of his own capacities. The boy's fixation on a fetish] was therefore essentially not the result of overgratification but of a specific traumatic absence of maternal empathy for the healthy grandiosity and the healthy exhibitionism of his forming independent self.
>
> (p. 79)

Although Kohut recognizes that insufficient frustration or "excessive gratification" may contribute to psychopathology, he suggests that the pathogenic factor is not the "overgratification" of some instinct, but the accompanying traumatic insufficiency of recognition and "gratification" of a selfobject need. In this context, it is instructive to recall an aphorism that Kohut (1977) introduced in a now-famous passage in *The Restoration of the Self*:

> Man can no more survive psychologically in a psychological milieu that does not respond empathically to him than he can survive physically in an atmosphere that contains no oxygen ... the analyst's behaviour vis-à-vis his patient should be the expected average one—i.e., the behaviour of a psychologically perceptive person vis-à-vis someone who is suffering and has entrusted himself to him for help.
>
> (p. 253)

There is an apparent contradiction between this view and the recognition of the therapeutically beneficial effects of frustration. In order to explore this contradiction intelligibly, it is necessary to consider the difference between "optimal" *frustration* and "traumatic" *frustration*, and *their* relationship to so-called "empathic failure."

Optimal Frustration and Traumatic Frustration

Let me say at once that the notion of empathic failure by parental selfobjects cannot by itself answer the question of what is traumatic, since it is likely that not all empathic failures lead to long-range deleterious effects on the psyche of the child. Indeed, since optimal frustration by selfobjects is regarded as essential to the growth and development of the self, empathic failure by selfobjects in childhood, as well as by the analyst as selfobject at a later stage, should according to this theory be welcomed. The central issue, both developmentally and in analysis, is what will lead to structural deficit or defect and what will be "optimal," in the sense of curative, leading to transmuting internalization of experience that is structure-building or fault-reparative?

The question still remains, however, what is "traumatic"? The earliest conception of trauma focused on isolated events, in particular on sexual seductions. The idea of trauma as the product of ongoing processes and relationships was not recognized before the contributions of such object-relations theorists as Balint, Winnicott, and Masud Khan (1963) with his notion of cumulative trauma. All would agree, however, that trauma involves a degree of intensity that is too great for the ego to master and has far-reaching effects on psychic organization. For example, Kris (1956) distinguished between "shock trauma," the effect of a single powerful experience impinging on the child, and "strain trauma," the accumulation of frustrating tensions. Kris, however, did not emphasize the quality of the relationship, but conceived these events as occurring within a drive-tension-discharge model (Kligman, 1983). Kohut and Seitz (1963) also regarded the quantitative factor as a distinguishing element of trauma, but they also suggested that the qualitative factor was significant:

> The differences between experience of traumatic and optimal frustration are differences in degree. It is the difference between one mother's harsh "N-o!" and another mother's kindly "No." It is the difference between a frightening kind of prohibition on the one hand, and an educational experience, on the other. It is the difference between one father's handling a child's temper tantrum by an equally hostile counter-tantrum and another father's picking up the child and calming him—firm but non-aggressive, and loving but not seductive. It is the difference between an uncompromising prohibition, which stresses only what the child must not have or cannot do, and the offering of acceptable substitutes for the forbidden object or activity.
>
> (pp. 369–370)

According to Balint (1969), there are three conditions or phases associated with the occurrence of trauma. In the first stage of the traumatic process, the relationship between the child and the potentially traumatogenic object must be characterized by a certain intensity and be a mainly trusting and loving one. Trauma occurs, in this situation, when the adult does something highly exciting, frightening, or painful, either once and quite suddenly, or repeatedly. This action may involve an excess of tenderness or cruelty, whether or not sexuality is involved, and may result in severe overstimulation of the child or, if the child's approaches are ignored, in rejection and deep disappointment. The first two phases outlined by Balint are necessary but not sufficient to produce trauma. In order for trauma to occur the adult must act with indifference toward the child's experience, whether excitement or rejection.

Balint's thesis goes beyond merely quantitative considerations pertaining to the degree or intensity of traumatic experience (i.e., the field of one-person psychology) to the study of the quality of object-relationship (i.e., the field of two-person or multi-person psychology). In this way, Balint extends the work of Ferenczi (1933) who suggested that the real shock to the psychic organization of the child who is interfered with sexually is the adult's betrayal of the child's trust. The trauma derives from the fact that the child's tender or playful love is mistaken for passion and either responded to or rejected and is not primarily due to the stimulation or frustration of the child's innate sexual drives.

Classical analysis, however, fails to make a meaningful distinction between the pathogenic and the pathogenic that is also traumatic—a distinction, I would suggest, that is of great clinical importance. This failure on the part of classical analysts and current object-relations theorists stems from their attempt to understand the effects of the environment in the context of a theoretical position that is essentially a one-person psychology, where excessive or pathological drives are regarded as the determinants of the psychopathology. From the self-psychological perspective, this is not an issue, as the theory presupposes that psychopathology results from a failure of environmental response to the needs of the child's developing self. Although Winnicott adopted this position quite early, he did not systematically explore its clinical significance. Self psychologists, on the other hand, have only recently adopted the insight of early object-relations theorists such as Balint regarding the specific quality of the relationship between a particular child and a particular parent as the context of pathogenesis, and that between a particular therapist and a particular patient as the context in which pathology is potentially resolvable. In both cases, the relationship is a product of the interaction of two vulnerabilities and two capacities, those of the parent and those of the child and, later, those of the analyst and those of his patient (Stolorow, Brandchaft, and Atwood, 1983).

It has never been our intention, as analysts, to either traumatize or frustrate our patients, however optimally, but to understand them. Consequently the notion of optimal frustration is not tenable as a working clinical concept; however, the idea of optimal gratification conceivably could be. For to be understood can be deeply gratifying and is perhaps the most important function performed for us by our selfobjects. It is possible that the gratification of being understood by one's selfobject is of central importance in the curative process. If internal structure could not be built and defect repaired through the experience of being understood, the analyst would be wasting much of his time doing good work instead of making calculated errors thought to lead to manageable disruptions between himself and the patient and, thus, to transmuting internalization through the associated optimal frustration and its understanding. This is obviously unsatisfactory, and brings to mind the so-called "corrective emotional experience" of Alexander (1956) in which the analyst adopted the role that he considered to be the opposite of that of the pathogenic nuclear object. This confusion can be resolved if we reflect that no one comes for understanding unless they feel they have not been understood. As analysts, we are constantly confronted with a complex spectrum of varying degrees and kinds of frustrated need for understanding, sometimes of a traumatic order. Our responses must satisfy (a better word, perhaps, than gratify) the frustrated need for understanding of a particular patient or they will not be helpful. We will, as therapists, make mistakes, if only as a result of the analytic inertia that is inherent in our technique and, thus, inadvertently trigger or intensify the patient's frustration. The patient, moreover, will inevitably reenact his frustration with us in an attempt to right the original wrong. In many, perhaps in the majority of instances, if we understand, as and when our patients need us to, frustration will not be a factor in the therapeutic process. We are not analytic machines, however, and upon the not infrequent occasions when we fail, when we are in a state of empathic lapse, or when our responsive understanding is not accurate, we will encounter a patient who is frustrated with us.

The term "optimal" means "a condition, degree or compromise that produces the best possible result" (Collins English Dictionary, 1979, p. 1032). Since our approach to psychoanalytic therapy is to do the best we can and we do not, indeed we cannot, set out optimally to frustrate our patients, I suggest that the idea of optimal frustration is really an after-the-fact metapsychological explanation of what happens when the analytic relationship breaks down, retrievably. From the patient's point of view, it breaks down when his selfobject needs are greater than the analyst's capacity to understand and respond at a particular moment.[2] Furthermore, the patient's apparent stubborn resistance and "negative therapeutic reaction" may not represent an intention to defeat the analyst, but are caused, at that moment, by the breakdown of the analyst's empathy and the patient's incapacity for reciprocal empathic resonance (Bacal, 1979; Brandchaft, 1983; Wolf, 1981). When, however, the "intersubjective disjunction" cannot be resolved, even by an honest scrutiny of countertransference, and a "decentered" (Stolorow, Brandchaft, and Atwood, 1983) perspective on the part of the analyst, it may be useful to consider whether the patient's feeling that he is not optimally responded to may be attributable to a traumatic injury or frustration that has caused a defect or deficit in the self, that is, whether he has been seriously hurt in a state of extreme vulnerability (Balint, 1968, 1969). I propose that an experience is traumatic to the psyche of the child if it has apparently caused a degree of defect or significant enfeeblement of the self, in our patients, that is not responsive to ordinary interpretative work. This operational definition of traumatic experience can be crucially important as a guide in our treatment of those patients for whom the resumption of selfobject relatedness, after disruption, is especially difficult to achieve, and sometimes impossible to restore by ordinary analytic work—even in instances where both patient and analyst agree they are grappling with the relevant issues.

Freud, "in the social matrix of his time ... felt constrained to publicly overemphasize restraint and austerity in analytic practice in order to mute criticism engendered by having placed sexuality, and particularly infantile sexuality, at the center of his scientific investigations" (Wolf, 1976, p. 104). While this was an understandable concern in Freud's day, I would agree with Wolf's (1976) assertion that "contemporary psychoanalysts need rather less constraint and more freedom to engage the analysand in the analytic process" (p. 104), because of the increasing numbers of patients whose pathology is the result of serious disorders of the self. The real "danger" inherent in the analytic situation is not the possibility that the analyst might respond sexually to his patient, as such behavior is governed by moral and ethical principles and cannot seriously be regarded as a valid part of the therapeutic process. The danger is rather that the analyst, by assiduously or rigidly avoiding any interaction with his patient except that of verbal exchange, may mistake a regressively repetitive transference for acting-in and repeat and perpetuate the childhood experience that caused the self defect or developmental arrest in the first place and, in this way, miss the patient's bid for a *creative transference relatedness*.

Freud's counsel to frustrate the patient's wish for libidinal gratification has, unfortunately, often been taken as a directive to block all satisfaction within the analytic situation. As Wolf (1976) noted,

> a misreading of this rule of abstinence creates a cold and critical ambience and will result in transference artifacts that are easily mistaken for derivatives of aggressive drives (p. 113) ... Ideally the psychoanalytic situation ought to be constructed in such a way as to yield the optimally facilitating ambience for the ongoing psychoanalytic process.
>
> (p. 111)

Interpretation and Therapeutic Relationship

Balint (1969) argued that we have

> two major therapeutic methods, one of which is interpretation and the other the creation of a therapeutic relationship between the patient and ourselves. Compared with the first, the techniques for the second method have been much less well studied and it is important that we should start investigating them.
>
> (p. 435)

The self-psychological understanding of the therapeutic process and its associated analytic technique more closely represents a synthesis of these two facets of therapy, "interpretation and relationship," than the traditional psychoanalytic model. There are, however, contradictions and inconsistencies still to be resolved.

For some time, Kohut was undecided as to whether interpretation or relationship is the fundamental therapeutic component in psychoanalysis. In *The Restoration of the Self*, Kohut (1977, p. 31) held that interpretation and insight are not in themselves what cure the patient, but are the means by which the essential curative factor, the beneficial structural transformation of the self, is effected. For example, Kohut described his work with Mr. M as follows:

> [The analyst's] attention is focused predominantly on the analysand's subjective transference experiences and, on the basis of his understanding of their form and content, [he] reconstructs the experiential world of the patient's childhood during the genetically decisive junctures … . In Mr. M's case, the essential psychological fact (the reactivation of the decisive genetic determinant …) was that he experienced his mother, and in the transference the analyst, as traumatically unempathic vis-à-vis his emotional demands and as unresponsive to them. True enough, the analyst might occasionally wish to point out (in order to retain a realistic framework—if, for example, because of the intensity of the frustrations he experiences in the transferences, the patient might seriously consider quitting the analysis) that the patient's expectations and demands belong to his childhood and are unrealistic in the present. And he might at the appropriate moment also wish to explain to the patient that the intensity of his childhood needs may have led to a distortion of his perceptions of the past (in Mr. M's case, to a falsification of his perception of his adoptive mother's personality). The essential structural transformations produced by working through do not take place, however, in consequence of such supportive intellectual insights, but in consequence of the gradual internalizations that are brought about by the fact that the old experiences are repeatedly relived by the more mature psyche.
>
> (pp. 29–30)

By reliving these early experiences *with the analyst* the patient transmutes (i.e., converts and assimilates) into his self structure the "anxiety-assuaging, delay-tolerating, and other realistic aspects of the analyst's image" (p. 32)—that is, the function of the analyst as a selfobject.

Although Kohut never explicitly addressed the issue of interpretation and relationship as complementary aspects of therapeutic work, the clinical process in psychoanalytic self psychology illuminates their interacting functions. In effect, Kohut emphasizes the curative effect of relationship.

If optimal frustration has not occurred here, but rather understanding and explanation, must we conclude that transmuting internalization and related structure building have not taken place and that the apparent therapeutic gain will be shown during the termination phase to be illusory? As I have already indicated, the patient brings *to* the analyst his frustration at not being understood so that any additional frustration caused by the analyst's lack of understanding cannot be regarded as optimal. In this situation, the interaction between the analyst and patient does not generate frustration; rather, the analyst recognizes the frustration that the patient brings to him and the patient feels understood by his response. In Wolf's (1981) terms, harmonious or reciprocal empathic resonance takes place between analyst and patient: "At the moment that I really understand what is going on in the analysand, I also know that he really understands what I am doing" (p. 7). The accuracy of the analyst's empathic insights is confirmed by the patient's expression of his own empathic grasp of the analyst's psychological activity at that moment. A process of transmutation of the analyst's functions into the patient has begun. The interaction has been optimal from both the analyst's and the patient's point of view and neither need question the appropriateness of the gratification he receives in this way.

As this suggests that frustration is not a necessary condition for transmuting internalization and real structure building to occur, what, if any, is the therapeutic element in the working through of "optimal" frustration? According to the clinical model emphasizing optimal frustration, the patient's reaction to the therapist's supposedly empathically derived communication (or silence) tells the analyst that he has not been attuned to his patient's psychological state. The patient's frustration is manifested in resistance[3] until, under favorable circumstances, the analyst is able to overcome his empathic lag (Bacal, 1979) and perhaps, in addition, achieve an increased awareness of some aspects of his countertransference. Finally, the process of mutative interpretation is completed by a careful analysis of the events that precipitated the disruption and, concomitantly, of the analogous childhood experiences.

In this situation, the analyst believes that his interpretation is empathically correct until the patient's response makes him reconsider its accuracy. Simultaneous with the correction and clarification of the transference disruption, the analyst is able to restore the previous harmonious selfobject relationship with the patient and, in the process, a transmuting internalization occurs.

If both the foregoing processes are therapeutic, what is the common curative element? It is, I believe, the patient's experience of the analyst's *optimal responsiveness*; and the quality of the therapeutic relationship at that moment confirms, for the analyst, that his response is usable by the patient. In the second example, the resumption of the harmonious selfobject relationship is therapeutic, not because the understanding of disruption is therapeutic, but because *understanding* is therapeutic.

Although interpretation is the principal means through which the analyst conveys optimal responsiveness to his patients, it may not be a sufficient or appropriate expression of responsiveness in every case. The continuing controversy among psychoanalysts as to what constitutes a valid addition or alternative to interpretation is due to our failure to evolve a framework for the systematic consideration of the *psychoanalytic* nature of the therapeutic relationship and how it relates to the interpretive process.[4] Acceptance of the importance of *relationship* for the analytic process has until recently been limited to the recognition of the part it plays in the so-called working or therapeutic alliance. Although Wolf's (1976) recognition of an analytic ambience that is therapeutic represents an important advance, most analysts consider the therapeutic aspects of relationship in treatment as a necessary evil, or at best, as a temporary parameter making possible the resumption of the "real" analysis. As analysts, we evade this issue because it raises the specter of transference and countertransference acting-in. Those of us who have extended the scope of psychoanalytic treatment to include the more serious disorders of severely traumatized people, however, have found an in-depth understanding of the analytically legitimate therapeutic aspects of our relationship with our patients increasingly important.

Optimal Responsiveness and the Developmental Line of Empathy

In his final address to the fourth annual self psychology conference, Kohut (1981) stated that the most important insight contained in *How Does Analysis Cure?* is that "analysis [ultimately] cures by giving explanations, i.e., interpretations ..." He maintained that the analyst must proceed from understanding to explanation, from showing that he is attuned to his patient's inner life, his feelings, thoughts, and fantasies, to the next step, interpretation. Kohut (1981) defined the advance from understanding to interpretation as a progression "from a lower form of empathy to a higher form of empathy," and described the analogous development within the individual with the following example:

> a child and the mother are in the park. The child was a young child who clung to the mother. The sun was shining, pigeons were walking around there. All of a sudden, the child felt a new buoyancy and daring and it moved away from the mother toward the pigeons. He goes three or four steps and then he looks back. The general interpretation of that is that he is anxious, he wants to be sure he can come back, to be encased in her arms, cradled, et cetera. That is true, but something more important is true. He wants to see the mother's proud smile; he wants to see her pride [looking] at him walking out now, on his own—isn't that wonderful—and at this moment, something extremely important had happened: a low form of empathy, a body-close form of empathy expressed in holding and touching ... is now expressed only in facial expression and perhaps later in words: I am proud of you, my boy.

Kohut (1981) believed that interpretation in psychoanalysis performs a parallel function for the patient as these events in the development of the child. In this process, the "bodily holding" or "merger" phase is superseded by a much higher form of empathy, verbal interpretation, which is a psychological message on a more evolved level of understanding. In the case of the severely damaged patient, this process may be a very prolonged one.

As we have already noted, Kohut was for some time undecided as to whether interpretation or relationship is the therapeutic component in psychoanalysis. Although he maintained at different times that it was not interpretation but the relationship that essentially cured, he still firmly believed in the healing capacity of insight. Kohut's (1981) recent view, that progress in the therapeutic process from understanding to interpretation represents a parallel advance on the part of the patient from a lower to a higher level of what he called the developmental line of empathy, integrates the two major methods of psychoanalysis and confirms the intuitive conviction of many analysts that interpretation and relationship are both curative. This is not merely an academic or semantic issue, but has practical implications for the way we respond as psychoanalysts and as psychoanalytic psychotherapists to our patients. Kohut (1981) felt that future research in self psychology should concentrate upon the continuum of empathic stages, "the developmental line of empathy,[5] from its early archaic beginnings to such high levels as barely touching, as barely still having any trace of the original holding that communicates the empathic understanding."

This issue, I believe, can be addressed most effectively in terms of the concept of optimal responsiveness. The analytic attitude that is here termed "optimal responsiveness" is described by Wolf (1976) as follows:

> The decision about a proper response to a patient's demand, be it experienced ever so subtly or directly, must depend upon a proper dynamic understanding of the current analytic situation, its transference implications, and the genetic background. It is thus no different from any other analytic understanding or intervention. Whether to comply enthusiastically or reluctantly, whether to refuse firmly or hesitatingly, or not to respond at all, these decisions belong to the armamentarium of alternative action to be used in accordance with one's total understanding of the analytic process. (p. 107)

Earlier, Winnicott (personal communication, 1967) expressed a similar concern when he stated that the analyst's true function is not to provide the correct interpretation, but to be available to respond with understanding that is appropriate and useful to his patient. In self-psychological terms, the analyst's response must be commensurate with the patient's level of self-selfobject organization or the degree of intactness, defect, or deficit within the self.

In the majority of cases this response is communicated largely through verbal interpretation. Changes in the patient population, however, require corresponding changes in the analyst's vocabulary of response. Kohut (1981) recognized the need on the part of analysts for greater freedom to respond to their understanding of their patients in a passage that, because of its controversial nature, has had insufficient attention from self psychologists who are understandably reluctant to adopt a position that might expose them, however unjustifiably, to accusations of engaging in the "corrective emotional experience" advocated by Alexander (1956):

> the more one knows, the less one needs to stick to some ritual anxiously, because one *knows* [my italics] what is appropriate and inappropriate. The question [relates] to treating patients with very severe self disorders who cannot possibly benefit from interpretations for [a very long time, perhaps even] many years. They do need an empathic understanding on the closest

> level we can muster. It does not mean we cannot naturally move slowly and gradually into higher forms of empathy[6] [the form of optimal responsiveness that we call explaining or interpreting to the patient] much later on.
>
> (Kohut, 1981)

Kohut (1981) supports this controversial view with a clinical example drawn from the lengthy analysis of an extremely vulnerable woman patient:

> She lay down on the couch the first time she came, having interrupted a previous analysis abruptly and she said she felt like she was lying in a coffin and that now the top of the coffin would be closed with a sharp click ... she was deeply depressed and at times I thought I would lose her, and that she would finally find a way out of the suffering and kill herself ... . [A]t one time at the very worst moment of her analysis during ... perhaps a year and a half, she was so badly off I suddenly had the feeling—you know, how would you feel if I let you hold my fingers for a while now while you are talking, maybe that would help. A doubtful maneuver. I am not recommending it but I was desperate. I was deeply worried. So I ... moved up a little bit in my chair and gave her two fingers. And now I'll tell you what is so nice about that story. Because an analyst always remains an analyst. I gave her my two fingers, she took hold of them and I immediately made a genetic interpretation—to myself. It was the toothless gums of a very young child clamping down on an empty nipple. That is the way it felt. I didn't say anything ... but I reacted to it even there as an analyst to myself. It was never necessary anymore. I wouldn't say that it turned the tide, but it overcame a very, very difficult impasse at a given dangerous moment and, gaining time that way, we went on for many years with a reasonably substantial success.

Kohut is not alone in responding to his patient in this way. Although few analysts have admitted to similar experiences,[7] Winnicott (1947) recognized the appropriateness in certain situations of this kind of intervention:

> There is a vast difference between those patients who have had satisfactory early experiences which can be discovered in the transference, and those whose very early experiences have been so deficient or distorted that the analyst has to be the first in the patient's life to supply certain environmental essentials. In the treatment of a patient of the latter kind all sorts of things in analytic technique become vitally important, things that can be taken for granted in the treatment of patients of the former type.
>
> (p. 198)

The important clinical issue raised by Winnicott concerns what response on the part of the analyst can be considered optimal in relation to the patient's level of organization of his self-selfobject relationships. This level, as one would expect, corresponds to the position the patient has achieved on the developmental line of empathy.[8]

The empty nipple for Kohut's patient was the antithesis of a selfobject that would satisfy her selfobject need (not only drive need) to suck. Other selfobject needs may require a responsiveness for which verbal interpretation will not do and we need to study the significance of these optimal responses for the patient, for example, the warmth provided by the analyst's blanket, or the thirst or faintness that elicits a drink,[9] as well as other needs that may be related to the "psychological survival of the self."

In my opinion, there is no such thing as a "parameter," an extraanalytic, or unanalytic, measure we adopt for a time in order ultimately to return to doing proper analysis in the traditional way. We must respond in ways that enable us to communicate understanding to the particular patient with whom we are working. That is analysis.

Optimal Responsiveness and the Repetitive and Creative Aspects of Transference

The concept of transference can be usefully reexamined in light of the idea of optimal responsiveness. As no one simply repeats pathological patterns and distortions, selfobject transferences are better understood as *creative aspects of transference*, since their aim is to forge a link with a selfobject that will be a better version of the old one. This is true of virtually every patient, but particularly significant with respect to severely traumatized individuals in whom the development of the self has been seriously impeded. These patients sometimes create what I have called a *fantasy selfobject* (Bacal, 1981) around a nuclear figure whose archaic idealization or mirroring function has virtually no counterpart in the patient's antecedent experiences.

The creative aspect of transference has to do with the area of illusion, the area of play, and what Winnicott (1951) called "the transitional object" and "transitional phenomena." The experience of this kind of illusion is necessary in order for dis-illusion to not become disillusionment and traumatic frustration in analysis. Then and only then will the inevitable dis-illusion with a new version of the old selfobject, now recognizable as "good-enough" in Winnicott's terms, become associated with the ability to tolerate the fact that one's fantasy may or may not always elicit the response for which one hoped. This, in my opinion, is the only frustration that can be considered "optimal," non-traumatic frustration that alternates and is interwoven with the building of developmentally essential illusion associated with experience of a new responsive selfobject. In this way, confidence in the possibility of a "good-enough" selfobject can begin to develop. In this way, an optimal experience with the analyst can occur in which self defect or faulty self structure is repaired and new self structure can be built. Both analyst and patient should feel that progress is resulting from this process. The patient should feel stronger and be able to deal more effectively with the stresses specific to his particular vulnerability. Similarly, disruptions of such an inordinately painful degree that the patient recurrently feels that he cannot go on with the analysis should not occur.

These ideas assume that there is a basic tendency toward growth and development in every individual that requires the optimal responsiveness of the selfobject in order to be realized. This is, I believe, the implicit assumption that underlies all psychotherapeutic efforts, whether psychoanalytic or not. The concept of "optimal frustration" mainly serves to give analysis respectability. It "proves" we don't think of ourselves as gratifying our patients when we treat them. Related to this image of the hard path that the patient must travel toward cure is that of fixation points of the libido and the idea that patients will adhere to these positions to which they have regressed unless confronted with reality or with the deleterious effects of their continuing to function in their archaic ways with objects. According to this perspective, unless patients are optimally frustrated and exhorted to progress they will simply be gratified by the understanding, demand more and more, and remain where they are. An even less fortunate outcome of "gratification" is said to be the so-called "malignant regression" (Balint, 1968) in which the analyst's accession to the patient's demands is thought to produce a spiral of negative, resistive, clinging, and increasingly demanding attitudes. In a previous paper (Bacal, 1981), I attempted to distinguish therapeutic regression from malignant regression on the basis of their genesis: therapeutic regression occurs as a result of accurate empathic responsiveness; while malignant regression occurs as a result of catastrophic selfobject failure in patients with particularly vulnerable selves. The latter tend to be those whose selfobjects have been predominantly fantasy selfobjects and who, as children, have been pervasively related to by their significant nuclear figures *as* selfobjects.

An optimal synthesis between the experience of the creative selfobject transference and the working through of the repetitive transference is necessary. Before he can usefully allow himself to experience the old unempathic selfobject in the new selfobject constituted by the analyst, the patient's self must become stronger as a result of a good deal of positive interaction with this new version of the old selfobject. Sometimes, even where the good selfobject is not of the order of a fantasy selfobject, the analyst may have to be experienced by the patient as a good selfobject separately from the old selfobject, and it is countertherapeutic to interpret this self-reparative move as "pathological splitting." Rather, it must be accepted as creative transference relatedness,[10] perhaps for some time. However, the split-off good selfobject in these cases *is* often the good *fantasy selfobject*; and, in this situation, when the experience of the split-off bad selfobject occurs in the transference, the patient may fragment dangerously. At these moments, the analyst virtually becomes for the patient the original traumatically unempathic or unavailable archaic selfobject (Bacal, 1981); and situations of this sort may be just barely retrievable. I believe that Kohut (1977) may have had something like this in mind when he suggested that defensive structures may sometimes usefully be left intact and that analytic working through in these cases will be carried out predominantly in the area of compensatory structures. The criticism that this would be merely supportive psychotherapy is undermined by the recognition that working through in the area of compensatory structures is related to the creative aspect of transference.

Resistance and Countertransference

A reexamination of resistance and countertransference will throw further light on the relevance of the clinical usefulness of the concept of optimal responsiveness. Resistance in classical analysis refers to the patient's inability or reluctance to participate in the analytic process co-operatively, that is, to free associate. The patient's silence, controlling, acting-in, or acting-out is attributed to his fear of the consequences of expressing his instinctual drives in relation to the analyst. From the perspective of self psychology, resistance to the analytic process is seen as reflecting a fear of retraumatization through repetition in the analytic relationship of traumatic childhood experiences. This fear is sometimes justified by the analyst's countertransference, of which the patient is usually aware, and which the analyst should not only analyze in himself but judiciously acknowledge to the patient. In some instances, in order for the inevitable frustrations of the patient by the analyst to be non-traumatic and even potentially useful by enhancing the patient's trust in the analyst and contributing to the working through process, the analyst will not only acknowledge this countertransference, but respond to the distress it occasioned with an explanation that his patient can manage and assimilate. Of course, the analyst must not burden the patient with his own problems.

The analyst works within the inevitable limits of his understanding and his countertransference. His personality will determine, to some extent, his capacity to provide an optimal therapeutic experience for his patient. An analyst who is committed to providing an ambience of replenishing deficits will not provide a patient who needs to engage in recurrent disruptions with his analyst (in order to repeat his pathological nuclear situations for the purpose of healing his self defects) with the analysis he requires. Alternatively, an analyst who is committed to the working through of optimal frustration (that is, transference disruptions) will provide the patient who needs developmental experience with a new selfobject and an understanding of this experience with an analysis that may be worse than useless. Often, of course, both are necessary for analytic progress. It is important for us to consider what I would regard as the clinical counterpart of Winnicott's (1952) assertion that "there is no such thing as a baby, ... [there is rather] a nursing couple" (p. 99), the idea that "there is no such thing as a patient, there is only an analytic couple." A good match between the analyst and the patient does not have to be present at the outset. It may evolve as a result of the analyst's willingness to scrutinize the intersubjective context in which his interactions with his patient occur (Stolorow, Brandchaft, and Atwood, 1983), and from his capacity to respond in a relevant way.

The following clinical example may help to illustrate and integrate the central concepts and issues we have been discussing.

In her first analytic session, Dr. M, a psychologist in her late 20s, reported a dream that she had not long after her initial interview with her analyst, which took place a few weeks prior to the beginning of the analysis. She prefaced her account of the dream by what was, in effect, an association to it: she said how much she appreciated the generous gesture of the analyst friend who called the prospective analyst to prepare the way for her referral. In the dream the friend appeared as a taxi driver and drove her to a bridge where he said that he had forgotten the analyst's phone number and address. As she searched in her purse for the directions, the contents, her money, and things she had on her mind fell out. Her son called "Mommy" to her and, as at home, everything was once again pulling at her.

Although the analyst recognized even then that the dream would have significance for the whole analysis, its meaning was only partially apparent at that time. The interpretation reached, although tentative and incomplete, was that, despite her hope that her relationship with the analyst (whom she associated with her analyst friend) would enable her to enter a world in which she might receive the generosity of which she felt deprived by her parents, she feared she would again be caught up in a relationship in which she would be traumatized by being exposed to and emptied by another's limitless needs and demands.

A few months after the analysis started, she began to convey to her analyst her increasing anxiety about her financial situation. Although she earned a very good salary compared to a number of her colleagues, she was having serious trouble maintaining her standard of living largely because of the meanness and vindictiveness of her estranged husband with regard to child support for her three children.

Proud of her ability to manage independently, it was with great difficulty, embarrassment, and hesitation that she asked the analyst for a small decrease in her fee. He agreed, and there soon followed a second request for a substantial decrease, a request that was associated with continuing anxiety about her ability to cope financially. The analyst was initially reluctant to comply with this second request and the situation was discussed over a number of weeks. Dr. M reacted to her analyst's reluctance with a complex mixture of desperate insistence, anger, increasing tension and anxiety, as well as with a continuing sense of shame at having to make the request. Attempts to analyze the issue led only to a heightening of the tension and the analysis showed signs of breaking down. Finally, the analyst acquiesced and told his patient that he was acceding to her implied request to pay nothing more than the amount that the national health insurance would reimburse her, until such time as she felt she could pay. He also explained that, while he knew that she was aware only of the economic determinants of her need and he was not denying the importance of these factors, he felt the psychological one to be paramount, although at the moment he was not completely cognizant of its significance.

After this, the impasse disappeared, and analytic work resumed. The unfolding of the significant issues and events of her childhood revealed that when she was three years old, her father, with whom she apparently had a close, idealized relationship, left the family and moved to a distant city. Her parents were divorced, and she was left with her mother, whom she experienced as deceiving and exploiting her throughout her childhood and young adulthood by repeatedly failing to fulfill implicit and explicit promises to meet her emotional and financial needs. Following the departure of her father, she saw him on only two occasions until her late teens, as he did not visit and would not send her a ticket to come to him. Their total contact was restricted to letters, which they exchanged about every two months. She maintained her idealization of him, however, and throughout her childhood, never stopped longing for him to come to her. He remained extremely important to her as a sustaining figure. Except for his answers to her letters, she alone sustained this sense of relatedness to him through her capacity to create for herself, where only the barest basis for such a creation ever existed, what I have called *a fantasy selfobject* (Bacal, 1981).

Within a few weeks of the analyst's accession to the patient's request, the analysis of its meaning also began. This analysis had not been previously possible while the analyst was committed to a method (which might be described as optimal frustration) of not complying but trying just to understand and interpret. It is not possible to fully elaborate here the analysis of this incident of the fees, which extended over months and continued from time to time over years—as, indeed, one may have guessed from the account of the initial preanalytic dream. The most significant meanings, which were focused in the transference, were her need to create a new selfobject relationship with her analyst as both the mother and the father who would respond with demonstrable generosity; her need to have tangible proof of being protected from becoming entangled in a trusting relationship with someone who would only take from her and drain her of all her resources; her need for the analyst to respond by demonstrating to her beyond a doubt that he would share her burden and that she could in this sense exercise some control over him (money had always been a symbol of control in her family). Deeper than her need to know that she would not have to bear all of the burden herself lay the need of the child within her not to have to feel she had anyone to care for, specifically, the analyst-mother-child. As the analysis proceeded, a lifelong, sometimes suicidal, depression lifted. Her shaky self-esteem and self-assertiveness strengthened impressively, her career moved forward, and she was able to show her talented and very creative work to others, including the analyst, for the first time in her life.

Ultimately, the analysis of the patient's request and of the analyst's eventual responsiveness to that request revealed what were perhaps their deepest meanings. The analyst, by responding to her request, provided her with the first incontestable experience in her life of someone considering her interests before their own. More than anything else, it meant that someone believed in her, that she was worthwhile investing in.

In this connection, let us consider Wolf's (1981) recommendations for treatment.

> ... ideally, the analyst by virtue of his empathy and his theoretical orientation, can recognize the legitimate selfobject needs underlying the archaic and distorted manifestations, manifestations that he experiences often with some discomfort also. This then leads to the next substep in achieving empathic resonance. The analyst explains and interprets the sequence of events to the patient. He corrects his own previous misunderstanding of the patient. Again, it is important to point out, that the disruption, like the preceding harmonious selfobject transference, are not new experiences with a new object for the patient. What is new is that the analyst does not respond in a manner of an ordinary social situation but responds by explaining and interpreting on the basis of an empathically informed understanding. Nor is such an explanation a gratification of a need—neither of a selfobject need, nor of an instinctual wish or need—except for the need to be understood. By again feeling understood, the empathic flow between analyst and analysand is restored.
>
> (p. 6)

I am in essential agreement with Wolf except, perhaps, on two counts. The first is that, while the disruption was not a new experience for this patient, the means of its restoration in the regressed selfobject transference was essentially new. Dr. M needed to effect a shift or change in her analyst in order to create a selfobject response that was significantly different from anything that she had previously experienced. Second, while there was what *could* be called a gratification of a selfobject need, I would suggest that it was the *responsiveness that was optimal* for the patient at the level of organization of her self-selfobject relationships, in other words, at the level of development of her inner experience of empathic responsiveness in relation to nuclear selfobjects.

Implicit in this understanding of analytic work is the recognition of the therapeutic significance of what I have called the *creative aspect of transference* and its associated archaic selfobject, which can, I believe, legitimately be regarded as a "fantasy selfobject" or as a "transitional selfobject."[11] The transitional selfobject can be viewed as a prestage of the transitional object, in effect, a selfobject created by the patient, partly out of himself (in fantasy) and partly out of a sense of pliable surroundings. It constitutes a necessary intrapsychic stage as a precondition for the apprehending of the concrete transitional object, such as a blanket or a teddy bear. (In a sense, it represents, "I know that I can create that inside me.") The fantasy selfobject is created by the patient when the environment provides almost nothing around which he can elaborate a need for the responsiveness he requires. Dr. M's demand for a response to a fantasy selfobject need was responded to optimally, which meant, at this level, that it was "gratified." Far from producing a malignant regression, this enabled the analysis to resume and to deepen.

Although the analyst did not subsequently raise the question of the fees, Dr. M herself brought it up from time to time. She wanted to pay a fee but continued to struggle with her anxiety about paying anything. At the same time, it was evident that she was testing the analyst to see whether he would require her to do so. One day, three years after the analysis began, she reported a "new fantasy" that she felt completed the dream that she had shortly before entering analysis. The fantasy concerned the part of the dream where all her money fell out of her purse and her analyst friend picked it up and returned it to her. She reflected at this moment that she had never paid the cab fare. Apparently, no one paid for the cab ride, which she thought symbolized her need for it not to cost her any more than it had already. She felt that no one took care of her, and remarked, "you can't fall apart when there is no one to take care of you." At that moment, the analyst learned that her disintegration anxiety, with which she was struggling when she needed him to reduce the fees, could not have occurred unless she felt there was a potential selfobject who might respond. She was afraid at that time that she would cease to exist personally, professionally, or in some other sense. She reminded the analyst of the enormous difficulty that she experienced in asking to see him during the recent summer break as she was convinced that he would tell her that he had given her enough, that she was selfish, and that she shouldn't ask for such a thing. On another occasion she referred once again to the part of the dream where all her money spilled out of her purse and her subsequent anxiety about the fee arrangement. The original fantasy underlying the dream seemed to be that if she paid her analyst, he would get all her money and she would starve, and if she didn't pay him, she would survive and he would have nothing. The new fantasy was that she could pay him something at some point and the amount would vary according to what she could afford. She experienced this fantasy as hopeful and accepted the analyst's interpretation that it expressed her feeling that the amount that he would have and that she would have could be regulated. Less than three months later, she offered, without anxiety and with a quiet pride, to pay a fee commensurate with her economic situation at that moment.

Kohut has indicated that some patients require a gesture of what he called "preliminary enactment" without which no further analysis can take place. While I would essentially agree that certain patients may need this in a preliminary phase (in this sense, the notion of a "transitional selfobject relatedness" is useful), I suggest that it should not be thought of as a stage to be overcome so that the real analytic work can begin. Rather, it should be regarded as central to analytic work with these patients at the level of the development of their experience of empathy.

Sometimes, for some patients, this need arises as a result of progress, as, to some extent, in the case of Dr. M. She told the analyst that the experience of having both her requests granted, particularly having her wish for an extra session during the holiday break gratified, enabled her to think about his limitations. The knowledge that she was in an atmosphere in which she could make requests, combined with the fact that she had grown stronger, enabled her to consider not only what she might ask for but also what she might or might not receive. She felt it was important for her to deal with the analyst's limitations and believed that his tolerance helped her to do so. She estimated his tolerance as falling somewhere between saying yes to one extra session, and refusing altogether. Her initial fantasy was to ask for all of them since the analyst was in town for the holiday, but she decided that he would probably refuse this.

I do not believe that the analyst's accession to his patient's request should be regarded as an "enactment" or a parameter. Although many would claim that it is indeed the latter, this seems to me an unnecessary apology on the part of analysts who struggle within the limits of their countertransference and their hard-won theories toward an intelligible flexibility in analytic work. *Rather, I would suggest that we reexamine the so-called "parameter" as a necessary aspect of the analyst's optimal responsiveness for his patient.* [12] In order to answer the question of what is optimal responsiveness for a particular patient at a particular time, I believe that we need to consider carefully the creative aspect of the selfobject transference. We need to remind ourselves that the selfobject transference is not predominantly a repetition, but rather is mainly an attempt at the creation of a new kind of relatedness with the frustrating nuclear object. *Fantasy selfobjects, fantasy selfobject relatedness*, and the specific examples of this that I think deserve to be called *transitional selfobjects* and *transitional selfobject relatedness*, are instances of the transformation of traumatic (often quite early) selfobject failures into *creative aspects of selfobject transference* by seriously injured patients. While the analyst need not intentionally enact a part different than the significant parent ("corrective emotional significance"), he does have to consider what response will be optimal in relation to the current level of his patient's specific developmental capacity to utilize empathic understanding of his selfobject needs for human relatedness. This will be therapeutic. If, however, the analyst does not wish to or feels he cannot respond to the archaic selfobject demand, no shame should attach to his refusal. Indeed, he may feel that to refuse will constitute an optimal response for that patient's growth. I would suggest, however, that there is less danger in responding to a regressed patient's suggestion as to how he needs to be treated than in refusing on the basis of the unproven thesis that the patient will develop if he is frustrated to the optimal degree.

While frustration is an inevitable part of life, I question whether the analyst can usefully regard it as "optimal" when he is working with his patients. This applies to gratification as well. Neither, per se, are appropriate considerations as part of a therapeutic process. They are legacies of a psychoanalytic morality, an intrusion into the clinical situation of a psychoanalytic ethic that regards the patient's "real" unconscious and conscious intent to be the discharge and satisfaction of instinctual drives. Responsiveness, rarely perfect, almost always flawed in some way, can be optimal and comprises the legitimate efforts of our analytic work.

What does the analyst do with those patients for whom his kind of responsiveness does not work? As I have suggested, it is important to recognize that some forms of responsiveness that are crucially therapeutic may entail responses that an analyst cannot or will not, for ideological reasons, provide. For example, the necessary response to patient X may be withheld by analyst Y either because he simply does not respond to "acting-in" or because the patient's need gives him countertransference difficulties. From this perspective, what is designated as optimal frustration may sometimes be a rationalization of countertransference inflexibility on the part of the analyst. While the therapist must be himself, he also needs to be flexible to a degree or he will be correspondingly limited in treating certain patients. Kohut understood his concept of an average expectable environment as the "normal human responsiveness" promoting the patient's analysis and growth.[13] I would like to stress that *this will be different for each person.*

Conclusion and Summary

My thesis is that if our analytic responsiveness is optimal (and I would define optimal as relative and specific to the particular patient, not simply a matter of degree as Kohut and Seitz viewed it) then our efforts will be growth producing. Selfobject relationships will mature and the self will become stronger and more free, flexible, and more resilient. An "optimal" frustration can only be optimal when it is optimal for something to be frustrated. It would be interesting to know what this might be. The view that optimal frustration alone produces internal structures is a hypothesis that needs to be challenged. As I believe I have shown, we cannot assume that all internalizing processes occur through frustration. In a good-enough situation, for example, identification and assimilation occur. Similarly the prior internalization of the parent/analyst as a responsive selfobject allows the child/patient to tolerate the former's inevitable unempathic responsiveness when it occurs, and to accept with less disturbance the limitations of the selfobject. This is particularly true in the case of patients whose relations with selfobjects in childhood have been traumatic.

It may well be that transmuting internalizations that occur without engaging transference frustrations are those where deficit (versus defect) is predominantly present, both self deficit and defect being ordinarily encountered together. This would be interesting to research in the psychoanalytic situation.

It is my belief that the notions of optimal frustration and optimal gratification can usefully be replaced by the concept of optimal responsiveness. Optimal responsiveness is an analytic concept that is distinct from the concept of the "parameter" and the "corrective emotional experience," which are devices that are essentially non-analytic, but deliberately planned and actively initiated by the therapist. The *optimal responsiveness of the analyst* is determined by the position of the patient on the developmental line of his self-selfobject relations, and on his position on the developmental line of internalization of, and capacity for, empathy. It is not simply part of the ambience (Wolf, 1976) or the "frame" (Pines, 1981). Nor is it just an expression of the therapeutic or working alliance. Rather, it is the analyst's job. Interpretation and relationship are only the component aspects of optimal responsiveness in psychoanalytic treatment.

Notes

1 In a letter dated a year later Kohut (1972, September 23) also makes the point that "the *drive-curbing* behaviour of the selfobject is in essence experienced by the child as a *narcissistic* injury [and therefore] ... structure formation is always due to a loss of the prestructural selfobject, not of the drive-curbing true object ..."
2 Stolorow, Brandchaft, and Atwood (1983) have discussed this issue in terms of dissonant intersubjective states between patient and analyst.
3 I understand resistance here as a variety of blockages of communication that are defenses not against drives, but against the anxiety of retraumatization (Wolf, 1981).
4 There are, in fact, two authors who more or less explicitly address this issue (Gill, 1982; Lichtenberg, 1982a, 1982b).
5 After preparing this chapter, I had the opportunity to read an interesting clinical paper by Charles Coverdale (1983), which deals specifically with this topic.
6 I am indepted to Dr. Bonnie Wolfe, who responded to my initial presentation of this material with the following comments: "It seems to me that the important issue is whether and how the analyst's empathy can be conveyed to the patient in a way that the patient can experience *as being responsive to him* [my italics]. Sometimes, the patient can discern the analyst's responsiveness only through gestures, tone of voice, or facial expression ... [and] attempts at verbal communication are experienced as unempathic and non-responsive to the patient's state ... I am [here also reminded of Dr. Basch's nice example of the parent lifting the baby and saying, "U-u-up we go." At a more developed state or stage, the patient may be able to utilize (and tolerate) responses that are more predominantly verbal; although this verbal responsiveness may need to be at a primitive level ("you feel that," "it hurts"). At a more advanced level, you may find responsivity in the reciprocal communication [cf. Wolf's (1981)] notion of reciprocal empathic resonance of abstract ideas about psychological functioning" (Wolfe, personal communication, 1983).
7 Freud apparently did the same for Marie Bonaparte (Bertin, 1982).
8 Compare Wolf's (1980) notion of the "developmental line of selfobject relations."
9 Eva Rosenfeld (1966) reported that Melanie Klein gave her a glass of sherry under similar circumstances during an analytic session.
10 Contrast this with the Kleinian notion of splitting as a way of protecting the good primordial part-object from one's inclination to attack and destroy it.
11 Winnicott described the transitional object as the "first not-me possession" (Winnicott, 1951), that is, something that is experienced as part of the world and yet as belonging to me, something about which it is not to be asked, who created it, me or mother?
12 I am grateful to Dr. Michael Basch (personal communication, 1983) for a number of helpful comments on reading the draft of this chapter. He suggests that a differentiation should be made between "transference of need" and the "transference of solution." "When there is a transference of need, a deficit, then the transitional selfobject relationship is called for; when, however, the patient demonstrates that he is bringing now inappropriate attempts of problem solving into the analysis, then these, I think, must be interpreted genetically, contrasting the analytic to the past situation,

rather than taking it for axiomatic that the analyst has made a mistake in his relation to the patient. To use your terms, optimal responsiveness on the part of the analyst is not limited to one or another position. Optimal responsiveness can involve the analyst's functioning as a transitional selfobject at one time, as an interpreter of the patient's past reality at another, and as an interpreter of the analytic or external situation at still another time. This, I think, is in complete agreement with your statement ... to the effect that there is no such thing as a parameter."

13 Kohut conveyed this notion in a conversation with me in 1978.

References

Alexander, F. (1956). *Psychoanalysis and psychotherapy: Developments in theory. Technique and training.* New York, NY: Norton.

Bacal, H. (1979). *Empathic lag in the analyst and its relation to "negative therapeutic reaction."* Unpublished manuscript.

Bacal, H. (1981). Notes on some therapeutic challenges in the analysis of severely regressed patients. *Psychoanalytic Inquiry*, 1, 29–56.

Balint, M. (1968). *The basic fault.* London: Tavistock.

Balint, M. (1969). Trauma and object relationship. *International Journal of Psycho-Analysis*, 50, 429–435.

Bernfeld, S. (1928). *Sisyphos, oder veber die Grenzen der Erziehung.* Vienna: Internationale Vereinigung fuer Psychoanalysis.

Bertin, C. (1982). *Marie Bonaparte: A life.* New York, NY: Harcourt, Brace, Jovanovich.

Brandchaft, B. (1983). The negativism of the negative therapeutic reaction and the psychology of the self. In A. Goldberg (Ed.), *The future of psychoanalysis* (pp. 327–359). New York, NY: International Universities Press.

Collins English Dictionary. (1979). London & Glasgow: William Collins.

Coverdale, C. (1983). Developmental lines in self psychology: Selfobject empathy and interpretation. In L. Hedges (Ed.), *Listening perspectives in psychotherapy.* New York, NY: Jason Aronson.

Ferenczi, S. (1933). Confusion of tongues between the child and the adults. *International Journal of Psycho-Analysis*, 30, 225–230.

Freud, A. (1946). *The ego and the mechanisms of defense.* New York, NY: International Universities Press.

Gill, M. (1982). *Transference in the divergent analytic schools.* Paper presented at the Annual Scientific Meeting of The Canadian Psychoanalytic Society, June.

Khan, M. (1963). The concept of cumulative trauma. In *The privacy of the self* (1974). New York, NY: International Universities Press.

Kligman, D. (1983). Psychic trauma revisited. Paper presented to the Psychoanalytic Extension Program, Toronto Psychoanalytic Society and Institute of Psychoanalysis.

Kohut, H. (1971). *The analysis of the self.* New York, NY: International Universities Press.

Kohut, H. (1972). Letters of September 12th and September 23rd, 1972. In *The search for the self* (Vol. 2, pp. 867–870). New York, NY: International Universities Press.

Kohut, H. (1977). *The restoration of the self.* New York, NY: International Universities Press.

Kohut, H. (1981). From the transcription of remarks presented by Heinz Kohut at the Conference on Self Psychology, Berkeley, California, October.

Kohut, H., & Seitz, P. (1963). *The search for the self* (Vol. I, 1978, pp. 337–374). New York, NY: International Universities Press.

Kris, E. (1956). The recovery of childhood memories in psychoanalysis. *Psychoanalytic Study of the Child*, 11, 54–88.

Lichtenberg, J. (1982a). *An experiential conception of what is curative in psychoanalysis*. Unpublished manuscript.

Lichtenberg, J. (1982b). *Transmuting internalization and developmental change*. Unpublished manuscript.

Pines, M. (1981). The frame of reference of group psychotherapy. *International Journal of Group Psychotherapy*, 31, 275–285.

Rosenfeld, E. (1966). Unpublished address to The British Psycho-Analytical Association.

Stolorow, R., Brandchaft, B., & Atwood, G. (1983). Intersubjectivity in psychoanalytic treatment, with special reference to archaic states. *Bulletin of the Menninger Clinic*, 47, 117–128.

Strachey, J. (1934). The nature of the therapeutic action of psycho-analysis. *International Journal of Psycho-Analysis*, 15, 127–159.

Winnicott, D.W. (1947). Hate in the countertransference. In *Collected papers* (1958, pp. 194–203). London: Tavistock.

Winnicott, D.W. (1951). Transitional objects and transitional phenomena. In *Collected papers* (1958, pp. 229–242). London: Tavistock.

Winnicott, D.W. (1952). Anxiety associated with insecurity. In *Collected papers* (1958, pp. 97–100). London: Tavistock.

Wolf, E. (1976). Ambience and abstinence. *The Annual of Psychoanalysis*, 4, 101–115.

Wolf, E. (1980). On the developmental line of selfobject relations. In A. Goldberg (Ed.), *Advances in self psychology* (pp. 117–130). New York, NY: International Universities Press.

Wolf, E. (1981). *Empathic resonance*. Panel discussion to the Conference on Self Psychology, Berkeley, California, October 4.

4 British Object-Relations Theorists and Self Psychology: Some Critical Reflections[1]

This survey of six major British object-relations theorists examines the ways in which their ideas anticipated self psychology. The work of Ian Suttie is first considered as a relatively undiscovered but significant member of this group. W.R.D. Fairbairn, Harry Guntrip, Michael Balint, and D.W. Winnicott introduced concepts that self psychology developed in its own idiom, none of which has been recognized by Kohut or his followers. A review of Melanie Klein's work suggests interesting parallels with Kohut's work but reveals essential incompatibilities in basic theoretical assumptions with regard to the nature of the relationship between the infant's self and its early environment.

The British theorists failed to systematize a psychology of the self in the way Kohut did, largely because they were unable to dissociate their theories from the prevailing moralistic view of narcissism; that is, maturity required that "narcissistic" object relations be relinquished. Kohut took the final step necessary for the development of a psychology of the self by eliminating the maturity-morality inherent in this view, and by recognizing "narcissistic" object relations as reflecting the psychological legitimacy of selfobject needs throughout life. The difficulty which these theorists had in disengaging their concepts from instinct theory is regarded as a less important determinant preventing them from developing a comprehensive psychology of the self. Some ways in which the work of these object-relations theorists can enrich self-psychological theory and practice are suggested.

The origin of infantile anxiety has been explained by an analyst with the following vignette:

> I once heard a three-year-old boy calling out of a dark room: "Auntie, speak to me! I'm frightened because it's so dark." His aunt answered him: "What good would that do? You can't see me." "That doesn't matter," replied the child, "if anyone speaks, it gets light." [The analyst continues:] Thus what he was afraid of was not the dark, but the absence of someone he loved; and he could feel sure of being soothed as soon as he had evidence of that person's presence.

DOI: 10.4324/9781003570806-5

This was written by Freud, in 1905, but it is an excellent illustration of the relevance of modern selfobject theory. This little story, however, appears only as a footnote to Freud's monograph, "Three essays on the theory of sexuality" (Freud, 1905, p. 224) and has little relevance to the work's central themes.

Just as Freud failed to develop his earlier discovery of the Oedipus complex, undoubtedly the first definitive psychoanalytic statement about object relations, into a fully articulated theory of the latter, he did not expand his understanding of the little boy's anxiety into a theory of self psychology.

While it is true that the antecedents of new ideas can generally be identified as relatively undeveloped points of view (virtually every one of *Freud's* ideas were previously anticipated in this way), such precursors should not be confused with those truly significant and relatively developed earlier views which the new ones reflect.

Kohut found a prophetic significance for his own work in the observation of William James: "First they will say it is all wrong, then that it is unimportant and trivial, and finally that they knew it all along" (Kohut, personal communication, 1977; Goldberg, 1984, p. xi).

Kohut has been criticized for not sufficiently considering antecedent theories when formulating his own. Kohut, however, had found that the attempt to integrate the existing psychoanalytic literature in his area of interest left him "floundering in a morass of conflicting, poorly based, and often vague theoretical speculation" (Kohut, 1977, p. xx). While Kohut may not have regarded the contributions of American psychoanalysis as relevant to his work, his familiarity with this literature is undeniable. However, a survey of his work suggests that Kohut, like many American analysts until fairly recently, was not so familiar with analytic developments in Britain. His references to British psychoanalysts throughout his works are not only scanty, but do not reflect an extensive understanding of their concepts.

There is no unified theory of "object relations," and perhaps no universal agreement as to which theories should be included under this rubric. Generally, the term seems to be applied to psychoanalytic theories which de-emphasize the importance of instinctual discharge in explaining human motivation and emphasize the significance of the psychological meaning of a broad range of feeling in human interaction. I have for some time been struck by the similarities between many concepts in self psychology and those in theories of object relations. In particular, I have been impressed by the remarkable ways in which the conclusions of certain distinguished British analysts are reflected in the central ideas of Kohut's work. The relationships between the British object-relations theorists and self psychology have not, in my view, been sufficiently studied.[2] In the following critical reflections, I would like to explore the question of whether the British object-relations theorists did in fact discover self psychology or, if they did not, why they failed to do so and, finally, to consider whether self psychology may be enriched by their perspectives.

I would like to begin this survey of object-relations theorists with Ian Suttie, who was a central figure in the early Tavistock group (Sutherland, personal communication, 1984) and whose ideas significantly anticipated the work of Fairbairn, Guntrip, Balint, and Winnicott, and with Melanie Klein who made more general contributions to this body of theory. Whereas Suttie's views represent an epistemological break with the traditional psychoanalytic theory of his day, Melanie Klein's significance is mainly as a transitional figure whose work does not unequivocally transcend drive defense psychology in favor of a consistent object-relations theory.

Ian Suttie

Ernest Jones recognized Suttie's brilliant originality when he made the difficult decision to reject his 1923 article submitted for publication in the *International Journal*. As Jones' biographer (Brome, 1982) remarks, "Critical material was one thing; revolutionary principles quite another" (p. 144). Suttie is now receiving belated recognition as one of the first significant object-relations theorists. Brome describes the essence of Suttie's perspective as "a systematic account of man as a social animal whose object-seeking behaviour was discernible from birth. It replaced Freud's dual instinct theory with a full object relations theory" (p. 144).

The degree to which Suttie's ideas also anticipated those of modern self psychology has been less appreciated. I will outline here only a few of the contributions he made in his remarkable book, *The Origins of Love and Hate* (1935).

Suttie's basic concept concerns what he posits as the individual's innate need for companionship:

> To my mind the most important aspect of mental development ... is the *idea of others and of one's own relationship to them* ... Man [for Freud] is a bundle of energies seeking to dissipate themselves but restrained by Fear. Against this I regard expression not as an outpouring for its own sake, but as *an overture demanding response from others*. It is the absence of this response, I think, that is the source of all anxiety and rage whose expression is thus *wholly purposive*.
>
> (Suttie, 1935, pp. 29–35)

In contrast to Freud's view of the infant mind as co-operating or competing instincts, Suttie saw it as dominated from the beginning by the need for a close relatedness to the mother, a need which, if thwarted, produced extremes of fear and anger (p. 16). For Suttie, "Earth hath no hate *but* love to hatred turned, and hell no fury but a baby scorned" (p. 23). The infant, in the beginning, experiences

> only its pleasure and goodwill, and these it gives freely ... [When it] discovers that the benevolence of others is whimsical or conditional and that its own gifts in turn are apt to be criticized and rejected ... [its] frustrated social love turns to anxiety ... and then to hate if the frustration is sufficiently severe.
>
> (p. 42)

Suttie's perspective on anger enabled him to identify the essential importance of what we now call *selfobject functioning*. Anger, for Suttie, was not a primary affect or an independent instinct nor simply a reaction to frustration or rejection, but "an insistent demand upon the help of others"—initially the mother—to remove the sources of frustration. Anger is "the maximal effort to *attract* attention, and ... must be regarded as a protest against unloving conduct rather than as aiming at destruction of the mother, which would have fatal repercussions upon the *self*" (p. 23, my italics).

Although Suttie offered no coherent conception of the "self," he seems to use the term throughout his work to refer to the psychological center of the individual. He thus understood hate as a standing reproach against the object which threatens the self with the anxiety of separation. "Its purpose is not death-seeking or death-dealing, but *the preservation of the self* from the isolation which is death, and the restoration of a love relationship" (p. 31, my italics).

He regarded the phases of psychosexual development as the product of the interaction between the child and its mother determined by the rearing practices of the culture, a conclusion reached independently by Michael Balint writing in Hungary in the same year. He rejected Freud's view of love as sublimated sexuality, and saw it as an affect whose primary quality was affectionate tenderness from the beginning. As a result of the prohibition which, in Suttie's view, has developed against tenderness in our culture (he called it a "taboo on tenderness"), sex is often a defensive substitute through which the forbidden yearning for tenderness is regularly expressed. He suggested that sexual intercourse is sometimes sought to restore a sense of the absence of difference between people; and he makes the point, here, that suckling and coitus are, in this respect, alike and unique "where there is as yet no doubt of 'welcome' or 'acceptance'" (p. 72). He thus anticipates the essence of both Michael Balint's theory of *primary love* and Heinz Kohut's notion of *archaic merger*.

Suttie's views on narcissism are very similar to those of Kohut. While he accepts the term as usefully descriptive of a form of behavior or a feeling state, he does not believe that it represents a phase in the development of love. He suggests that what Freud mistook as the narcissism of the infant was not a "love of self" but a mixture of primitive states of satisfaction and increased perceptions of, and interest in, itself—in its own body and in its own immediate concerns—as a result of the ministrations of the mother (pp. 32 and 37).

Suttie also identifies a particular quality of relatedness which is difficult to comprehend in selfobject terms, a quality exemplified by the feeling of the analyst who is primarily interested in the welfare of his patient, or by the mother in her infant:

> I consider that the child wakes up to life with the germ of parenthood, the impulse to "give" and to "respond" already in it. This impulse, with the need "to get" attention and recognition, etc., motivates the free "give and take" of fellowship.
>
> (p. 58)

Melanie Klein

Although the aspects of Kleinian theory which I will highlight will not do justice to the complexity of Melanie Klein's ideas, they will permit me to bring into focus those of its elements which demonstrate, for the most part, its sharp differences from self psychology. Her work constitutes a fully articulated object-relations theory which posits the existence of a primitive ego at birth, "driven by instincts and anxiety to form primitive object-relationships in phantasy and reality" (Segal, 1973, p. 14). Thus, in contrast to Suttie, who made a radical departure from Freudian metapsychology toward a true object-relations theory, Klein shares Freud's view of instincts as the motivational force for object relations. In contrast to Kohut, who emphasized the importance of the psychic *reality* of the child's experience with selfobjects, Klein emphasized the child's unconscious *fantasies* about his objects.

Although Klein retains the terms id, ego, and superego, these do not figure in her work as they do in classical analysis. Rather, she focuses upon what she terms the paranoid-schizoid and depressive positions. These are regarded not only as stages of infant development but as specific configurations of object relations, with their associated anxieties and defenses which, to some extent, persist throughout life in everyone.

Klein fully accepts the significance of the death instinct as formulated by Freud. Her basic position is that the struggle to establish a good internal object—which is regarded as the basis for health as well as the criterion for a successful analysis—will be strongly opposed by the death instinct. The individual's psychological life is dominated by this conflict, in one way or another, from the beginning to the end of life.

The infant, threatened by the destructiveness of the death instinct, protects itself through the mechanism of projective identification. This process involves the splitting off of the part of the self, or ego (these terms are generally used synonymously by Klein) containing the death instinct and the projection of this rejected aspect of the self into the primordial part-object, the mother's breast (as well as into the father's penis, which the breast is imagined to contain). The mother's breast, now containing these parts of the infant, is therefore experienced, when reincorporated by the infant, as destructive as well as destroyed. Despite Segal's view that "a normal infant does not spend most of his time in a state of anxiety" (p. 35), Kleinian theory sees the newborn as significantly struggling with the fear "that the persecutory object or objects will get inside the ego and annihilate both the ideal object and the self" (p. 26). The difference between this perspective and self psychology which sees the baby as born into a matrix of potentially supportive selfobjects, whose positive regard reflects the potentially wonderful virtual self of the infant, is clear. Klein's infant must protect itself from the felt repercussions of unsuccessful attempts to externalize its self-destructiveness. Nevertheless, Klein's concept of projective identification suggests Kohut's idea of the vertical split, according to which the self splits in protective reaction to a world which *may* be experienced as inimical under adverse environmental circumstances. For Klein, idealization of the object is at this stage a totally defensive strategy adopted in order to keep the good object protected from the persecutory object; and good experiences with "external" objects (mother, father, and others) only minimally mitigate the terrors of this situation.

In normal development, the paranoid-schizoid position is largely superseded by the depressive position, which is characterized by the infant's recognition of, and capacity to apprehend, his mother as a whole person and to accept his ambivalence toward her. Here, idealization also plays a developmental role. This position is reached not only as a result of the increasing strength of the ego through maturation, but also through an increasing ability to possess and identify with a "strong ideal object" (Segal, 1973, p. 67). Idealization then becomes the basis of the belief in the goodness of objects and of oneself, and is a precursor of good object relationships. This view is similar to that of self psychology. However, the depressive position was so named by Klein mainly because it is marked by the depressive anxiety that the forces of the death instinct will destroy the loved and ideal mother. This anxiety is alleviated only by the infant's hope that his reparative impulses will tip the balance.

Projective identification, according to Kleinian theory, is not only defensive, but, like introjective identification, the earliest form of empathy (Segal, 1973, p. 36) and an important mode of communication (Rosenfeld, 1983). Despite certain similarities between the concepts of empathy and projective identification, it should be remembered that projective identification, as usually understood clinically, derives its motivation from the attempt to extrude the death instinct, and still indicates a persecuting internal object. Although empathy, as defined by self psychology, constitutes an essentially neutral function of the self—the way in which we apprehend the inner life of another—its usual source, as Kohut recognized (1981), derives from compassionate and well-intentioned purposes. When material in the clinical situation is interpreted as a projective identification, this can be regarded, from the perspective of self psychology, as an empathic lag on the part of the analyst. At that moment, the analyst, in an experience-distant mode, is experiencing himself as the target of a process which originates in the analysand's need to rid himself of intolerable links with archaic unempathic selfobjects.

The concept of envy, as understood in Kleinian theory, can be contrasted with certain concepts in self psychology with which it has important points of contact. Although related to admiration, envy has, for Klein, a destructive, spoiling intent. Envy is constitutional, operative from birth and, if severe, can interfere with the maintenance of the ideal object, which provokes envy and is therefore attacked and destroyed. The growth of the ego, or self, is thus also seriously impeded, since its development largely depends on the internalization of the ideal object and the ego's identification with it. Although this latter hypothesis is one with which self psychology would essentially agree, the therapeutic factor would be conceived as the transmuting internalization of selfobject function. In so far as envy also entails a wish to possess the goodness of the object, or to be as good as the admired object, it signifies a painful failure in this regard. However, envy between the self and the object cannot, according to Klein's theory, be intelligibly bridged by positive experience, since this simply generates a greater degree of envy of the object that provides the good experience. From the perspective of self psychology, on the other hand, this separation is not produced by an innate envious destructiveness, but by the failure of the idealized selfobject to include the admiring child as part of the adult world. This failure of responsiveness on the part of admired selfobjects to the child's desire for recognition can produce intractable envy and operate significantly at all phases of development, including psychoanalysis, to interfere with individual creativity and the development of personal growth. This is a very subtle process and can become exacerbated in the analytic situation if the patient's devaluation of the analyst, or attempts to spoil what is "good" in the analysis, are interpreted in Kleinian terms, as further manifestations of destructive envy or defenses against it (Segal, 1973, p. 45), rather than recognized as the reaction of the analysand to the frustration of being unable to elicit the longed-for mirroring responses from the idealized analyst. If, however, the analysand as a child was exposed to *unidealizable* selfobjects, a self defect will occur associated not only with a tendency toward bitterness, disappointment, and denigration, but also with a selfobject transference requiring perfection in the analyst, in conjunction with painful envy, on the basis of an *intensified* need to idealize the object. This desperate, compensatory idealization never really "takes" and, therefore, cannot lead to any strengthening of the self. If *this* kind of envy is not properly understood, it may result in an almost insurmountable psychological gap between the regressed patient and the analyst.

Although Klein does not link narcissism with envy, Segal suggests that it is implicit in her theories:

> The way primary envy is described by Melanie Klein is as a spoiling hostility at the realization that the source of life and goodness lies outside. To me, envy and narcissism are like two sides of a coin. Narcissism defends us against envy (as was described by Rosenfeld and others).
>
> (Segal, 1983, p. 270)

Segal seems to move tentatively in the direction of self psychology, when she adds, "If one believes in a prolonged narcissistic stage [as normal], envy would be secondary to disillusionment" (p. 271). (Presumably, Segal means disillusionment in one's own omnipotence.) It is not a significant shift in perspective, however, as she concludes that all persistent narcissism is essentially a way of dealing with the pain and dangers of a primary envious destructiveness based on the death instinct and envy.

Klein's "internal objects" have been likened to Kohut's "selfobjects." While both are seen as intrapsychic, and thus "internal," Klein regards internal objects largely as a product of phantasy which the infant experiences as concrete and which comprise good and bad objects, and Kohut understands selfobjects as the product of the child's actual experience with external objects which function to sustain the self and enhance its development. (The only way that self psychology has of talking about the experience of bad selfobjects is to refer to the failure of selfobjects.) Although there are important similarities between Klein and Kohut, their fundamental theoretical positions are irreconcilable, because the self of self psychology develops in consequence of the infant's internalization of function of selfobjects which are generally experienced as empathically responsive, and the self of Kleinian psychology develops as a result of the internalization of repaired objects whose goodness thus survives the infant's enviously destructive unconscious phantasies.

W.R.D. Fairbairn

Although he did not found a school and does not have an organized following, Fairbairn came closest of all the British object-relations theorists to *systematizing* a theory of object relations which constituted a significant departure from the Freudian framework. Living in Edinburgh, he worked in virtual isolation, so that his profound and original contributions to psychoanalysis represent a considerable achievement.

Ernest Jones had apparently softened a little during the 29 years since he rejected Suttie's views, for he wrote in his preface to Fairbairn's (1952) book, *Psychoanalytic Studies of the Personality*:

> If it were possible to condense Dr. Fairbairn's new ideas into one sentence, it might run somewhat as follows. Instead of starting, as Freud did, from stimulation of the nervous system proceeding from excitation of various erogenous zones and internal tension arising from gonadic activity, Dr. Fairbairn starts at the centre of the personality, the ego, and depicts its strivings and difficulties in its endeavour to reach an object where it may find support … All this constitutes a fresh approach in psycho-analysis which should lead to much fruitful discussion.
>
> (Jones, 1952, p.v.)

What Jones accurately identifies as the essence of Fairbairn's views is clearly central to Heinz Kohut's "psychology of the self," which might be seen as a fulfillment of Jones' prediction, some 20 years later. Yet, there is not one reference to Fairbairn in Kohut's work.

Like Freud before him, and Kohut after, Fairbairn initially concentrated his investigations upon a specific illness. In Fairbairn's case, this was the schizoid condition, or schizoid factors in the personality, which he defined as splits in the ego, and regarded as virtually universal. Indeed, he regarded repression itself as a schizoid phenomenon (Fairbairn, 1944).

Fairbairn, like Klein, retained aspects of Freud's instinct theory. However, he rejected Klein's view of the central importance of instincts in relationships and described libido as primarily object-seeking. He focuses upon the nature of the individual's relationships with objects, what he termed "object-relationships." Like Suttie, Fairbairn recognized that, "although Freud's whole system of thought was concerned with object-relationships, he adhered theoretically to the principle that libido is primarily pleasure-seeking ..." (p. 126). Fairbairn suggested that what Freud was describing as the libidinal aims of various erotogenic zones, oral aims, anal aims etc., were not really aims at all, but modes of dealing with objects and that "the real libidinal aim is the establishment of satisfactory relationships with objects ..." (1946, p. 138).

> Thumb-sucking ... represents a technique for dealing with an unsatisfactory object-relationship; and the same may be said of masturbation ... Autoerotism is essentially a technique whereby the individual seeks not only to provide for himself what he cannot obtain from the object, but to provide for himself an object which he cannot obtain.
>
> (Fairbairn, 1941, pp. 33–34)

Fairbairn's use of the term "libidinal" in this context reflects the difficulty entailed in disengaging psychoanalytic theory from the metapsychology of instinct. Like Kohut prior to 1971, he tended to retain the established terminology. The real challenge for Fairbairn was to find a conceptual framework that could describe the motivational force for the all-important link to the object or, in other words, to conceptualize the function of the object. His concept of *dynamic structure* represents an important step toward the evolution of a psychology of the strivings of a central self. According to this theory, which Fairbairn regarded as fundamental to all his work, the ego is not driven by instincts or drives, but is the source of its own energy; and instinct is not the stimulus to psychic activity, but consists in characteristic activity on the part of a psychical structure (1946).

Fairbairn, however, did understand the importance of the function of what we now call a selfobject. In 1943, he concluded, from his extensive experience of war neuroses and psychoses, "that the most distinctive feature of military breakdowns is separation-anxiety ... for ... the dependent individual can find no substitute for his accustomed objects under military conditions (the sergeant-major proving a very poor substitute, e.g., for an attentive wife)" (p. 80).

Fairbairn did not realize the full significance of this observation because he held, like most theorists at that time, an essentially moral perspective on narcissism. While his view of personal growth as a progression from immature to mature dependence accords with selfobject theory, he believed the overcoming of narcissism to be a necessary condition of this process. It remained for Kohut, in his study of narcissistic personality disorders, to demonstrate that the legitimizing of selfobject functioning in the analytic situation decreases the self's sense of pervasive urgency in its dependence on the response of the selfobject.

Fairbairn, like Suttie, regards the capacity to give as innate. He views it, however, as more characteristic of the stage of mature dependence than the stage of infantile dependence. If the narcissistic attitude between the self and object is relinquished, the capacity to give matures. Although there is little discussion of giving in self psychology—Wolf's concept of reciprocal empathic resonance perhaps comes closest (Wolf, 1980)—the individual with a self strengthened by responsive selfobjects is seen as maturely dependent in Fairbairn's sense. He is predominantly oriented toward giving (Fairbairn, 1941, p. 39) or, in self-psychological terms, capable of functioning in a healthy way as a satisfactory selfobject for others. Self psychology has, perhaps, been distracted by its passionate war against the pervasive moralism which it believes to be inherent in classical psychoanalytic theory, from undertaking the systematic study of this area.

Fairbairn seems to share Kohut's sense that the manifestations of distorted sexuality are products of the experience of the failure of selfobjects and constitute attempts at restitution of the self-selfobject relationship. Fairbairn describes it as follows: "Where relationships with outer objects are unsatisfactory, we also encounter such phenomena as exhibitionism, homosexuality, sadism, and masochism; and these phenomena should be regarded as in no small measure attempts to salvage natural emotional relationships which have broken down" (1941, p. 40). He returned to this issue at a later date, when he concluded, "From the point of view of object-relationship psychology, explicit pleasure-seeking represents a deterioration of behaviour ... since libidinal need is object-need, simple tension relief implies some failure of object-relationships" (1946, pp. 139–140).

Self psychology has been criticized for minimizing the importance of the instinctual, for example, the strictly sexual or lustful in the psychology of child development except as breakdown products of the self due to selfobject failure. Fairbairn, on the other hand, has no difficulty integrating these elements in his theory of object relationships. He believes that as the child becomes aware of the genital discrepancy between his parents and as his own physical needs are increasingly experienced in genital terms, the child's need for the mother comes to include (in fantasy) a need for her vagina, and the need for the father, a need for his penis. But he maintained that "[the] *strength* of these physical needs for his parents' genitals varies ... in inverse proportion to the satisfaction of his emotional needs. Thus, the more satisfactory his emotional relations with his parents, the *less urgent* are his physical needs for their genitals" (1944, p. 122, my italics). This latter view accords well with self psychology. Fairbairn's understanding of the physical need which the child experiences for the parents' genitals as not simply a symptom or breakdown product, but as a step in the development of the self, can contribute significantly to self psychological understanding of the need for selfobject recognition of the child's developing sexuality.

Fairbairn clearly anticipated Kohut's concept of "self-state" dreams; dreams which, in contrast to Freud's sense of dreams as only wish-fulfillment, depict the current psychological condition of the self—usually, its state of vulnerability. In referring to the dreams of a particular patient, Fairbairn noted that:

> [there] were a number which defied all efforts to bring them into conformity with the "wish-fulfilment" theory, and which [the patient] came to describe quite spontaneously as "state of affairs" dreams, intending by this description to imply that they represented actually existing endopsychic situations.
>
> (p. 99)

This view represents a more radical departure from Freud's position than that of Kohut, who recognized that some dreams are wish-fulfillments. Fairbairn maintained that "dreams are *essentially* not wish fulfillments, but dramatizations or 'shorts' (in the cinematographic sense) of situations existing in inner reality ..." (p. 99, my italics). The situations to which he refers are clearly relationships between the self and its internalized objects.

Harry Guntrip

A review of Guntrip's work leaves little doubt that, although he did not evolve a systematic framework for a psychology of the self, he was the first explicitly to emphasize the importance of placing the self, which he regarded as the core of the individual (and which he used synonymously with the term, "ego"), at the center of psychoanalytic theory. For Guntrip, "the one fundamental thing that matters to human beings is to possess a stable experience of themselves as whole and significant persons" (1968, p. 399).

Guntrip builds on the perspectives of Fairbairn and Winnicott. He undertook the task of clarifying, systematizing and popularizing Fairbairn's work and, indeed, extending it. About the now famous protest of Fairbairn's patient, "You're always talking about my wanting this or that desire satisfied; but what I really want is a father," Guntrip remarks: "the reason why the patient wants a father (and needs an analyst) is that without a satisfactory relationship with another person he cannot become a developing ego" (p. 174). His view that "*'radical' psychotherapy must aim, not simply at the resolution of specific conflicts, but at the fundamental regrowing of the ... whole personal self ...*" (p. 317) is significantly close to the essence of the self psychological theory of therapy.

Guntrip shared Fairbairn's interest in the schizoid condition which affects individuals who, in Winnicott's sense, have not had good-enough mothering and who suffer from a sense of emptiness, isolation and alienation from their world. The schizoid condition, as Guntrip understood it, does not concern relations with others so much as the question of "whether one is or has a self" (p. 148). What Guntrip means by a "self" is Winnicott's idea of "basic ego-relatedness." In thus using an object-relational term to indicate the *self*, Guntrip has captured what seems to me to underlie the concept of the "cohesive self" of self psychology, that is, a self which has been strengthened by assimilating into its structure (through transmuting internalization) a sense of a good-enough connection with its selfobjects. With this apparent paradox, Guntrip has progressed beyond an object-relations theory which focuses upon the relationship with others, toward a psychology of the self in the sense that Kohut meant.

Guntrip adopts Fairbairn's view of the central importance of separation anxiety to which the infant is particularly exposed as a result of his primitive, undeveloped psychological organization. Since the infant "cannot retain his primitive wholeness for more than a short period in the absence of mother ... separation anxiety ... is a pointer to the ... worst fear, fear of the loss of the ego itself, of depersonalization, and the sense of unreality" (p. 128). Guntrip is here undoubtedly describing the condition which Kohut later identified as "disintegration anxiety" of the self (Kohut, 1977, p. 104) in the face of significant selfobject failure. Guntrip, like Fairbairn, emphasizes that the infant attempts to protect itself through a schizoid process which causes a split in the ego. If, for example, the infant is seriously neglected by the mother and cannot elicit an adequate response from her, he must escape the empty environment by means of mental withdrawal (p. 128). Guntrip asks us to recognize not only the faulty or deficient function of significant objects but also to look closely at the intrapsychic defensive reactions of the self to selfobject failure—including even "fragmentation" *as a defense*. Kohut discussed defensive splitting of the self in *The Analysis of the Self*, where he understood "vertical splitting" to be maintained by disavowal and "horizontal splitting to be maintained by repression" (Kohut, 1971, p. 285). Yet except for Newman's (1980) article on defenses and Basch's (1983) paper on disavowal, a consideration of defenses has not figured significantly in current theorizing in self psychology until the publication of Kohut's most recent monograph (Kohut, 1984).

Self psychology has focused mainly on the *precipitants* for psychic disruption in the face of environmental failure specific to the child's selfobject needs as this is believed to be most useful clinically. It recognizes the resulting states of disturbed functioning within the self as weakening and, in severe instances, "fragmenting." But is this all that happens? Winnicott, as we shall see, addressed this in terms of a "false self" which conforms superficially and protects the "true self," which hides. Fairbairn described and Guntrip elaborated upon the concept of "disunited psychic functioning" according to which the self does not fragment, but splits into three parts, or egos, which function in dynamic relation to one another in persistent and characteristic ways (Guntrip, 1968, p. 188). The infant who is repeatedly made aware of his helplessness through parental rejection or intolerance of his weakness and dependency comes to share the critical adult attitude toward his own immaturity. He comes to experience his primary needy self as a part of his whole self which can be split off, repressed, or destroyed. The initial unity of the psyche is disrupted and Fairbairn identifies three distinct ways in which it now functions. The *libidinal ego*, the original needy, object-seeking and ego-developing infant psyche in a state of fear and unsatisfied need (p. 188), is actively persecuted by the *anti-libidinal ego*, which can be compared to Freud's sadistic superego. This "internal saboteur," as Fairbairn originally called it, despises the libidinal ego for its weakness and immaturity and attempts to crush its spontaneous needs and creative relatedness to the object. As Guntrip indicates, "It produces a psychical condition in which *natural maturing* becomes impossible" (p. 188). Yet, he recognizes that this anti-libidinal ego "must be respected as the patient's desperate struggle to keep himself functioning in the absence of genuine help" (p. 190). The functioning of the libidinal and anti-libidinal egos is largely repressed and unconscious. In contrast, the *central ego* is the conscious aspect of the self which tries to conform to the requirements of the outer world, sacrificing spontaneity and creativity to achieve security. It is similar to Winnicott's conception of the false self.

The bad object is initially internalized in an attempt to control it, and defensively split into an "exciting object" and a "rejecting object" which, for the most part, function on an unconscious level. The exciting object, to which the libidinal ego is related and obstinately attached, represents the aspect of the parents which stimulates but never satisfies the child's need for love and caring, and the rejecting object represents the critical, denying, angry aspects of the parents with which the anti-libidinal ego allies itself to "suppress those of [the child's] needs which go unmet" (Guntrip, 1966, p. 235).

Fairbairn and Guntrip's understanding of disunited psychic functioning can contribute to self psychological awareness of the nature of severe resistance to the therapeutic process. The patient's resistance to the longing experienced by the libidinal ego or true self to reach out to a safe selfobject, insofar as it constitutes a fear of retraumatization, is exacerbated by this process of intrapsychic splitting.

Guntrip believes that conflicts over sex, aggression, and guilt—in addition to the significance they might have at the level at which they are operating—are used as a defense against experiencing the self as small, weak, cut-off, and unreal, and to forestall the necessity for further defensive withdrawal, regression, and depersonalization "in order to preserve the very existence of the self" (p. 129). Guntrip maintains that man's predilection for attributing his troubles to the possession of powerful and resistant animal instincts stems from his preference for regarding himself as bad rather than weak:

> The reason why patients hold on with such tenacity to their Kleinian world of internal bad objects and their Freudian inner world of oedipal conflicts of sex and aggression, is that their external object-relations have become so weakened by early schizoid withdrawal inside, that they are compelled to maintain a world of internal fantasied objects to keep their ego in being at all.
> (pp. 128–129)

Guntrip introduced the concept of the "regressed ego" as the ultimate schizoid defense. In the face of significant failure in responsiveness of external objects, "the living heart" of the self takes flight into regions deep within the personality, making meaningful relations with others impossible.

Thus, while Freud regards hate as one of the basic attitudes toward the environment, and as secondarily engendering fear, Guntrip, like Suttie and Fairbairn, maintains the opposite view: "Human beings hate because they are afraid ... It is fear that makes it impossible to love, and the conflict between love and fear is the fundamental problem" (p. 386). Thus, Guntrip's view on aggression is identical to Fairbairn's and remarkably similar to that of Kohut. He does not believe in a primary destructiveness and regards destructive attitudes and behavior as essentially reactive or protective:

> … in twenty-five years of psychoanalytic therapy I have not come across any case of unanalyzable aggression, that is, I have always found that all forms of aggressive reaction were defensive reactions to fears, anxieties, insecurities, feelings of underlying weakness, and especially basic feelings of isolation … The frustration-aggression theory is the only one supported by clinical observation.
>
> (Guntrip, 1971, pp. 129–131)

Michael Balint

Although Balint does not explicitly include the notion of the *self* in his theoretical formulations, a number of his major contributions to psychoanalysis are clearly reflected in some of the central concepts which later emerged in self psychology. I will discuss three of these: his critical appraisal of the psychoanalytic theory of the pregenital organization (Balint, 1935); his concepts of "primary love" and "primary object" (Balint, 1937, 1968); and the "basic fault" (Balint, 1968).

In his "Three essays on the theory of sexuality" (Freud, 1905, p. 198), Freud wrote that "[the pregenital] phases of sexual organization are normally passed through smoothly, without giving more than a hint of their existence. It is only in pathological cases that they become active and recognizable to superficial observation" (p. 198). Freud, however, identifies the pathogenic factor in a footnote added in 1920: "The differences separating the normal from the abnormal can lie only in the relative strength of the individual components of the sexual instinct …" (Freud, 1905, p. 205, footnote added in 1920).

Balint was in complete agreement with Freud's observation that normal children do not exhibit signs of pregenital sexuality except as a playful or ephemeral manifestation. In this regard, he shared Ferenczi's view that tenderness, and not passion or erotism, is the natural expression of love on the part of children. As we have already seen, Suttie recognized this as well. Balint, however, disagreed with Freud's understanding of overt manifestations of pregenital sexuality in childhood as arising from biological factors. He considered all these phenomena—which psychoanalytic theory describes as "oral," "anal," "oral-sadistic," "anal-sadistic," "phallic object relations," or "negative Oedipus complex," and regards as natural phases of normal development—to be artefacts, in effect, products of the child's upbringing. He finds significant support for this assertion in the fact that they are treated as such in analytic practice and "analysed, understood, interpreted, and resolved" (Balint, 1935, p. 44). He adopts a similar perspective on hate and aggression which "have their explanation in the child's individual history … [in the absence] of good, loving understanding between the child and the grown-ups around him …" (p. 45).

There is little here that is not reflected in Heinz Kohut's theory of development which understands healthy psychological growth as dependent upon phase-appropriate responsivity to the child's selfobject needs and that significant selfobject failure leads to the distortion of the personality and the expression of isolated or aberrant sexuality or destructiveness.

Kohut expressed these ideas in 1977. Balint, a little ahead of his time, first presented these revolutionary ideas in a paper to the Vienna Psycho-Analytical Society in 1935. No-one took them seriously.

The psychoanalytic world treated the next development in his thought, two years later, with the same lack of interest. It was, nevertheless, a major revision of psychoanalytic theory. He rejected the concept of a primary narcissism and argued in favor of the idea that, in the earliest phase of its life, the infant is not turned inward on itself, but is, from the beginning, in a state of primitive relatedness to another object (Balint, 1937, p. 82).[3] The wishes of this primary object are felt by the infant to be identical to his own and his aim is to be loved and satisfied by the object without having to give anything in return. Balint called this state of relatedness *primary love*, or *primary object-love*, and suggested that its inevitable disruption produced two reactions in the infant in the attempt to reinstate it. One reaction is the detour of narcissism through which the child attempts to give to himself what he previously experienced in relation to the primary object. Narcissism thus arises out of the child's need to reestablish the primary relationship. The second is the route of active object-love through which the child attempts to please the object in order that he be satisfied in return. Therefore, for Balint, what is clinically observable as "narcissism" is the result of a frustration in relation to an object, and is "always a protection against the bad or only reluctant object" (Balint, 1937, p. 82). Narcissism is always secondary. Kohut's initial description of the selfobject relationship as "narcissistic" is, from this point of view, incorrect, since "selfobject relatedness" is not reactive or defensive. Similarly, Balint's primary object love is not "narcissistic" but the equivalent of early and reciprocal self-selfobject relatedness between the infant and the mother. Perhaps, if Kohut had been aware of Balint's concept of a primary object-relatedness which is *not* in its essence either narcissistic or object-instinctual, he might also have abandoned Freud's theory of primary narcissism, as it was not relevant to his selfobject theory of self psychology. He would not then have had to consider a "developmental line of narcissism" as distinct from a developmental line of love.[4] Kohut's core concepts really have nothing to do with "narcissism," which is simply one of the illnesses that result if the child's relationships with its primary objects break down.

Balint proposed that pre-oedipal configurations have sufficient, significant identifiable characteristics in common to justify a name of their own. The term he suggested was the level, or area, of the *basic fault*. The oedipal area is characterized by conflict, and associated with experiences occurring in a triangular relationship, in which "adult language is an adequate and reliable means of communication" (Balint, 1968, p. 16); the area of the basic fault is much simpler and more primitive. Here, conflict is not the essential dynamic force; experiences occur within a two-person relationship, and "adult language is often useless or misleading in describing events ... because words have not always an agreed or conventional meaning" (pp. 16–17). For our purposes, I will be considering only two of these conditions—the quality of the relationship and the nature of the dynamic force operating within it.

The characteristics of the two-person relationship in the area of the basic fault are derived from the disruption of the state of primary love, or primary object relationship. In this state, as I have already noted, the needs of the infant and his maternal object are perceived by the infant as identical. Because the adequacy and willingness of the object's responsiveness are taken for granted, the satisfaction of the subject's needs produces a tranquil sense of well-being, while frustration evokes a disproportionately intense reaction, which Balint describes as "highly vehement and loud symptoms" (p. 17). The patient may experience "a feeling of emptiness, being lost, deadness, futility" (p. 19) and the sense that the frustration associated with the analyst's response was intentionally inflicted upon him.

Conflict is not the issue at the level of the basic fault, but something more elementary—a discovery which partly contributed to Balint's use of the word "basic."[5] The notion of "fault" arose not only from its metaphoric association with the geological term, but more importantly from the way so many patients described it.

> The patient says that he feels there is a fault within him that needs to be put right ... there is a feeling that the cause of this fault is that someone has either failed the patient or defaulted on him, and ... a great anxiety invariably surrounds this area, usually expressed as a desperate demand that this time the analyst should not—in fact must not—fail him.
>
> (p. 21)

The patient experiences this fault as "a kind of deficiency ... something missing either now, or perhaps for almost the whole of the patient's life" (pp. 21–22). Balint felt that the origin of the basic fault lay in a discrepancy—a lack of fit—between the needs of the *specific* child and the capacity of the people in his early environment to provide them.

It is evident that much of this is compatible with self psychology. For example, Balint recognized the genesis of the condition, now called selfobject transference, in the structural defects within the individual which result from the significant failure on the part of primary objects to fulfill their expected function. Similarly, he understood what Kohut later termed disintegration anxiety, as the patient's fear that the analyst's failure to redress the deficiency would repeat the infantile trauma and provoke almost unbearable anxiety.

Balint did not believe, however, that the nature of the transference was solely attributable to the analysand's early life experience. Although Kohut recognizes this as well, it was Balint who first emphasized that its appearance in the clinical situation is very much a product of the interaction between a *particular* patient and his *particular* therapist. In this regard, he anticipated the work of Stolorow, Brandchaft, and Atwood (1983) on intersubjectivity, a concept which plays a crucial role in the therapeutic process. He maintained that, instead of attempting to interpret the regressive needs of the patient, the analyst should work with them—that is, that he accept these needs and allow his patient to maintain them in the analytic situation (Balint, 1968, p. 163). This is the therapeutic position essentially advocated by Kohut. For Balint, successful therapy involved allowing the patient to regress, where necessary, in the transference up to and even beyond the particular form of object relationship which caused the deficiency state associated with the basic fault in the first place.

While there are clearly many similarities between Balint's ideas and those of Kohut, there are significant and important differences. Balint, for example, places the time-frame of significant, primary object relationships at an early, ill-defined, ephemeral stage in the life of the infant, while Kohut regards the optimal satisfaction of selfobject needs to be important for development throughout life. There is another, perhaps more important, distinction which explains why Balint did not evolve a framework for a psychology of the self. While self psychology regards analytic progress as the strengthening of the self through the transmuting internalization of the analyst's selfobject functions, Balint speaks of a "new beginning" which results from the development of "new patterns of object relationship to replace those *given up*" (Balint, 1968, p. 166, my italics). Thus, beyond the area of the basic fault, beyond the level of the earliest relationships of the infant to its primary environment as manifested in the transference, Balint unmistakeably introduces a "maturity- or reality-morality" (Kohut and Wolf, 1978, p. 423) into the therapeutic process. Balint understood that the patient's regressive manifestations reflect the nature of the object relationship he needs to establish with his analyst. Yet, he would ultimately convey, in one way or another, that this regression is "primitive" and appropriate to an earlier time, that is, that the patient must ultimately adjust to reality, take responsibility for his life, and grow up. The "work of conquest" is necessary in order to change "an indifferent or possibly hostile object ... [into] a co-operative partner" (Balint, 1968, p. 74), and the most effective way of accomplishing this is *to tune in to the needs of the object*. Thus, while Balint was not concerned with the renunciation or taming of instinct, he tacitly regarded an obstinate regression in a patient as a narcissistic defense, not against the development of object-love in Freud's sense, but against the development of a relatively selfless concern for the object and a realistic appraisal of life's possibilities for himself. In other words, since the expectation of selfobject functioning is *legitimate* only in primitive states, Balint could not fully accept the significance of his discovery of the primary object, or selfobject and its functioning.

D.W. Winnicott

Reviewing Winnicott's writings, based upon his work in pediatrics, child analysis, and with deeply regressed patients, one immediately recognizes much that is reflected in the central concepts of self psychology, so that one is surprised to learn that Kohut was not directly and substantially influenced by his work. While Winnicott did not explicitly formulate the notion of the self as a supraordinate organizing concept for understanding the individual, his predominant area of interest was unquestionably the healthy and pathological development of what is regarded as the *self* in self psychology today. Like the other theorists we have discussed, he also uses the term "ego" interchangeably with "self." Winnicott was particularly interested in distinguishing between what he called the *True Self* and the *False Self*. The true self is present at the inception of primitive mental organization simply as "the summation of sensori-motor aliveness" (Winnicott, 1960a, p. 149). It then becomes the psychological sense of the several ways in which a particular individual experiences himself as being both alive and real—if you like, authentic. Later the true self can be regarded as equivalent to psychic reality. The essence of the true self is exemplified by the actor who can be both himself and play a role. The false self, on the other hand, is exemplified by the individual who is "completely at a loss when not in a role, and when not being appreciated or applauded ..." (p. 150). Winnicott regards the applause as the acknowledgement of the person's existence, which the false self cannot otherwise feel. This experience of personal acknowledgement is essentially what both Kohut (personal communication, 1979) and Winnicott (1967a) mean by the concept of mirroring. It is not "grandiosity" which the child needs confirmed, but a recognition of his uniqueness, of his creative capacity, that is, of his true self. Self psychology has not developed an adequate vocabulary to express this idea and has tended to rely upon notions such as "archaic grandiosity" (Kohut, 1977, p. 82) and "healthy layers of the grandiose-exhibitionistic self" (p. 53); terms which do not really do justice to Kohut's insight. Although Kohut realized the inadequacy of these concepts (personal communication, 1979), he failed to evolve a more precise and descriptive terminology. In this connection, Winnicott could also have provided him with the basis for a clearer distinction between vertical and horizontal splits. The vertical split—with its so-called infantile or archaic grandiosity—can be regarded as false self organization. The horizontal split, which Kohut initially identified with "unfulfilled archaic narcissistic demands" of the ego (1971, p. 185), and came to regard as the selfobject needs of an "incompletely organized nuclear self" (1977, p. 213), can be described as the repression of the true, or *real* self. There is a significant parallel between Winnicott's idea that the false self protects the true self and Kohut's recognition that analysis initially occurs on the level of the vertical split (where the false self prevails) and subsequently on the level of the horizontal split (where the true self components of the personality begin to form selfobject transferences).

While Freud, Suttie, Fairbairn, Guntrip, and Balint recognized the importance of selfobject functioning, Winnicott developed a deeper understanding of it. For example, he noted the paradox that "[the] basis of the capacity to be alone is the experience of being alone in the presence of someone" and further, that this capacity develops as "the ego-supportive environment is introjected and built into the individual's personality ..." (Winnicott, 1958, p. 36). This clearly represents the beginning of a psychological framework based on the central importance for personal growth of selfobject functioning. He suggested that the mother's ability to meet the primitive needs of her infant in those few weeks prior to and after birth, which is derived from a state of "primary maternal preoccupation" (1956) and which is really a state of enhanced maternal empathy, is facilitated by the infant's capacity to experience her as a *subjective object* (1962, p. 57). For Winnicott, the subjective object is "the first object, the object *not yet repudiated as a not-me phenomenon*" (1971, p. 80). It can be contrasted with the *transitional object*, which is the first *not-me* possession, a symbol of the baby and the mother (1951, p. 229).

Winnicott regards the cohesion of the early self as dependent upon "the fact that the mother holds the infant, sometimes physically, and all the time figuratively" (1960a, p. 145). The "good-enough mother" (p. 145) or the "ordinary devoted mother" (1949) enables the true self to become a reality by meeting the infant's omnipotence and giving it meaning (1960a). The idea of meeting the infant's omnipotence is as unfortunate as Kohut's concept of "archaic grandiosity" (Kohut, 1977, p. 82). What Winnicott means is that the good-enough mother functions as a selfobject for the infant to validate his creative gesture as his own and give it meaning. This formulation would be rejected by some self psychologists, yet it represents what, I believe, Kohut might have developed if he had integrated the valid aspects of Winnicott's work with his own creative contributions. Kohut's view of the enfeebled or fragmented self as a reaction to selfobject failure could also be enriched by the addition of Winnicott's idea of the false self, which is not necessarily weak or fragmented, but has compromised its genuineness by *adapting* to selfobject shortfall through *compliance* with environmental demands.

While self psychology recognizes that lustful appetites can be one of the expressions of a healthy self, insofar as it is otherwise concerned with "the instincts," it considers them in terms of the emergence of isolated drives as disintegration products of a fragmenting self. Although it is clear that Winnicott did not mean the satisfaction of instincts when he referred to the satisfaction of infant needs, he remained committed throughout his work to the importance of the instincts of destructiveness and sexuality for infant development. He regards these as significant and strengthening for the self, however, only in the context of what he called "ego-relatedness" (Winnicott, 1958, pp. 32–34), which exists between an infant and a mother who recognizes the child's psychological immaturity. The concept of ego-relatedness is just one aspect of the maternal function that Winnicott called "holding," in which the environment is empathic and responsive to the whole spectrum of the infant's needs

(1960b, pp. 44 and 49). Winnicott stressed that it is only when the infant's ego gains strength that instinctual demands are experienced as part of the self, rather than felt to originate from without. When the infant's self is not yet strong enough to include them, id-excitements can be traumatic and will, in any case, have no meaning.

Winnicott believed that the infant harbors, as an intrinsic part of its self, a primary—although not angry—destructiveness. The mother's survival of this destructiveness enables the infant eventually to apprehend her as an entity in herself, and not as a "subjective object" (1969, pp. 89–94). At this point, the infant can utilize her, in self-psychological terms, as a selfobject. Winnicott's subjective object seems to correspond to Kohut's selfobject with which the self is in a state of archaic merger. The process identified by Winnicott would not be considered valid, however, by self psychology since it reflects the idea of a primary destructiveness. Winnicott's understanding of the importance of the infant's recognition of the mother's separateness is not as incompatible with self psychology as first appears, though, since Kohut's early view that the selfobject is necessarily experienced as part of the self seems now to have been abandoned by self psychologists. These areas need theoretical clarification, and further study of Winnicott's ideas may be helpful.

Winnicott's perspective on the pathogenic factor in abnormal maturation is the same as that of Kohut. Without engaging in moral judgment, Winnicott attributes the genesis of the false self and other forms of personality distortion to varying degrees and kinds of environmental failure (1962, pp. 58–60). He also shared Kohut's awareness that the strength of the self and the fulfillment of its potential are not only dependent upon its location within a matrix of phase-appropriately responsive selfobjects from birth to death, but that inevitable non-traumatic frustrations (Kohut's so-called "optimal frustrations") also play a significant role in development and in analysis. He described this process as a developmental shift which progresses from the *absolute dependence* of the small infant to the stage of *relative dependence* which is characterized by the adaptation of the infant to the gradual failure of responsiveness on the part of the mother, to the final stage which he calls *toward independence*. During this stage, which extends through adolescence and adulthood, the parents are still needed in phase-appropriate ways (1965, pp. 91–92). At this point, however, the individual can do without the actual care he needed in childhood because he has introjected the memories of care and has developed a sense of confidence in the environment (1960b, p. 46). "In ever-widening circles of social life the child is identified with society, because local society is a sample of the child's personal world as well as being a sample of truly external phenomena" (1965, p. 91). The close adaptation of the mother to her infant's needs which was essential in the beginning for healthy development will be increasingly unnecessary as the infant's mind is able "to allow for failures in adaptation. In this way, the [infant's] mind is allied to the mother and takes over part of her function" (Winnicott, as quoted in Davis and Wallbridge, 1981, p. 53). Winnicott has identified, here, the developmental value of inevitable non-traumatic frustration and what I have referred to as *optimal responsiveness* (Bacal, 1985). He has, in effect, defined the selfobject of self psychology and the transmuting internalization of its function into self-substance and, thus, anticipated the way analysis cures according to Heinz Kohut. It should be recognized, however, that although Winnicott noted the importance of these factors for the maturational process, Kohut developed them into a systematic theoretical model.

Conclusion

It should be evident by now that, with the exception of Melanie Klein, the British object-relations theorists I have been discussing made considerable progress toward a psychology of the self as central to psychoanalysis. They did not evolve a coherent and systematic self psychology, however, because they retained an essentially moral conception of the maturation process. Kohut took the final step necessary for the development of a psychology of the self by eliminating the maturity-morality inherent in earlier views of psychoanalysis and by recognizing "narcissistic" object relations as reflecting legitimate needs of the self in relation to its selfobjects throughout life.

Loyalty to Freud's metapsychology of instinct was not as significant a factor in the failure of these theorists to articulate a full self psychology as has been assumed. Apart from Klein, they did not regard instinct theory as central to the understanding of the psychopathology of object relationships or the development of the self. While Fairbairn continued to use aspects of the language of instinct theory, his formulations represent a radical departure from orthodox psychoanalytic theory and a significant step toward the development of a psychology of the self. Guntrip, in further developing Fairbairn's work, largely dispensed with this language.

Although there are significant parallels between Klein's and Kohut's ideas, their positions are essentially incompatible since, in Kleinian terms, the most significant determinant of states of the self is constitutional envy and the death instinct, and in self psychology it is the quality of interaction between the self and its selfobject environment.

In a number of areas, a careful examination of the work of British object-relations theorists would contribute to the development of self psychological theory and practice. For example, self psychology has much of value to say about the legitimate needs of the deprived child for selfobject responsiveness, but has paid less attention to the development of the individual's capacity to be responsive to the needs of others. It is tacitly assumed that if the child is exposed to a sufficiently empathic milieu in childhood, his capacity for concern will develop, a view similar to Suttie's belief that the germ of "parental feeling" is a basic impulse, present from birth. For Balint, in contrast, this capacity originates as a complex strategy to elicit the desired response from the object. Klein and Winnicott regard the child's concern as an attempt to mitigate through reparation the anxiety produced by his own destructive impulses and fantasies. Grotstein (1983) has recently suggested that Kohut's recognition of the role of the mother's empathic regard toward the infant in maturation and

Klein's emphasis on the infant's reparative attitude toward the mother be integrated as complementary aspects of a "dual-track" theory of personal growth (p. 175). Klein's perspective, however, presupposes the operation of a primary destructiveness, an assumption rejected by self psychology. Winnicott's description of an infantile destructiveness which constitutes a significant factor for maturation, represents, however, a challenging concept for self psychology. The mother's survival of the infant's destructiveness enables him to apprehend her as a separate object, a necessary condition of his ability fully to utilize what self psychology would regard as her selfobject functions.

While self psychology has relegated instinctual life to a subsidiary affect system, both Fairbairn and Winnicott recognize its function in the development of the child's relatedness to his parents. Guntrip understands conflicts over sex and aggression as a defense against states of schizoid loneliness by a self which feels largely deserted by an unresponsive world of objects.

Self psychology has primarily focused upon the importance of selfobject failure and regarded the resulting splitting and fragmenting of the self as less significant phenomena in the therapeutic process. The work of Fairbairn, Guntrip, and Winnicott, however, demonstrates the usefulness of examining the highly organized reactions within the self to the failure of selfobjects. A deeper understanding of these reactions can increase our appreciation of patients' attempts to protect themselves against retraumatization and add a dimension to our skills in dealing with resistance.

I have not dealt here with the work of Marion Milner, Margaret Little, Masud Khan, and John Bowlby, all British analysts whose contributions also point significantly toward a psychology of the self and its relationship with selfobjects as central to our theoretical and clinical concerns in psychoanalysis.

The belief that Kohut discovered self psychology solely through the systematic use of empathy in the clinical situation without theoretical presuppositions is generally regarded today as scientifically impossible. A history of Kohut's struggle in evolving self psychology would surely confirm Winnicott's observation that, "*it is not possible to be original except on a basis of tradition*" (Winnicott, 1967b, p. 99). Nevertheless, most advances in our field have been made and will continue to be made by therapists who enter their consulting rooms with de-idealized theories which they are willing to modify or abandon when they hear better ones from their patients.

Summary

This survey of six major British object-relations theorists examines the ways in which their ideas anticipated self psychology. The work of Ian Suttie is first considered as a relatively undiscovered but significant member of this group. The work of W.R.D. Fairbairn, Harry Guntrip, Michael Balint, and D.W. Winnicott demonstrates the introduction and development of many concepts which reflect essential theory in self psychology, none of which has been recognized by Kohut or his followers.

The British theorists, however, failed to systematize a psychology of the self in the way Kohut did, largely because they were unable to dissociate their theories from the prevailing moralistic view of narcissism. The *psychological* legitimacy of *selfobject* relations throughout life could not be placed at the *center* of theory, since maturity required that "narcissistic" object relations be relinquished. The difficulty which these theorists had in disengaging their concepts from instinct theory is regarded as a less important determinant preventing them from developing a comprehensive self psychology.

A review of Melanie Klein's work suggests interesting parallels with Kohut's work, but reveals essential incompatibilities in basic theoretical assumptions with regard to the nature of the relationship between the infant's self and its early environment.

Some ways in which the work of these object-relations theorists can enrich self-psychological theory and practice are suggested.

Notes

1 MS received January 1985. Copyright © Institute of Psycho-Analysis.
2 For important exceptions to this trend see: Grotstein, 1983, in press; Robbins, 1980; Sutherland, 1980.
3 He was to point out later that, in effect, this was Freud's original view (Balint, 1968, pp. 35–36).
4 Current self psychological theory seems to have returned to the idea of a single line of development involving the relationship between the self and its selfobjects. There is no theory of object love in self psychology as there is in classical psychoanalysis; rather, "love" is either subsumed within the notion of the supportive responsivity of selfobjects, or regarded as a subsidiary affect system influencing the quality of the relationship between the self and its selfobjects.
5 The term "basic" also indicates that the influence of the basic fault extends widely to include "the whole psychobiological structure of the individual" (Balint, 1968, p. 22).

References

Bacal, H.A. (1985). Optimal responsiveness and the therapeutic process. In A. Goldberg (Ed.), *Progress in self psychology* (pp. 202–226). New York, NY: Guilford Press.

Balint, M. (1935). Critical notes on the theory of the pregenital organizations of the libido. In *Primary love and psycho-analytic technique* (1952, pp. 49–72). London: Hogarth Press.

Balint, M. (1937). Early developmental states of the ego: Primary object love. In *Primary love and psycho-analytic technique* (1952, pp. 90–108). London: Hogarth Press.

Balint, M. (1968). *The basic fault*. London: Tavistock.

Basch, M.F. (1983). The perception of reality and the disavowal of meaning. *Annual of Psychoanalysis*, 11, 125–153.

Brome, V. (1982). *Ernest Jones: Freud's alter ego*. London: Caliban Books.

Davis, M., & Wallbridge, D. (1981). *Boundary and space: An introduction to the work of D.W. Winnicott*. New York, NY: Brunner/Mazel.

Fairbairn, W.R.D. (1941). A revised psychopathology of the psychoses and psychoneuroses. In *Psychoanalytic studies of the personality* (1952, pp. 28–58). London: Tavistock.

Fairbairn, W.R.D. (1943). The repression and the return of bad objects (with special reference to the "War Neuroses." In *Psychoanalytic studies of the personality* (1952, pp. 59–81). London: Tavistock.

Fairbairn, W.R.D. (1944). Endopsychic structure considered in terms of object-relationships. In *Psychoanalytic studies of the personality* (1952, pp. 82–136). London: Tavistock.

Fairbairn, W.R.D. (1946). Object relationships and dynamic structure. In *Psychoanalytic Studies of the Personality* (1952, pp. 137–151). London: Tavistock.

Fairbairn, W.R.D. (1952). *Psychoanalytic studies of the personality*. London: Tavistock.

Freud, S. (1905). Three essays on the theory of sexuality. In *The standard edition of the complete psychological works of Sigmund Freud*, Volume VII. London: Hogarth Press.

Goldberg, A. (1984). *Introduction*. In H. Kohut, *How does analysis cure?* (pp. xi–xiii). Chicago, IL: University Chicago Press.

Grotstein, J.S. (1983). Some perspectives on self psychology. In A. Goldberg (Ed.), *The future of psychoanalysis* (pp. 165–201). New York, NY: International Universities Press.

Grotstein, J.S. (in press). Self psychology in perspective. To be published in J. Reppen (Ed.), *Self psychology: A critical evaluation*, New York, NY: Analytic Press.

Guntrip, H. (1966). The object-relations theory of W.R.D. Fairbairn. In *American handbook of psychiatry* (Vol. 3, pp. 230–238). New York, NY: Basic Books.

Guntrip, H. (1968). *Schizoid phenomena, object relations, and the self*. London: Hogarth Press.

Guntrip, H. (1971). *Psychoanalytic theory, therapy, and the self*. London: Hogarth Press.

Jones, E. (1952). *Preface to W.R.D. Fairbairn's psychoanalytic studies of the personality* (p. v). London: Tavistock.

Kohut, H. (1971). *The analysis of the self*. New York, NY: International Universities Press.

Kohut, H. (1977). *The restoration of the self*. New York, NY: International Universities Press.

Kohut, H. (1981). Transcription of remarks at the 4th Annual Conference on Self Psychology. Berkeley, California, October.

Kohut, H. (1984). *How Does Analysis Cure?* Edited by A. Goldberg and P. Stepansky. Chicago: Univ. Chicago Press.

Kohut, H., & Wolf, E. (1978). The disorders of the self and their treatment. International Journal of Psychoanalysis, 59, 413–441.

Newman, K. (1980). Defense analysis and self psychology. In A. Goldberg (Ed.), *Advances in self psychology* (pp. 263–278). New York, NY: International Universities Press.

Robbins, M. (1980). Current controversy in object relations theory as outgrowth of a schism between Klein and Fairbairn. *International Journal of Psychoanalysis*, 61, 477–492.

Rosenfeld, H. (1983). Primitive object relations and mechanisms. *International Journal of Psychoanalysis*, 64, 261–267.

Segal, H. (1973). *Introduction to the work of Melanie Klein*. London: Hogarth Press.

Segal, H. (1983). Some clinical implications of Melanie Klein's work: emergence from narcissism. *International Journal of Psychoanalysis*, 64, 269–276.

Stolorow, R. D., Brandchaft, B., & Atwood, G. E. (1983). Intersubjectivity in psychoanalytic treatment, with special reference to archaic states. *Bulletin of the Menninger Clinic*, 47(2), 117–128.

Sutherland, J.D. (1980). The British object relations theorists; Balint, Winnicott, Fairbairn, Guntrip. *Journal of the American Psychoanalytic Association*, 28, 829–860.

Suttie, I.D. (1935). *The origins of love and hate*. London: Kegan Paul, Trench, Trubner.

Winnicott, D.W. (1949). The ordinary devoted mother and her baby. In *The child and the family* (1957, pp. 3–78). London: Tavistock.

Winnicott, D.W. (1951). Transitional objects and transitional phenomena. In *Collected papers* (1958, pp. 229–242). London: Tavistock.

Winnicott, D.W. (1956). Primary maternal preoccupation. In *Collected papers* (1958, pp. 300–305). London: Tavistock.

Winnicott, D.W. (1958). The capacity to be alone. In *The maturational processes and the facilitating environment* (1965, pp. 29–36). London: Hogarth Press.

Winnicott, D.W. (1960a). Ego distortion in terms of true and false self. In *The maturational processes and the facilitating environment* (1965, pp. 140–152). London: Hogarth Press.

Winnicott, D.W. (1960b). The theory of the parent-infant relationship. In *The maturational processes and the facilitating environment* (1965, pp. 37–53). London: Hogarth Press.

Winnicott, D.W. (1962). Ego integration in child development. In *The maturational processes and the facilitating environment* (1965, pp. 56–63). London: Hogarth Press.

Winnicott, D.W. (1965). *The maturational processes and the facilitating environment* (pp. 83–92). London: Hogarth Press.

Winnicott, D.W. (1967a). Mirror-role of mother and family in child development. In *Playing and reality* (1971, pp. 111–118). London: Tavistock.

Winnicott, D.W. (1967b). The location of cultural experience. In *Playing and reality* (1971, pp. 95–103). London: Tavistock.

Winnicott, D.W. (1969). The use of an object and relating through identifications. In *Playing and reality* (1971, pp. 86–94). London: Tavistock.

Winnicott, D.W. (1971). Creativity and its origins. In *Playing and reality* (pp. 65–85). London: Tavistock.

Wolf, E. (1980). On the developmental line of selfobject relations. In A. Goldberg (Ed.), *Advances in self psychology* (pp. 117–130). New York, NY: International Universities Press.

5 The Selfobject Relationship in Psychoanalytic Treatment

It is generally agreed that the selfobject concept is the cornerstone of the self-psychological perspective in psychoanalysis. So central is it that Basch has suggested that the proper designation of self psychology should be "selfobject theory of motivation." In this chapter, the author draws attention to the relational nature of the selfobject experience in psychoanalytic treatment. He identifies the selfobject relationship as more than simply a static background experience of the patient against which therapy is effectively conducted. He suggests that it is a continuous dynamic experience that arises from a complex interaction between analyst and analysand and is integral to the ongoing therapeutic process. He also submits that it is variously experienced, quite legitimately, by both participants and that this will have a significant effect on the course of the therapy.

It is generally agreed that the *selfobject* concept is the cornerstone of the self-psychological perspective in psychoanalysis. So central is it that Basch has suggested that the proper designation of self psychology should be "selfobject theory of motivation." In this chapter, I draw attention to the relational nature of the selfobject experience in psychoanalytic treatment. I identify the selfobject relationship as more than simply a static background experience of the patient against which therapy is effectively conducted. I suggest that it is a continuous dynamic experience that arises from a complex interaction between analyst and analysand and is integral to the ongoing therapeutic process. I also suggest that it is variously experienced, quite legitimately, by both participants and that this will have a significant effect on the course of the therapy.

Kohut formulated the concept of the selfobject[1] when he began to apprehend his patients' complex mental states consistently from the vantage point of their subjective experience by using what he called vicarious introspection, or empathy. What he discovered was that his patients did not seem to experience him as an object toward whom they directed their conflictual wishes over the discharge of instinctual drives; rather, they appeared to need responses from him that would evoke and affect their sense of self. He was, as it were, a "*selfobject*" whom they needed to experience in certain ways: as confirming their sense of vigor and perfection; as a figure of calmness, infallibility, and omnipotence with

DOI: 10.4324/9781003570806-6

whom they could merge; and as someone who was silently present but, in essence, like them. Kohut (1971) regarded the appearance of these recurrent, identifiable configurations, which he called "transferencelike structures" (p. 25), as variously indicating not only the emergence of selfobject needs for mirroring, idealizing, and twinship or alterego responses, and the experiencing of those needs as being met, but also the expectation that the analyst would respond to those needs. What I want to draw attention to here is the fact that the selfobject is a multi-faceted concept that implies not only the experience of need and the experience of function provided by the other, or "object,"[2] but also *the experience of a relationship*, and that it has done so since the beginning of self psychology. My conceptualization of a *selfobject relationship* is an intrapsychic experience of another who can be counted upon to provide essential selfobject functions. The cohesiveness of the self is reinforced by the expectation that this other will respond optimally to one's selfobject needs. There is a sense of ownership of this other that is associated with a sense of entitlement to his or her optimal responsiveness, both of which may operate to some extent on an unconscious level (see Bacal and Newman, 1990, pp. 233, 252). In other words, a selfobject relationship is one in which a relatively stable sense of the object's availability as a selfobject prevails. There is a bond with the analyst, at the center of which is the sense that the analyst will be with the analysand in the way he or she needs the analyst to be.

While the selfobject "transference"[3] is commonly referred to as a tie or bond, that is, as a selfobject relationship (see Kohut, 1984, pp. 49–52), the only allusion to its functioning as a selfobject relationship in the clinical situation has been as the necessary background against which therapeutic work is carried out in the foreground (see Stolorow, Brandchaft, and Atwood, 1987, p. 26). Recently, however, the selfobject relationship is becoming recognized not merely as some vague, friendly, or supportive connection but, rather, as an experience that is at the very center of the therapeutic process. Thus, Wolf (1988), in his recent description of the selfobject, regards it "as being neither self nor object, but the subjective aspect of a self-sustaining function performed by a *relationship* of self to objects who by their presence or activity evoke and maintain the self and the experience of selfhood" (p. 184, emphasis added). It is also significant that Stern (1985) regards the selfobject as a "term for a variety of ongoing functional *relationships* with others that are necessary to provide the regulating structures that maintain and/or enhance self-cohesion" (p. 242, my emphasis).[4]

I have described how the ideas of certain British object relations theorists anticipated the relational aspect of the selfobject experience (Bacal, 1987; Bacal and Newman, 1990): Ian Suttie's emphasis on the importance of companionship, security, and the psychological responsiveness of the mothering figure resonates strongly with the concept of the selfobject. Aspects of Bowlby's attachment relationship are strongly reflected in the selfobject concept, as Lichtenberg (1989) has noted in his schema of motivational systems. Bowlby's concept of the attachment figure also recognizes the specificity of the selfobject.

That is, it implies the experience of a relationship with an important other: it is not that any selfobject experience with anyone will do; it is *that* therapist whom the patient misses or whose absence results in the patient's falling apart. Balint (1968) and Winnicott (1954), in particular, described certain characteristics of archaic relatedness that appear almost identical to those of Kohut's archaic merger or mirroring selfobject relationship[5] in patients who are in deeply regressed states in analysis. Indeed, since they have Winnicott, it is only quite recently that British analysts have formally acknowledged that self psychology has something to offer them.[6] And self psychologists besides myself are now paying more attention to some of their ideas: one of the more sophisticated self-psychological analogues of Winnicott's view that the infant cannot be considered by itself but, rather, as part of the infant–parent unit is reflected in Stolorow and Atwood's (1992) notion of the "myth of the isolated mind."

And yet, despite the commonalities between the views of certain British object relations theorists and those of self psychology, the intrinsic nature of the selfobject relationship significantly sets it apart from any other relational concept in psychoanalysis. In order to appreciate this fully, we must return to Kohut's earliest conceptualization of the selfobject in 1971.

While Kohut (1971) initially thought of the selfobject as subserving a narcissistic experience, he defined selfobjects as objects that "are either used in the service of the self ... or are themselves experienced as part of the self" (p. xiv). He also brought a completely fresh attitude to the concepts of narcissistic needs and narcissistic experiences. Because he regarded them as reflecting neither a fixation, a defense, nor an intensification of self-love but, rather, an attempt at repairing a developmental deficit through a relationship with him, he could respond to them as psychologically legitimate. Just as Freud had conferred a sense of legitimacy upon the analysis of sexuality 50 years before, so too did Kohut confer a sense of legitimacy upon the analysis of narcissism (see Wolf, 1988, pp. 6–8), opening up important new territory for therapeutic work. Until then, analysts, including the British object relations theorists, only accepted the archaic needs of patients when they were in seriously regressed states; they responded to the archaic longings of all other patients in ways that emphasized their developmental age *inappropriateness*, displaying what Kohut came to call a "maturity-morality." Kohut, in contrast, introduced the concept of the selfobject to denote the analysand's selfobject needs, experiences, and expectations of the other's responsiveness as psychologically appropriate, or legitimate, without reference to the level or degree of the patient's regression.[7] In doing so, he transformed the way we view the psychoanalytic relationship and the way we treat our patients.

However, when Kohut also characterized the selfobject experience as the analysand's *expectation* of control over the other and his function as being more like the control that grown-ups would expect to have over their own body and mind, he went much further (see Kohut, 1971, p. 32). I emphasize the word expectation, as I believe that its implications have been insufficiently appreciated. Kohut was, in effect, sanctioning the patient's sense of natural entitlement to certain basic human responses from the analyst as a parental figure in the transference. Today, we are less interested in the question of whether or not analysands experience the selfobject as part of their physical self, and, since Stern's work, we tend to think they do not. I would agree with Morton Shane (1991) that the idea of the *psychological* inclusion of the analyst in the patient's sense of self is as intrinsic to the selfobject concept in use today as it is to Kohut's conceptualization in 1971, but I would regard this as meaning that patients feel they have a basic sense of entitlement to the analyst's selfobject responsiveness. This sense of natural entitlement to the responsivity of the significant other is to be distinguished from the urgent, intense, agitated, controlling, and sometimes extravagant expressions of entitlement that, in fact, belie a deficiency or disturbance in a natural sense of entitlement.[8] I believe that its restoration and its increasing strength and stability are major determinants of the decrease in the intensity, urgency, and anxiety associated with the experiencing of selfobject needs over time; in other words, its development is associated with the maturation of selfobject relationships. If one has a confident expectation that one is entitled to ongoing selfobject relationships[9] with significant others, the self is stronger and feels more prepared to respond reciprocally to the comparable selfobject need of others.

In self-disordered patients, this sense of basic entitlement is seriously disturbed and may contribute significantly to the persistence of feelings of being hopelessly bad and inadequate. Without this sense of entitlement, the patient feels psychologically alone, an experience that people with severe narcissistic personality disorders and borderline conditions sometimes suffer from terribly. In other words, I am suggesting that the experience of this basic sense of entitlement is a precondition for experiencing a selfobject relationship, a relationship in which patients feel that they can count on the selfobject responsiveness of their analyst. There is for the patient an important sense of ownership of the other and a concomitant sense of specialness within the self; the selfobject is the *self's* object. I believe that this sense of ownership is also at the heart of what has been called "basic trust."

I have elsewhere described the therapeutic effect of a self-psychological analysis as a "corrective selfobject experience" (Bacal, 1990). The therapeutic process through which this experience occurs is the establishment and regulation of a selfobject relationship,[10] which is, in effect, a joint creation on the part of the analyst and the analysand. Equating the therapeutic process with the mutually created evolution of the selfobject relationship reframes a perspective that others have advanced in different ways. As Lachmann and Beebe (1992) have pointed out, a number of authors such as Gill, Hoffman, Mitchell, Stolorow, Brandchaft, and Atwood have discussed the interactive contributions of analyst and analysand that shape transference, and they themselves have proffered the view that the mutual regulation between the contributions of both participants can transform the patient's experience and psychic structure (see also Beebe, Jaffe, and Lachmann, 1992). Analogous views include

Terman's (1988) concept of a "dialogue of construction," Paul Tolpin's (1988) definition of the therapeutic task as "optimal affective engagement," and Lessem and Orange's recent (1993) hypothesis that the emotional bond that develops as a result of interactions between the patient and the therapist constitutes the central curative determinant of psychoanalysis.

I should now like to outline my conception of the respective contributions of the patient and the analyst to the creation of the experience of a selfobject relationship. In doing so, I am also describing what I regard to be the central elements of the therapeutic process. The selfobject relationship is, in effect, experienced by both analyst and analysand. Let us first consider the contributions of the analysand to his or her experience of this relationship:

1 The transference of unmet needs motivates analysands, despite their fears and defenses, to put the therapist in the role of provider of essential psychological functions for the sustenance of the self.
2 Antecedent selfobject relationships, especially in childhood, are also transferred onto the therapist, and they, too, incline the patient to believe that a selfobject relationship with the therapist is possible. I would include here the sense of a right to the selfobject ministrations of a parent figure, what I have called a natural sense of entitlement, which is transferred from the experiences of the early interactions that confirm it.
3 The capacity of analysands to create in phantasy a figure who is imbued with qualities that would justify their trust also contributes to their experience of a selfobject relationship with their therapist. The exercise of this capacity is a major determinant of the experience of idealization. To the extent that the capacity derives from prior selfobject experience, it may operate somewhat like the evoked companion described by Stern (1985), that is, like a "self-regulating other [that] becomes 'present' in the form of an active memory" (p. 116). It is important to recognize, however, that it predominantly reflects the analysand's capacity for creative imagination. I have found it useful to conceptualize a "phantasy selfobject" when the patient's experience of his or her contribution to the experience of the relationship with the analyst as selfobject appears to be based largely on this capacity, that is, on the mobilization of imagos of responsive selfobjects that the patient has already substantively created in childhood. These imagos serve to substitute and compensate for unbearable experiences of deprivation that patients feel they must continue to disavow; without them the experience of a selfobject relationship would likely not be possible. A patient of mine recently explained to me, during a period when she was finding the courage to experience her despair and hopelessness, "You make a phantasy because you don't have the real thing." This patient, and others, also taught me that any selfobject relationship that does develop largely on the basis of phantasy will be delicate and therefore particularly susceptible to disruption.

The essence of the analyst's contributions to the patient's experience of a selfobject relationship is his or her optimal responsiveness to those of the patient (see Bacal, 1985, 1990; Bacal and Newman, 1990). As we know, the therapist's optimal responsiveness may take many forms. It includes the provision and/or interpretation of a variety of verbal and non-verbal selfobject functions. It also includes a willingness to collaborate on the task of working through disruptions in the selfobject relationship between the two participants. It may entail an inquiring attitude or a quiet non-inquiring presence, an echoing confirmation, or a confrontational challenge. Its form will be determined not only by the issues that the patient and the analyst are working on but also by the strength of the patient's self, and by the patient's operative level of developmental achievement, which Basch (1991, 1992) has described.

The therapist's ability to respond optimally to the patient will be determined partly by his or her own prior experiences of selfobject relationship. It is also significantly influenced by his or her capacity for creative imagination, or phantasy. The mild idealization of the patient by the therapist, which Kohut believed to be an essential ingredient of an effective treatment, is likely fueled by the exercise of this capacity. It is as if the therapist is saying, "You, my patient, are a special person who is entitled to this special relationship that we have together."

The complexity of the interactions between the patient and therapist that constitute the experience of a selfobject relationship for the patient also results in the therapist's experiencing a selfobject relationship with the patient (Wolf, 1980). The therapist, too, brings unmet selfobject needs and prior selfobject experiences into the relationship with his or her patient, and these engender expectations that the analysand will respond in certain ways. Since it is agreed that the participants have come together for the psychological benefit of the patient, our customary attitude toward the therapist's selfobject needs is that they are to be regarded as countertransferences to be understood. Insofar as the therapist is fortified by his or her extra-analytic selfobject relationships and can decenter from these selfobject needs, he or she will be able to contribute effectively (i.e., be optimally responsive) to the patient's need for a selfobject relationship in therapy. When the analyst cannot fulfill this function, we recommend supervision or more personal analysis. This perspective is valid, ethical, and safe, but it ignores what we all know but have somehow found it awkward to discuss with each other: The therapist's experience of a selfobject relationship with the patient not only is pervasively operative in every therapeutic relationship but constitutes a precondition for the therapist to respond in ways that will enable the patient to experience a selfobject relationship with him or her. Analysts regularly *expect* analysands to respond in a number of ways that are, in fact, self-sustaining or self-enhancing for the therapist, such as honoring their commitment to ongoing regular sessions, for which a fee is paid, for a process in which *both* patient and therapist expect the patient to make some progress over time. These are only a few of the more evident selfobject functions that analysts consciously expect from the analysand, which they usually experience in their selfobject relationship with the analysand and which they tacitly, and sometimes explicitly, regard as preconditions for their effective analytic functioning. There are others that operate at an unconscious level; it is likely that a good deal of what we call countertransference corresponds to the analyst's experience of the thwarting of his or her selfobject needs that are *ordinarily* met in the selfobject relationship with the analysand. Perhaps Stolorow and I might agree to call this "intersubjective optimal responsivity." In any event, there is a certain essential mutuality or reciprocity in the analytic selfobject relationship. This is a topic that deserves further explication and illustration, which I will offer on another occasion (see Bacal and Thomson, 1993).

Notes

1 Initially, the word was hyphenated. Kohut removed the hyphen between *self* and *object* to "express more unambiguously the fact that we are dealing not with an adhoc construct but with a viable concept which we hope will find an enduring place in analytic thought" (in a letter to the *International Journal of Psycho-Analysis* on September 9, 1978).

2 The selfobject concept is used to refer both to certain needs of the self as well as to experiences of their being met by others. These needs and experiences of the function of others fundamentally include the evocation of the sense of self and the reconstitution of the sense of self after it has been shaken or lost. Other ubiquitously recognized selfobject needs and experiences include self-esteem regulation, affect attunement, affect containment, tension regulation, soothing, and vitalization. Curiously, these selfobject needs and functions have not yet been given the status of the three others. Stolorow and Atwood (1992) have recently described a "self-delineating selfobject function" (pp. 27, 49), which will likely become accepted as of equal importance to the three described by Kohut.

3 I put "transference" in quotes because I believe that Kohut's initial designation of selfobject transferences as "transferencelike structures" (Kohut, 1971, p. 25) is correct insofar as they include much more than transference.

4 In effect, Stern's (1985) view of the normal infant is that its "life is so thoroughly social that most of the things the infant does, feels, and perceives occur in different kinds of relationships" (p. 118).

5 For further illustrations of analogous conceptualizations to the selfobject relationship in the writings of the British object relations theorists, see Bacal and Newman (1990).

6 During the summer of 1992 a colloquium was held in London between members of the Independent Group of the British Psycho-Analytical Society and members of the National Council for Self Psychology (see also Mollon, in press).

7 Some self psychologists, such as Basch (1991), would retain the designation *selfobject* to refer to the optimal responses that only the endangered self requires of the therapist and would distinguish this sharply from the cohesive self's relationship to objects. I have argued, in contrast, that in practice we are always dealing with a *relatively* cohesive self (Bacal, 1991). This usually presents as a relatively weakened or fragmented self; however, we do regularly encounter situations where patients who are progressing in analysis, and whose self is becoming stronger, paradoxically need, because their sense of self is under increased strain at that time, the experience of selfobject responsivity that is above and beyond the usual in order to soar to new heights of efficacy and freedom.

8 George Kriegman (1988) has classified attitudes of entitlement in a way that is very similar to the one I am describing here.

9 Compare Howard Levine's (1979) "sustaining object relationship."

10 In a certain sense, Kohut held a comparable view. He believed that it was not the interpretation that cured the patient but, rather, the therapeutic relationship that led to an empathic bond between the patient and the analyst. He understood the process to entail microrelationships between the self and its selfobjects that lead to the building of psychological structure through the process of transmuting internalization of optimal frustrations (see Kohut, 1977, pp. 31–32). I agree with Kohut that effective therapy entails the experience of the self's relationship with selfobjects, but I view the genesis of that relationship quite differently.

References

Bacal, H.A. (1985). Optimal responsiveness and the therapeutic process. In A. Goldberg (Ed.), *Progress in self psychology* (Vol. 1, pp. 202–227). New York, NY: Guilford.

Bacal, H.A. (1987). British object-relations theorists and self psychology: Some critical reflections. *International Journal of Psycho-Analysis*, 68, 81–98.

Bacal, H.A. (1990). The elements of a corrective selfobject experience. *Psychoanalytic Inquiry*, 10, 347–372.

Bacal, H.A. (1991). Notes on the relationship between object relations theory and self psychology. In A. Goldberg (Ed.), *The evolution of self psychology: Progress in self psychology* (Vol. 7, pp. 36–44). Hillsdale, NJ: The Analytic Press.

Bacal, H.A., & Newman, K. (1990). *Theories of object-relations: Bridges to self psychology*. New York, NY: Columbia University Press.

Bacal, H.A., & Thomson, P. (1993). *The psychoanalyst's selfobject needs and the effect of their frustration on the treatment: A new view of countertransference*. Presented at the 16th Annual Conference on the Psychology of the Self, Toronto, October 31.

Balint, M. (1968). *The basic fault*. London: Tavistock.

Basch, M.F. (1991). Are selfobjects the only objects? Implications for psychoanalytic technique. In A. Goldberg (Ed.), *The evolution of self psychology: Progress in self psychology* (Vol. 7, pp. 3–15). Hillsdale, NJ: The Analytic Press.

Basch, M.F. (1992). *The selfobject concept: Clinical implications*. Presented at the 15th Annual Conference on the Psychology of the Self, Los Angeles, October 10.

Beebe, B., Jaffe, J., & Lachmann, F. (1992). A dyadic systems view of communication. In N. Skolnick & S. Warshaw (Eds.), *Relational psychoanalysis* (pp. 61–81). Hillsdale, NJ: The Analytic Press.

Kohut, H. (1971). *The analysis of the self*. New York, NY: International Universities Press.

Kohut, H. (1977). *The restoration of the self*. New York, NY: International Universities Press.

Kohut, H. (1984). How does analysis cure? (A. Goldberg & P. Stepansky, Eds.). Chicago, IL: University of Chicago Press.

Kriegman, G. (1988). Entitlement attitudes: Psychological and therapeutic implications. In V. Volkan & T. Rodgers (Eds.), *Attitudes of entitlement* (pp. 1–21). Charlottesville, VA: University Press of Virginia.

Lachmann, F., & Beebe, B. (1992). Reformulations of early development and transference: Implications for psychic structure formation. In J. Barron, M. Eagle, & D. Wolitzky (Eds.), *Psychology and psychoanalysis* (pp. 133–153). Washington, DC: The American Psychoanalytic Association.

Lessem, P., & Orange, D. (1993). *Emotional bonds: The therapeutic action of psychoanalysis revisited.* Presented at the 16th Annual Conference on the Psychology of the Self, Toronto, October 31.

Levine, H. (1979). The sustaining object relationship. *The Annual of Psychoanalysis*, 7, 203–231.

Lichtenberg, J.D. (1989). *Psychoanalysis and motivation.* Hillsdale, NJ: The Analytic Press.

Mollon, P. (in press). *The fragile self and the search for mirroring: The structure of narcissistic disturbance.* London: Whurr.

Shane, M. (1991). Selfobject or self-regulating other. In A. Goldberg (Ed.), *The evolution of self psychology: Progress in self psychology* (Vol. 7, pp. 31–36). Hillsdale, NJ: The Analytic Press.

Stern, D. (1985). *The interpersonal world of the infant.* New York, NY: Basic Books.

Stolorow, R.D., & Atwood, G.E. (1992). *Contexts of being: The intersubjective foundations of psychological life.* Hillsdale, NJ: The Analytic Press.

Stolorow, R.D., Brandchaft, B., & Atwood, G.E. (1987). *Psychoanalytic treatment: An intersubjective approach.* Hillsdale, NJ: The Analytic Press.

Terman, D. (1988). Optimum frustration: Structuralization and the therapeutic process. In A. Goldberg (Ed.), *Learning From Kohut: Progress in self psychology* (Vol. 4, pp. 113–125). Hillsdale, NJ: The Analytic Press.

Tolpin, P. (1988). Optimal affective engagement: The analyst's role in therapy. In A. Goldberg (Ed.), *Learning From Kohut: Progress in self psychology* (Vol. 4, pp. 160–168). Hillsdale, NJ: The Analytic Press.

Winnicott, D.W. (1954). Metapsychological and clinical aspects of regression within the psycho-analytical set-up. In *D.W. Winnicott: Collected papers* (pp. 278–299). London: Tavistock.

Wolf, E. (1980). Empathy and countertransference. In A. Goldberg (Ed.), *The future of psychoanalysis* (pp. 309–326). New York, NY: International Universities Press.

Wolf, E. (1988). *Treating the self: Elements of clinical self psychology.* New York, NY: Guilford.

6 The Psychoanalyst's Selfobject Needs and the Effect of Their Frustration on the Treatment: A New View of Countertransference

This chapter explores the psychoanalyst's "selfobject" needs—emotional needs that, when unmet, may disrupt the therapist's effectiveness in treatment. Countertransference, where the therapist's feelings toward the patient impact the therapeutic process, is central to this exploration. Traditionally viewed as either a therapeutic hindrance or asset, countertransference is here reframed to consider how analysts' unmet selfobject needs can interfere with their empathy and responsiveness. The author argues that these needs are inherently relational, and acknowledging them may enhance, rather than hinder, therapy. The author also includes clinical examples, illustrating how the frustration of selfobject needs can lead to counterproductive reactions such as shame or anger, affecting both the analyst's and patient's experiences. The author advocates for therapists' self-awareness and suggests that such acknowledgment can mitigate negative impacts, fostering a balanced therapeutic relationship.

We are aware of the multiple and complex definitions and conceptualizations of "countertransference" in the literature (see especially definitions and references in Rycroft, 1972; Moore and Fine, 1990) and we will not review them here. Historically, psychoanalysts have variously held two contradictory views on countertransference. One view is that it constitutes feelings on the part of the analyst that may interfere with the patient's therapy. The other is that it may be a valuable asset in the treatment process. Both these views of countertransference parallel, to a large extent, analysts' views of transference—that it may be an interference, a resistance, to the analysis and that it may serve as a major vehicle for the analytic process. Freud (1910) identified countertransference as an impediment to the effective treatment of the patient. This view persisted, for the most part, until 1950, when Heimann (1950) proffered a new definition and a novel perspective on countertransference. She regarded countertransference as comprising all the analyst's feelings toward the patient, and she argued that the analyst's emotional response to his patient provided him with one of his most useful tools for understanding the patient's unconscious. Sandler (1976) extended Heimann's idea to include the process whereby the analyst becomes alerted to important experiences within the patient by becoming aware of certain roles that the patient induces within the analyst. This process repeats significant early relationships for the patient.

DOI: 10.4324/9781003570806-7

Because of the difference in the role of the analyst from that of the patient in the treatment process, the psychology of the analyst has been relatively neglected. If we agree with Sullivan (1953) that "*everyone is much more simply human than otherwise*" (p. 32), then as therapists we must surely assume that we are made of the same psychological stuff as our patients. That is, we therapists, too, bring a relational history, a cumulative representation of our lived experience of interaction to the analytic situation. This puts us in a psychological position not unlike that of our patients, despite the difference in our roles.

Kohut, interestingly, took a similar view to that of Freud when he described the "narcissistic" countertransferences as interfering with the establishment of the narcissistic transferences. Kohut (1971) understood how the analyst tends to react in particular ways to these transferences:

> The analyst's own narcissistic needs ... may make it difficult for him to tolerate a situation in which he is reduced to the seemingly passive role of being a mirror of the patient's infantile narcissism, and he may, therefore, subtly or openly ... interfere with the establishment or the maintenance of the mirror transference.
>
> (p. 272)

And "the rejection of the patient's idealizing attitudes is usually motivated by a defensive fending off of painful narcissistic tensions ... which are generated in the analyst when the repressed fantasies of his grandiose self become stimulated by the patient's idealization" (p. 262). Wolf (1979, 1980) and Kohler (1984/1985) have elaborated on Kohut's views, using the new terminology of the "selfobject." The selfobject transferences refer to the need of the patient for self-restorative and self-sustaining responses from the analyst. Wolf (1979) coined the term "selfobject countertransferences" to denote the counterpart in the analyst of the selfobject transferences of the analysand, whether or not they are evoked by the analysand. That is, the analyst, too, has selfobject needs that are mobilized as a result of participating in the analytic process (see Wolf, 1980).

Kohut's introduction of the new language was more than a change in terminology. It underscored his view that so-called narcissistic phenomena reflect the frustration and distortion of a basic sort of psychological need—indeed, a *healthy* need of the self in a relational context. As Kindler (1991) has explicitly stated in his fine paper on the subject, every individual has at his core a need to be mirrored or affirmed. However, while the *analysand's* needs for selfobject responsiveness from the analyst have become increasingly accepted as psychologically legitimate, the *analyst's* selfobject needs in relation to the analysand, although they are understandable, have in practice continued to be regarded as largely undesirable. They are unfortunate reactions from which the analyst should attempt to decenter. In other words, we are still defining certain experiences of the analyst as "unhealthy." To put it plainly, the analyst should be ashamed of them. They constitute a problem that simply needs to be overcome. A large part of the problem is that analysts are, in effect, pretty good at disavowing their feelings when their selfobject needs are not met. We are not simply implying that "analysts are people, too" who have selfobject needs. We are, more importantly, also saying that because this is so it constitutes a very practical issue for the treatment of the patient. We have scarcely begun to explore the various ways in which the analyst's experience of his or her needs in relation to the patient and their satisfaction, frustration, or distortion affect the treatment process.

In this chapter, we will offer a new perspective on "countertransference." This perspective, in effect, supports the conceptual usefulness of restricting the usage of the term to refer to the interference with the analyst's therapeutic function. (This has, in fact, become the most common usage of the term.) We propose the view (see also Bacal, 1994) that the analyst's self is ordinarily sustained in his work by ongoing selfobject responses of the analysand, and we will argue that his or her analytic function may be substantially interfered with (i.e., countertransference reactions occur) when these selfobject needs are significantly frustrated. We will also suggest that the analyst's therapeutic function is enhanced as a result of his lessened requirement to protect himself or herself against the awareness of these needs. We will, further, suggest ways in which this goal may be attained—ways that centrally entail deactivating the sometimes disabling sense of shame that may accompany the awareness of our selfobject needs in relation to our patients.

We would affirm Wolf's view (1979) that, while we may have gained much from our personal analyses, none of us is entirely free from sensitivities, vulnerabilities, and longings that arise from personal and professional frustrations or injuries, both past and present. We plead for a measure of tolerance for the ubiquity of a wide range of inevitable shortcomings in the personalities of analysts. We do not of course condone the enactment by the analyst of selfobject needs or of any other needs in relation to the patient that are ethically unacceptable. When we speak of empathic failures or failures in optimal responsiveness, we are placing these against the background of the expectable performance of a committed therapist at the level of his or her experience and training. Having said this, we must acknowledge that all of us attempt to defend ourselves from the repetition of disruptive experiences and their disturbing affects—especially that of shame—with anyone, including with our patients.

Gunther (1976) emphasizes this perspective in his understanding of countertransference reactions. He sees them as enactments whose purpose is to restore the "narcissistic" equilibrium of the analyst that becomes disturbed in interactions with the analysand. They are symptoms of the reassertion of the analyst's narcissistic needs. Wolf (1980) was the first to explicitly recognize the bidirectional nature of selfobject neediness in the analytic process and to recognize its value and its liabilities as it is experienced by the analyst. Kohler (1984/1985), on the basis of the work of Beebe and Sloate, and Sander have described the complex interactions between the therapist's and the patient's selfobject needs as analogous to the interactions of the mother-child pair. Thomson (1991, 1993) has extensively illustrated how selfobject disruption in the analyst in relation to the analysand provides a particular opportunity to study how this may have contributed to the derailment in the patient. Bacal (1994) has recently suggested that

> The therapist's experience of a selfobject relationship with the patient is not only pervasively operative in every therapeutic relationship but it constitutes a precondition for the therapist to respond in ways that will enable the patient to experience a selfobject relationship with him or her. Analysts regularly *expect* analysands to respond in a number of ways that are, in fact, self-sustaining or self-enhancing for the therapist.
>
> (p. 28)

We submit that the complexity of these experiences requires conceptualization that the term "countertransference" simply does not do justice to at all. We believe that certain processes operating in the analyst that affect the patient may be usefully conceptualized in terms of the meeting of selfobject needs or the frustration of selfobject needs. We concur with Wolf that the term "empathic resonance" usefully describes the situation when the analyst effectively undergoes a controlled regression along with the patient in his efforts to remain attuned to him. However, to regard this as an aspect of countertransference—a term that commonly designates an interference with the therapeutic process—is conceptually confusing. This limited regression is in the service of the therapeutic relationship. Our understanding of empathic resonance is similar to Balint's understanding of the harmoniously regressive archaic experience which he termed "primary love" or "primary object-love" (1937, 1968) as it occurs within the analytic dyad—an experience not dissimilar to Kohut's conception of the archaic selfobject twinship transference.[1] A basic sort of alterego selfobject relatedness[2] is mobilized in the analyst (I know how you feel because I have had, or am having, similar experiences of my own). In this regression, the analyst may also have a complementary experience to the patient's selfobject experience (I sense your need, for example, to be special, and I do experience you in that way). Thus, in exercising his or her capacity for vicarious introspection, the analyst may experience comparable or complementary needs of his own as being met by the patient. We would add, parenthetically, that the need to give that is activated in the analyst—for example, to respond to the selfobject need of his analysand—may be one of the deepest and most vitalizing needs of his self (cf. Ian Suttie, chapter 1 in Bacal and Newman, 1990, pp. 19–20, and in chapter 3, this book).

In her recent study of the subjective and intersubjective determinants of *optimal responsiveness* (see Bacal, 1985), Estrella (1993) noted that the mutuality of subjective experiences contributes significantly to therapists' attunement and empathic resonance. She found that "the psychotherapist's attunement to his or her own subjective pain and corresponding resonance to their particular patient's pain may have contributed significantly to their being optimally responsive," especially around instances of loss. We do not think that experiences such as these are properly included in the idea of "countertransference."

Wolf (1980) has suggested that the analyst's experience of the intensification of his selfobject needs may be used as signals to alert him to an impending derailment of the therapeutic process. We would propose the term "signal disruption in the analyst" to denote the analyst's experience that his selfobject needs are not being met, but when his self maintains its stability and cohesiveness. When the analyst has what we traditionally call a countertransference reaction, the analyst's selfobject needs that are ordinarily being met by the patient during their interaction are now being frustrated, and his sense of self is concomitantly threatened or shaken—or worse. This selfobject disruption in the analyst will affect the analyst's capacity to attune and to respond optimally to the patient. If analysts insist on retaining the term "countertransference" (which they probably will do), we believe that it should refer to these reactive or disjunctive[3] phenomena that affect the analyst's therapeutic function. These run "counter," if you like, to the selfobject "transference" needs of the analysand in the treatment.

It must be emphasized that the therapist's selfobject needs do differ from those of the patient insofar as they are represented through his or her therapeutic function. The most common selfobject need of the therapist is for mirroring of his function according to whatsoever way he conceives this function. If he conceives it as a caring attitude, he needs to be affirmed for this. If he conceives his function in terms of cognitive understanding, he needs affirmation for this. If, for example, he needs to idealize the patient, then he can feel wonderful if he perceives his patient as having special attributes. He may see his function as providing a holding, enlivening, reliably receptive ambience, for which he unconsciously needs affirmation. In the course of the analysis many of these needs are ordinarily met by the patient's attendance, his arriving and leaving on time, lying on the couch while he is there, staying awake, supplying associative material, listening to interpretations, paying a fee, picking up the tab for missed sessions, and so on—that is, conforming, more or less, to the routines of the analytic situation. In this situation, the analyst is usually no more aware that these routines may embody selfobject needs than he is of the air he breathes. To some extent, the analyst's training makes him take the meeting of these expectations for granted.

In his training of general practitioners for psychotherapeutic work, Balint (1964) referred to the "apostolic mission or function" of the doctor—"that every doctor has a vague, but almost unshakably firm, idea of how a patient ought to behave when ill … . It was … as if he had a sacred duty to convert to his faith all the ignorant and unbelieving among his patients." Balint added: "Although this idea is anything but explicit and concrete, it is immensely powerful, and influences … practically every detail of the doctor's work" (p. 216). We believe that these expectations derive not only from therapist's training—some may say, from his or her indoctrination—but also from the therapist's unmet selfobject needs that he brings to the patient in the therapy situation. Personal analysis may enable the therapist to engage some of these needs, but unless they are addressed more directly (as we shall discuss in a moment), they may remain largely unconscious and thus pose a potential interference with the therapist's efficacy. Therapists' enhanced awareness of how their psychological needs and vulnerabilities have become organized into their professional working persona will enable them to become clearer about the limits to their capacity for optimal responsiveness to any particular patient.

Perhaps the therapist's predominant need is for affirmation of his capacity to understand and, in many instances, for his caring, humanistic motivation. We suspect that this need by therapists to be seen as decent, well-motivated human beings in their work is both pervasive and unacknowledged, yet it is difficult for analysts when they are thought to be anything but that by their patients. This need may reflect an inadequate working through of the "darker" or "nastier" sides of the analyst in his own analysis. Conversely, an analytic experience in which the dark side was all too vigorously attended to may repeat a trauma of the therapist's childhood. These experiences may leave the therapist with significant unmet needs that he or she brings into the consulting room. For some therapists, the meeting of such needs is at the center of their general raison d'être. The therapeutic work with their patients may serve to repair defects in self-structure that arose from a requirement to accede to the archaic selfobject needs of their caretakers.[4] The self-esteem and self-cohesion of these therapists will depend on their success in fulfilling the needs of their analysands (see Stolorow and Atwood, 1992).

When a patient becomes seriously disrupted, the analyst's selfobject needs may become significantly frustrated; in particular, the analyst may experience a loss of the sense of efficacy. He may also experience dysphoric affects such as anger, inadequacy, disappointment in himself, and shame.

Clinical Illustration: Tina

A situation that illustrates a number of these issues arose with Tina, an accomplished and successful young architect. Tina had a mother who was continuingly and grossly out of tune with her affiliative-attachment needs, and who had been so, apparently, from Tina's early infancy. In her analysis, Tina railed bitterly, angrily, and despairingly against her mother's insensitivity, cruelty, and her near-total dismissal of the validity of her daughter's complaints. As she regressed in the transference, which was largely positive in an idealizing way, she began to experience the holiday breaks as quite intolerable. And on more than one occasion, she experienced herself dissociating and fragmenting during breaks in ways that profoundly distressed her. However, she never appeared ill enough to justify hospitalization, nor was she at all interested in taking medication. The analyst responded by offering what he regarded as appropriate transference interpretations—essentially that she experienced him as repeating the neglect of her mother and deserting her as her mother and others had done in the past. Tina did not contest these interpretations, but they were of no help in relieving her painful symptoms.

As time went on, and each break produced the same horrendous distress, Tina began not only to rebuke the analyst for leaving on his holiday, but to imply that he should not be going, because of what it did to her. The analyst experienced a conscious resistance within himself to accepting the validity of his patient's request, that is, that the only way that he felt he could remedy the situation was never to take a holiday. He needed to feel that, despite her dissatisfaction, he was being a good therapist for Tina and he also needed to feel free to take a holiday. In other words, selfobject needs of the analyst that Tina had easily met all along, and of which the analyst had been quite unaware, were now being significantly frustrated. It should be mentioned that Tina never appeared to want to go on holiday with the analyst—in which case he would have had *more* problems—and she was quite uninterested in phoning him as a substitute for his being with her.

The analyst eventually stopped attempting to explain (i.e., to interpret) the reasons for Tina's self-disruption during breaks, because he thought that she had gone off the deep end around this issue and that it was time to draw her attention to the "reality" of the situation—that it was quite unrealistic of her to expect him not to go on holiday, and that he would simply not entertain the idea seriously. This did not help either. The analyst was now torn between a sense of outrage and a sense of inadequacy, shame, and guilt. He was angry that the patient would deprive him of his right to something that was important and necessary to him, and that in doing so she was being outrageously excessive in her demands. He also felt inadequate as a therapist—nothing he could say was useful and his patient was, by her account, being made worse by the analysis and regarded him as a bad, cruel, and uncaring person. He liked and admired Tina, and generally felt good about his ongoing work with her. He did not, however, know what to do to remedy the situation as she experienced it. Tina left the analysis after four years but returned some months later for psychotherapy because she felt unable to hold onto a man. She consciously decided to avoid the regressive experience of analysis that would render her vulnerable to trauma at holiday breaks, but she referred, reproachfully, to the "failed" analysis—which failed, as she saw it, because of the analyst's inadequacies. Indeed, it would take several years more for the analyst to "get it," an achievement that, as Wolf (1980) has conveyed, would come from the growing strength and therefore decreasing vulnerability and neediness of the analyst's self. The analyst had to be able to accept that his responses were not good enough for the patient without experiencing a disabling sense of shame. Paradoxically, of course, this acceptance made him a better analyst for Tina.

It is useful to discover—to really discover—that one's selfobject need to be recognized by the patient as a good-enough therapist is common to all therapists, and that this need never completely disappears. This therapist's recognition and acceptance of the need enabled him to begin to provide Tina with what she *really* needed from him—the deep-going validation that she had been right all along, that he *was* insensitive to her needs and therefore was cruel to her. He placed his need for a holiday above her pain and he deserted her, like all the men in her life and like her mother, too. She was right—he didn't care about her all *that* much. She was, as she put it, "only" a patient, and he was "only" an analyst. She didn't need to experience his blame or his shame or his guilt. In taking his holiday, he had made the choice, at that moment, to put the needs of his self before those of Tina's. In other words, when she reproached him, all he had to do was to say "uh huh" and *mean* it, and she felt understood. Following this acknowledgment, Tina's reproaches to the analyst for his unresponsiveness to her suffering when he went on holiday did not recur.

When the selfobject needs and expectations of the analyst are met by the analysand, a situation of mutual regulation—a kind of harmony, as we have described it—prevails in the analytic ambience. At these times, the analyst may feel a variety of self-syntonic emotions, such as friendliness, concern, mild idealization, sympathy, compassion, and also sometimes anger or attraction of a regulatable degree toward the patient. However, when, for whatever reason, the analyst's needs are not met, he may experience the painful and even visceral sensations of disrupted self-states that can undermine his therapeutic function. These disruptions include distancing, disinterest, hostility and hatred, contempt, eroticism, prolonged boredom, sleepiness, or even falling asleep.

In the following example, the analyst experienced frustration of his need to feel that he had a function as a therapist. He was also frustrated in his need to experience himself as supplying care for the patient.

Clinical Example: Sarah

For many months, Sarah, a young woman analysand, repeatedly asserted, often vehemently, that there was no relationship and that the analysis was meaningless. Despite this she attended regularly. The analyst reacted to Sarah's assertion by interpreting it as a resistance to transference. He repeatedly told her that she was avoiding her feelings and needs regarding the therapist. The only effect of this was that the patient reasserted, with even more passion and distress, that there was no relationship. She became disillusioned with the analysis and indeed with life itself. At one point, she cried, "Analysis is totally useless. Why do you let me come? It's a big sadistic tease." One day, in great despair, Sarah left a message on the analyst's answering machine telling him the analysis was hopeless and she would not be returning. Galvanized into action by fears of the patient's committing suicide, as she had attempted to do several times in the past, the analyst contacted her and was able to arrange an emergency double session. The analyst now began to sense that he had not been attuned to his patient's aversive state, and that he must set aside his preoccupation with defenses against transference. For the first hour or so, Sarah expressed her desperate and disillusioned state with great affective intensity. Then, perhaps sensing, via the analyst's murmurs of assent, that he was more attuned, she became calmer. She then spoke with much emotional pain of her father's unavailability. She recalled climbing up onto his lap as a small child only to experience him as "a hard wooden chair."

As the session drew to a close, she spoke of her former therapist in the following words: "I did not meet his needs. He needed to do good. He needed to have an impact." The therapist almost immediately recognized that these comments also referred to himself and fit well with his attitude of the previous few months. He now recognized that his argumentative interpretive activity, rationalized as theoretically sound, had masked a frustrated selfobject need—a "countertransference reaction," if you like. During that period he had had to avoid awareness of his need to have a function, to be an "analytic somebody." He had thus failed to attune himself to his patient's need to work through, in transference, a repetition of her aversive experience of an unresponsive and unavailable father.

In the vignette just described, the analyst attempted to satisfy his need for efficacy[5] by repeated interpretations of his patient's need to deny her transference feelings toward him. Interpretation has been accorded such a high and unquestioned value in analytic practice that we have lost sight of—or perhaps never saw—how intrinsic it is to the analyst's assertion of his role as an analyst. A little self-analysis will demonstrate that most of us tend, at times, to step up our interpretive activity when we feel less effective with our analysand. We may then interpret simply to assure ourselves that we have a function. As training analysts, we often urge our students to make interpretations, especially transference interpretations. We believe that transference interpretations are not infrequently offered when the analyst feels unengaged with the patient. In one such instance, the analyst found himself drifting off during a patient's silence. He then experienced the urge to interpret that the patient was removing himself from the analyst and was thus making it difficult for the analyst to stay with him. Fortunately, the analyst was able to recognize that his own needs for stimulation and a sense of functioning were at odds with the patient's need to use him through silence, and that he would only experience the interpretation as the analyst's need for the patient to accommodate to him.

We are all familiar with the patient who continues to associate, apparently doing his own analysis, but who leaves the analyst out of his associations for long periods. Such a patient will not only tend to make the analyst sleepy (McLaughlin, 1975; Dender, 1993) but will also tend to elicit transference interpretations, or interpretations about his or her resistance to transference. In our view, these interpretations are motivated unconsciously by a specific deprivation in mirroring: a depletion has occurred in the analyst's experience of being recognized, of being seen. The significance and utility of his existence as an analyst are simply not acknowledged. An ongoing selfobject need the analyst has generally come to count on his patient to meet is no longer being provided and the analyst feels useless and devitalized. The analyst then interprets in order to bring himself front and center. Although some patients may be able to shrug off such interpretations as simply incorrect, others may experience them as a disruptive transference repetition of the intrusive archaic selfobject needs of a significant caretaker.

Clinical Illustration: Tom

Tom, a young psychologist in analysis, regularly talked on without pause and without any reference to the analyst. Tom clearly liked and admired his analyst, and the analyst quite liked Tom, who was upbeat and who struggled bravely and insightfully with the many problems in his personal relationships. The analyst, however, usually felt so bored and sleepy he could hardly stay awake. He rarely had the opportunity to make an interpretation; in any event, it did not appear necessary to do so, as Tom articulated everything the analyst regarded as relevant. In short, the analyst felt *unengaged* and *irrelevant* to Tom's therapeutic experience. However, Tom idealized the analyst's skills, and he would, from time to time, refer to "our relationship," which, he implied, he valued very much.

Whereas the analyst felt he needed to give *some* interpretations in order to be useful, the analysand admired the analyst's capacity (as the analysand experienced it) to appreciate his ability to understand himself. What no doubt helped the analyst to avoid interpretations (that is, confrontations) that the analysand was "resisting" the transference was that the patient was improving steadily, which provided him with a sense of satisfaction, if not a sense of efficacy. When he did, on rare occasions, offer such interpretations, the patient seemed to shrug them off: they were neither useful nor disruptive.

Late in his life, Winnicott (1971) came to the conclusion that he had often prevented or delayed deep change in his patients by his need to interpret. And Casement (1985) states: "I was often tempted to interpret just to reassure myself that I was still able to think and to function in the session, when things seemed chaotic, but I had to learn to refrain" (p. 177). We would add here that when the analyst reassures a patient, his underlying need is sometimes actually to reassure himself.

We have referred to the significance of shame in the therapist's experience of frustration and disruption of self-cohesion, and in particular to the difficulties in facing shame. Here is a vignette that illustrates this vividly.

Dr. S sought her analyst's help in connection with a distressing reaction she had to a psychotherapy patient who had been recurrently talking about discontinuing treatment. Dr. S had responded to her patient's talk of terminating his recently begun, once-weekly therapy sessions by telling him that, in her view, he should not only not quit but that he should come five times a week. Immediately after saying this, she felt suffused with an inexplicable sense of intense shame. There is no question that her shame was partially in reaction to her sudden awareness of what she had done. That is, asking her patient to do something that she realized he was quite unprepared to do made her feel foolish both to him and to herself—and to her analyst, when she reported it to him. She was also understandably reluctant at first to permit the analyst to include the vignette in this chapter, because, like most therapists, she did not quite believe that everyone, including her analyst, had had the same kinds of experience. There was more to understand, though.

Dr. S's patient had been suffering keenly as a result of the recent abandonment by his wife. His wife had begun an affair with her husband's boss and had moved in with him along with the patient's three children. The patient was trying now, with considerable difficulty, to live a new life on his own while continuing in his role as father on a part-time basis. Dr. S had been empathically resonating with his strongly disavowed—and intense—feelings of shame about his wife's abandonment. Dr. S had had similar feelings in comparable circumstances—some of which she had never completely owned. Dr. S was not new to experiences of abandonment. Prominent among them was the loss of her father—to whom she had believed she was special—who left home when she was a little girl. In addition, she was currently facing the painful possibility of losing her boyfriend. Her patient's talk of leaving stirred up disavowed feelings of shame associated with her experiences of abandonment. She could empathize with her patient and respond optimally to him as long as he did not do the same thing to her that others had done—and what his wife had done to him. When her patient announced his intention to leave her, she lost her empathic resonance with him because she had in part unconsciously apprehended him as *the* selfobject who must not desert her. The shame surfaced when she tried to get him to be with her even more frequently. She was, in effect, expressing her unconscious, unrequited love to her abandoning father, whose leaving she had been powerless to prevent.

Dr. S also came to see that her disavowed sense of shame, and that of her patient, was due to a feeling of inadequacy. Neither of them had felt able to maintain their regard for their idealized partners who had failed them (for the patient, this was his therapist, his wife, and his family; for the therapist, it was her patient, her boyfriend, and her father) and, in consequence, they were unable to retain their sense of self respect. The commitment of her patient to the therapy unconsciously represented (that is, symbolized) for the therapist the partial but significant redressment of a lifelong disillusionment in an idealizing need and that of a mirroring need to be special again. The therapist had made herself vulnerable to shame because she needed to disavow her selfobject needs in relation to her patient. Had she been able to understand and accept them, she would likely have been able to offer her patient a considered therapeutic *response* instead of *reacting* to the "signal disruption" that his talk of leaving elicited.

This therapist's experience is not unique. Variations of her story about the significance and meaning of the relationship with her patient are common currency among therapists. We would claim that the patient's commitment to the treatment meets a universal idealizing selfobject need of therapists and a universal need of therapists to be mirrored as being effective and special to their patients.[6]

Thus, the situation for the analyst is essentially the same as it is for the analysand: If the analyst cannot accept the psychological legitimacy of her selfobject needs in relation to the patient, she will be affected in the same kinds of ways as the patient, her needs will intensify and she may act them out, very likely in relation to the partner who has frustrated them—her patient. If we must protect ourselves from the shameful awareness of our needs in relation to our patients, we will not be able to resonate empathically or respond optimally to their comparable, disavowed needs. If, however, the analyst can accept the psychological legitimacy of these needs, it will significantly enhance his therapeutic function (see Bacal and Newman, 1990; Bacal, 1994). This is, in effect, what happened when Dr. S worked this through in this way with her analyst. In other words, when her sense of shame about these needs and expectations in relation to her patient decreased, her defenses against them also relaxed; as a result, she could then extend the same empathy and acceptance to both herself and her patient.[7]

We believe that it is only recently, in particular because of the work of Broucek (1991), Morrison (1989, 1994), and Wurmser (1981), that the ubiquity of shame in human experience is becoming recognized. The therapist is no less liable to experiences of shame and to those defenses against shame experience that Morrison has described. But these experiences also offer us the opportunity for fresh self-inquiry, self-understanding, and self-acceptance. There are a variety of ways of pursuing this. "More analysis" is often the prescription for such problems, and it can help. Formal consultation or supervision is another. These tasks can also be very effectively accomplished if the therapist's analyst is prepared to respond directly to the therapist's discussion of his or her therapeutic work during the analytic sessions. In this way, the analyst can offer his immediate understanding of his analysand's countertransference reactions as they relate to the frustration of her selfobject needs in the work with her patient. This, in effect, characterized the way that Dr. S's training analyst worked with her, a method of supervision that was regularly offered by Ferenczi, Balint, and others to trainees at the Budapest Institute of Psychoanalysis.[8]

Another effective approach is to seek out opportunities for open exchange with trusted colleagues. The exploring and sharing, in a collegial ambience, of experiences about the effects of frustration of our selfobject needs and disruptive states can be enormously useful. We regularly find that, as a result of these exchanges, we have less propensity to feel ashamed of our "failures"; at least, shameful feelings do not *inhibit* our self-inquiry. In effect, the discovery that these experiences are indeed universal appears to be especially helpful in enabling therapists to become freer to respond optimally to their patients. These discussions can be undertaken with especial effectiveness in groups of therapists—for instance, in the so-called Balint-type groups, whose ambience facilitates the forthright engagement of problematic intersubjective issues (or "countertransference" problems). In this situation, the discrepancy between the faulty therapist and the supposedly non-faulty therapist is greatly diminished. In addition, the evolving bond of trust between members mitigates the shame of disclosing one's selfobject needs and the defenses against them. Concomitant with such a process, one's self undergoes significant strengthening.

There are some difficult or adversarial situations, however, that may particularly strain an analyst's capacity to maintain an empathic stance and benign bond with his patient. As one of us (H.B., in Bacal and Newman, 1990) has observed:

> [W]hen ... certain of the analyst's selfobject needs surface and he perceives his patient as, so to say, "violating" his expectations or acting upon him beyond the threshold of his tolerance, [t]his may precipitate a reaction in the therapist that can trigger or exacerbate a disruption of the patient's sense of selfobject relatedness to him.
>
> (p. 269)

Such situations, when the patient becomes disrupted and perhaps enraged, may reverberate back onto the analyst, resulting in further frustration of his psychologically legitimate needs for self-enhancing or self-restorative responses from his patient. Now the analyst may experience a spectrum of painful feelings such as rage, hatred, anxiety, profound discouragement, and loss of self-esteem. He also experiences the pressure of the requirement that he decenter from such feelings in order to remain in empathic contact with the patient. This, however, may be easier said than done, for it may seem to him that it demands that he totally disavow authentic aspects of his affective experience. We may ask whether self psychology demands too much of the analyst by requiring him to maintain the empathic stance at all times, which sometimes would seem to entail the complete renunciation of his or her selfobject needs. We allow, and indeed often encourage, children, parents, and patients to feel entitled to protest when their needs are not met. The long-suffering analyst tends to disallow himself such latitude. Moraitis (1993) has recently observed that

> [I]n order to achieve his objectives the analyst must forfeit his personal needs to the maximum degree possible, so that he can place himself or herself in the service of his patient and his science.
>
> I believe such demands are unrealistic and unwarranted. They place the analyst in the defensive position of claiming altruistic motives he usually questions in others and of disclaiming in himself the very needs he helps his patients to acknowledge and satisfy.
>
> (p. 343)

Is it not the analyst's natural and perfectly human need to protest against the assault on his own sense of self? No doubt in the vast majority of instances such protest would not be expressed openly. But the right to give covert—and sometimes even overt—expression to his own aversive attitude may help protect the analyst from injury and, having acknowledged his legitimate needs, enable him to continue working with his patient.

For a long period in the analysis of a young woman, *every* interpretation the analyst made disrupted her. She angrily and contemptuously dismissed almost all his interventions. The analyst now, himself, became disrupted. He began to experience increasing degrees of mortification, shame, and disappointment in himself. He strove valiantly to restore both the patient's and his own self-esteem by searching for the "right" interpretation. This was all to no avail. Finally he withdrew in discouraged silence. As his own vitality and cohesion were undermined, so did this reverberate on the patient in a vicious circle. This analyst was unable to accord himself the right to protest, even inwardly, at the patient's failure to affirm him. It was only with the aid of a consultant that he was able to begin to tolerate her disillusionment. The problem of this analyst with this patient is one that might especially lend itself to the kind of group discussion and support that we have suggested.

Winnicott (1947) recognizes that the analyst will, at times, hate the patient, especially the regressed patient (p. 195). He regards it as important that the analyst acknowledge this hate to himself and tolerate both the patient's hate and his ingratitude. Winnicott is, in effect, implying a significant selfobject need on the part of the analyst that is being deeply frustrated by the patient. In our experience, if the analyst accommodates to the analysand on a continuous basis in order to avoid the patient's experiencing intolerable trauma in the transference,[9] the hate engendered in the analyst by the prolonged frustration of his selfobject needs will inevitably interfere at times with the analyst's therapeutic function.

We recognize that not all analysts find adversarial situations difficult or disaffirming. In fact, some analysts feel mirrored or stimulated by the cut and thrust of an aversive encounter, as do some patients. The different personalities and theoretical approaches of analysts indicate great variation in their selfobject needs and expectations. The number of permutations and combinations in mutual selfobject needs, and frustrations of such needs, in the psychoanalytic situation must be infinite.

Stolorow and Atwood (1992) emphasize that sustained empathic inquiry must include the therapist's continual reflection on his ongoing subjective processes (i.e., as part of the intersubjective field). We believe it should be possible for an analyst to become practiced in monitoring his self states as they are affected by those of the patient and by the effects of external factors on his life.

We have argued that the analyst's self states are significantly affected by his selfobject experience in relation to the patient. In other words, what enables the analyst to carry out his therapeutic task—what, so to speak, keeps the analyst going—centrally includes responses on the part of the analysand that provide the analyst with selfobject experience.[10] The recognition that it is psychologically legitimate for the therapist to have these needs and that their frustration contributes to countertransference reactions will not only alter our conceptualizations of the therapeutic process but will also enhance our capacity to respond optimally to our patients.

Notes

1 Balint's concept of primary love is similar but not identical to Kohut's archaic merger transference. In the archaic merger transference, the other is experienced as part of the self. Primary love does not necessarily entail a loss of boundary; rather, the object is experienced as having similar or complementary needs as the subject (e. g., the baby experiences her need to feed and be held as identical or complementary to the mother's need to feed or hold the baby).

2 Basch (1992) regards the alterego, or twinship selfobject experience, to be basic to human relationships.

3 Countertransference reactions that involve the analyst's needs may also be conjunctive (or "collusive"). This may occur when the analyst tacitly—or even explicitly—encourages the patient to hope for the fulfillment—or enactment of—unmet needs of the analyst that correspond to those of the patient. In these instances (which are often unconsciously motivated), the analyst may sometimes find himself offering more than he can deliver. These reactions may thus also run counter to the therapeutic needs of the patient.

4 This requirement corresponds to the vertical split situation described by Kohut (1977) and to the false self reaction described by Winnicott (1960; see also Bacal and Newman, 1990).

5 According to Wolf (1988), "*Efficacy need* is a person's need to experience the self as an effective agent, that is, capable of eliciting a selfobject response" (p. 181).

6 The patient's commitment to the treatment likely also meets the need for attachment to a significant other—a need that is in many ways similar to the need for selfobjects (see Bacal and Newman, 1990).

7 Gunther (1976) recommends that the analyst use "selective empathy" with himself as a means of monitoring his defenses and disturbances. Gunther's emphasis is on the expectable "narcissistic" difficulties that analysts will encounter when doing analytic work. We affirm his observations; our additional emphasis, however, is upon the ongoing selfobject functions that are ordinarily supplied by the analysand to the analyst, and the effects of their frustration.

8 In Hungary, at the Budapest Psychoanalytic Institute, this was the usual form of supervision. When Balint emigrated to England from Hungary in the late 1930s, he offered this form of supervision to his trainee analysands at the British Institute of Psychoanalysis. He supervised the student's first training case during the student's own analytic hours. In this way, the student's countertransference problems could be addressed with more immediateness, richness, and effectiveness than in the standard form of supervision, where the unconscious determinants of the student's countertransference can only be touched on by the supervisor. Dr. S was, in fact, worked with in this way.

9 We are referring here to trauma that tends to occur when the analysand regresses to pathognomonic, genetically related disruptions in the transference—what Balint called "the basic fault" (Balint, 1968; Bacal and Newman, 1990).

10 Lessem and Orange (1992) suggest that the mutuality of selfobject experience is associated with an increasingly solid bond of seeker and healer. That is, the therapeutic process is enhanced by the patient and analyst both experiencing the other as providing selfobject functions.

References

Bacal, H.A. (1985). Optimal responsiveness and the therapeutic process. In A. Goldberg (Ed.), *Progress in self psychology* (Vol. 1, pp. 202–226). New York, NY: Guilford.

Bacal, H.A. (1994). The selfobject relationship in psychoanalytic treatment. In A. Goldberg (Ed.), *A decade of progress, progress in self psychology* (Vol. 10, pp. 21–30). Hillsdale, NJ: The Analytic Press.

Bacal, H.A., & Newman, K.M. (1990). *Theories of object relations: Bridges to self psychology*. New York, NY: Columbia University Press.

Balint, M. (1937). Early developmental states of the ego: Primary object-love. In *Primary love and psycho-analytic technique*, new and enlarged ed. London: Tavistock.

Balint, M. (1964). *The doctor, his patient & the illness* (2nd ed.). London: Pitman.

Balint, M. (1968). *The basic fault*. London: Tavistock.

Basch, M. (1992). *Practicing psychotherapy*. New York, NY: Basic Books.

Broucek, F.J. (1991). *Shame and the self*. New York, NY: Guilford.

Casement, P. (1985). *Learning from the patient*. New York, NY: Guilford.

Dender, J.M. (1993). *The phenomena of sleepiness in the analyst*. Presented at the 16th Annual Conference on the Psychology of the Self, Toronto, October 31.

Estrella, C. (1993). *Optimal responsiveness: An exploration of the subjective and intersubjective experiences of psychotherapists*. Unpublished PhD dissertation, California Institute for Clinical Social Work.

Freud, S. (1910). The future prospects of psychoanalytic therapy. In *Standard edition* (1957, Vol. 11, pp. 139–151). London: Hogarth Press.

Gunther, M.S. (1976). The endangered self: A contribution to the understanding of narcissistic determinants of countertransference. *The Annual of Psychoanalysis*, 4, 201–224.

Heimann, P. (1950). On countertransference. *International Journal of Psycho-Analysis*, 31, 81–84.

Kindler, A. (1991). Mirror transference and the need for confirmation. Presented to the Toronto Psychoanalytic Society, October 9.

Kohler, L. (1984/1985). On selfobject countertransference. *The Annual of Psychoanalysis*, 12/13, 39–56.

Kohut, H. (1971). *The analysis of the self*. New York, NY: International Universities Press.

Kohut, H. (1977). *The restoration of the self*. New York, NY: International Universities Press.

Lessem, P., & Orange, D. (1992) *Emotional bonds: The therapeutic action of psychoanalysis revisited*. Unpublished.

McLaughlin, J.T. (1975). The sleepy analyst: Some observations on states of consciousness in the analyst at work. *Journal of the American Psychoanalytic Association*, 23, 363–382.

Moore, B., & Fine, B. (1990). *Psychoanalytic terms and concepts*. Binghamton, NY: The American Psychoanalytic Association & Yale University Press.

Moraitis, G. (1993). The analyst's quest for self-consciousness. *Psychoanalytic Inquiry*, 13, 333–347.

Morrison, A. (1989). *Shame: The underside of narcissism*. Hillsdale, NJ: The Analytic Press.

Morrison, A. (1994). The breadth and boundaries of a self-psychological immersion in shame: A one-and-a-half person perspective. *Psychoanalytic Dialogues*, 4, 19–35.

Rycroft, C. (1972). *A critical dictionary of psychoanalysis*. New York, NY: Penguin.

Sandler, J. (1976). Countertransference and role-responsiveness. *International Review of Psycho-Analysis*, 3, 43–47.

Stolorow, R.D., & Atwood, G.E. (1992). *Contexts of being: The intersubjective foundations of psychological life*. Hillsdale, NJ: The Analytic Press.

Sullivan, H.S. (1953). *The interpersonal theory of psychiatry*. New York, NY: Norton Library, William Alanson White Psychiatric Foundation.

Thomson, P.G. (1991). Countertransference in an intersubjective perspective: An experiment. In A. Goldberg (Ed.), *The evolution of self psychology: Progress in self psychology* (Vol. 7, pp. 7–92). Hillsdale, NJ: The Analytic Press.

Thomson, P.G. (1993). The influence of the analyst's narcissistic vulnerability on his work. *Psychoanalytic Inquiry*, 13, 348–364.

Winnicott, D.W. (1947). Hate in the countertransference. In *Collected Papers of D.W. Winnicott* (1958, pp. 194–203). London: Tavistock.

Winnicott, D.W. (1960). Ego distortion in terms of true and false self. In *The maturational processes and the facilitating environment* (1965, pp. 140–152). London: Hogarth Press.

Winnicott, D.W. (1971). *Playing and reality*. London: Tavistock.

Wolf, E.S. (1979). Transferences and countertransferences in the analysis of disorders of the self. *Contemporary Psychoanalysis*, 15, 577–594.

Wolf, E.S. (1980). Empathy and countertransference. In A. Goldberg (Ed.), *The future of psychoanalysis* (pp. 309–326). New York, NY: International Universities Press.

Wolf, E.S. (1988). *Treating the self*. New York, NY: Guilford.

Wurmser, L. (1981). *The mask of shame*. Baltimore, MD: Johns Hopkins Press.

7 Shame

The Affect of Discrepancy—Commentary on Chapters 1, 2, and 3

This chapter is a reflective commentary on the experience of shame as it relates to feelings of discrepancy, particularly in relation to oneself and expectations. The author examines shame through the lens of psychoanalytic theory, exploring how an individual's perceived inability to meet personal or external expectations can lead to feelings of inadequacy and self-doubt. He reflects on theories by Freud, Broucek, and Balint, proposing that shame arises from a disruption in "primary relatedness"—a fundamental connection between self and others that is integral to self-esteem. This early relatedness, when disrupted, creates what Balint termed a "basic fault" in the psyche, manifesting as shame when there is a disjunction between self-perception and external judgment.

Prologue and Process

I approach the task of responding to these three chapters with some hesitation. I am invited to offer not a detailed critique of the articles, but to write about the thoughts they evoke in me. For some while, I believed I had nothing to add to what the authors have written in these fine, comprehensive, and scholarly essays. It takes but a moment of self-scrutiny to realize that not only am I a little anxious about the task before me, but also my procrastination is due to signal shame. Thus far, I am validating the authors' views through my own experience. Since I cannot think of anything to say myself, however, I reflect on the disruptive feelings occasioned by my apparently undoable assignment. Gradually it dawns on me that my feelings constitute a gateway to ideas that could enrich the views of Broucek, Lansky, Morrison, and Stolorow on the essential nature and development of the shame experience, with whose perspectives I basically agree. But I am a little ahead of my subjective process. I am still not sure at this point that I can do this.

I am aware that the experiences I am describing certainly arise from the threat of exposure to others, and to myself; that I will be unable to meet the authors' and their readers' expectations, as well as my own. The shaming judgment of inadequacy or failure would come from both within and without. At this point, I realize I have added but a small nuance to what the authors have amply stated. So, I still feel a little shaky about whether I can contribute

DOI: 10.4324/9781003570806-8

anything that would justify the requested submission of even "10 to 15 pages (double spaced)." Have they not said it all?

As I temporize and torment myself with the specter of possible failure, I realize that I am especially interested in—as well as troubled by—a particular aspect of my experience, a distressing sense of *discrepancy* between what I feel I can do and what I and the authors expect of me. I begin to feel a bit better since I have, in effect, reduced the discrepancy a little by discovering that I may have something to say after all. I think my experience of distress reflects a threat to the integrity of my self that arises from the possibility that I may be unable to bridge the *gap* [1] between what, at this moment, I feel I can do and what I and they require of me—the discrepancy between who I feel I am at this moment and what I and they would like me to look like in print (ultimately, the "narcissistic image" of who I am as a thinker and author)—when my words are printed or, worse still perhaps, when I have no words at all to submit for printing. Yet this dynamic, too, I sadly reflect, has also been at least partly enunciated in one way or another by the authors and by others. At the same time, I am comforted by the discovery that I am on to something, since a reread of the three chapters yields innumerable examples in which experiences of discrepancy of one sort of another are associated with shame experience. I decide I need some help.

I consult a respected colleague about my plight, and I share with him some theoretical ideas that support my contention that a central underpinning of the shame experience lies in the felt inability to do away with painful experiences of discrepancy. Not only does he aver that he has a similar view, he is sure that I will be able to develop my ideas into a good commentary. He also adds to the theoretical model that I have been thinking about that would give substance to our shared view. I feel quite a bit better now. I reflect that I have received an abundantly optimal response from my colleague. I have not only been mirrored, twinned, shared with, and materially confirmed by a respected other. I have also been responded to in such a way as to narrow the gap between what I felt I was (a non-author in this context) and how I needed to experience myself in order to try to create something worthwhile. In other words, I have got a bit of therapy for my persistent and paralyzing signal shame. After one last delay in which I drive to a shop to purchase a new cartridge for my printer, I am ready to write. Now that the discrepancy between what I would like to accomplish and what I feel I can achieve is substantially decreased, I realize that there is so much to respond to in these beautiful essays that I only regret that I must restrict my comments, on this occasion, to this single theme.

Theoretical Perspectives on Discrepancy as It Relates to the Shame Experience

Some of the theory I propose that is relevant to the perspective on shame that I am emphasizing has been mentioned by the authors of these three papers. For example, Lansky and Morrison (Chapter 7) point out that:

> self-conscious appraisals of ourselves that are *discrepant* with our aspirations, standards for lovability, and sense of competence, worthiness, and excellence generate shame, ... shame, then, is inextricably bound to the problem of narcissism—lovability, acceptability, selfhood—which depends on external or internal acceptability or recognition.
>
> (italics added)

And, as they point out, Freud (with Breuer and in other early works) implied a remarkably up-to-date formulation of shame as a defense against awareness of pain and of exposure associated with anticipation of disapproval and rejection both in the eyes of the self and of others.

Morrison and Stolorow also suggest that shame is frequently the affective experience in narcissistically *disjunctive* intersubjective interactions in the treatment situation. The difference (disjunction?) between me and the authors is that I would place discrepancy, or disjunction, at the center of my theoretical perspective on the shame experience.

I especially wish to draw attention to Broucek's questioning the validity of Freud's theory of primary narcissism, whose validity is also cast in doubt by Morrison and Stolorow. Instead of "an initially unrelated infant driven only by the need to relieve drive tension and who only gradually and reluctantly differentiates self from other," Broucek posits that the infant exists in a state of fundamental relatedness to a primary caretaking other by way of an innate understanding of the affective code and the utilization of that understanding to bring about mutual affective attunement with the caretaker. He calls this state *primary communion* and posits that the infant exists in this state prior to the development of objective self-awareness (OSA), which he defines as "an awareness of oneself as an object for others and through the mirroring of the observing others, taking oneself as an object of reflection (objectifying oneself)." His view is that OSA "is not only a prerequisite for more developed forms of shame experience but is a source of shame in its own right" (p. 23). He observes that the acquisition of OSA appears to result from the interplay of the maturation of the central nervous system, conflicting viewpoints, and disjunctive affectivity.

I find it interesting and useful in the present context to observe that Broucek, in identifying the earliest experience as one of "primary communion"—communion is defined (by the American Heritage Dictionary) as "the act or an instance of sharing, as of thoughts or feelings"—affirms in essence Balint's (1937, 1968) original, extensive conceptualization of the infant's quality of relatedness to its early environment; and that Broucek also describes how certain aspects of "the acquisition of OSA"—especially the occurrence of "conflicting viewpoints" and "disjunctive affectivity"—has a striking correspondence to the determinant of the "basic fault," described by Balint (1968) as the disruption of concordant relatedness between the infant and his primary caretaker. Broucek states: "The appearance of OSA means the end of primary communion."

Balint (1968) repudiated Freud's theory of primary narcissism. He argued that the experience of birth, when the baby must breathe, disrupts a state of relatedness that the fetus has with its intrauterine environment, which he called a "harmonious interpenetrating mixup." (This idea has points of contact with Grunberger's "monad," which Morrison and Stolorow describe.) Balint contends that aspects of the early extrauterine environment also normally become primary substances or objects that the infant can take for granted. The air surrounding him, with which he will have a new interpenetrating mix-up—that is, where the boundary between the air that is part of him and that which is not cannot be delineated with certainty—and certain objects, beginning with the mothering figure, assume for the infant varying degrees of the quality of such primary substances in the early stages of postnatal life. Balint posits that, in this situation, the wishes of this primary object are felt by the infant to be identical to his own; for example, the mother is experienced as wishing to love and satisfy the infant just as much as he wishes this from her. Balint called this state of relatedness with primary objects primary love, or primary object relationship. Winnicott's (1958) concept of "ego-relatedness" has analogous meaning. Whether we call this primary love, the monad, ego relatedness, primary communion, archaic selfobject relationship (Kohut) or (my preference) *primary relatedness*—a designation that I think more accurately reflects contemporary perspectives and that Broucek actually comes within a hair's breadth of using—it identifies the earliest situation not as "narcissistic" (in the sense of the infant's being self-preoccupied)[2] but as *relational*. That is, the earliest situation is not one of primary narcissism but is, rather, relational in the particular respect that it is characterized not only by mutual affective attunement but also—and perhaps at least as significantly—by affective sharing, that is, important experiences of a lack of discrepancy between the infant and the mothering figure.

I believe that experiences of this state of relatedness sufficient to enable their integration into the fabric of the self are essential for the establishment of the child's basic, quiet sense of entitlement to, and therefore expectation of, selfobject responsiveness. Balint (1968) theorized that traumatic disruptions of these states of primary love—what I am calling primary relatedness—leave a wound in the psyche that he called the "basic fault." The notion of "fault" arose not only from its metaphoric association with the geological term but, more importantly, from the way so many patients described it.

> The patient says that he feels there is a fault within him that needs to be put right ... there is a feeling that the cause of this fault is that someone has either failed the patient or defaulted on him, and ... a great anxiety invariably surrounds this area, usually expressed as a desperate demand that this time the analyst should not—in fact must not—fail him.
>
> (p. 21)

What Balint unfortunately leaves out, in this otherwise vivid description of the patient's experience of the basic fault—which is analogous, as I have observed elsewhere (Bacal and Newman, 1990), to Kohut's (1977) understanding that the primary defect in the self is consequent to disruption of an archaic selfobject relationship[3]—is that it is invariably associated with profound *shame*. What I am drawing attention to here is that the basic fault—this defect in the self with which such shame is associated—is brought about by a significant *discrepancy* between the selfobject needs of the individual and the capacity of those in his environment to respond to them. In the idiom of Stolorow, Brandchaft, and Atwood (1983, 1987), we may speak of archaic intersubjective disjunction. We must, of course, recognize that there are other reactions to the awareness of the interruption of primary relatedness which may have profound implications for our understanding not only of the individual but also of the relationship between the individual and the group and of the relationship between groups. Consideration of this reaction is beyond the scope of my discussion; I will just mention that this awareness may produce not only painful feelings of discrepancy but also experiences of separateness and difference that may or may not become involved in conflict and that may or may not evoke shame. That is, we eternally and variously seek both a sense of togetherness and a sense of separateness, both a sense of identity with others and a sense of distinctiveness in relation to others, each of which may become problematic under certain circumstances. Interestingly, probably the most prevalent circumstance in which they are inclined to become problematic is in situations of discrepancy, or intersubjective disjunction.

Balint (1968) further suggested that inevitable disruption in the experience of primary love—what I am calling primary relatedness—produced two reactions[4] in the infant in the attempt to reinstate it. One reaction is the detour of "narcissism," through which the child attempts to give to himself what he previously experienced in relation to the primary other. The second is through the route of active object-love[5] through which the child attempts to please the other so as to be satisfied in return.

Here, parenthetically, but importantly, we must recognize that the definition of narcissism as love of self is inaccurate. Narcissism should, rather, be defined as inordinate self-preoccupation. This self-preoccupation may manifest self-love or protest self-admiration; but its latent content is self-loathing, and it is replete with intense needs for certain kinds of relatedness, as both Balint (1968) and Kohut (1971, 1977) have described. "Narcissistic" reactions to painful, shameful discrepancy constitute attempts to avoid shame by shunning threatening experiences of mutual relatedness. When rudely ejected from the garden of Eden, we yearn for but are intensely wary about and exquisitely sensitive to offers of blissful togetherness that might reawaken our longing for paradise but may also result in re-injury to wounds that have not yet healed.

Morrison and Stolorow depict these issues vividly in their description of Kohut's idea of the vertical split, to which they offer important conceptual corrections, as well as useful advice about the optimal response to what they call *defensive grandiosity*. In keeping with my line of theorizing, I propose that we use the term *defensive narcissism* rather than *defensive grandiosity*. Narcissism, as Morrison notes, may be expansive or contracted, but it is always a reaction to the threat or experience of failure of the deeply yearned-for but even more deeply feared primary relatedness, a longing that hides beneath the "horizontal split." That is, narcissism, as Balint argued, is always secondary, that is, defensive; and shame is the affect that motivates narcissistic avoidance of genuine and trusting human relatedness. It is the affect of discrepancy in relation to the "other"—whether this discrepancy centers on a wish to be admired or a wish to be loved—from within or from without. The task of reducing these experiences of debilitating discrepancy constitutes one of the most important challenges to the optimal responsiveness of the therapist (see Bacal, 1985, in press).

Notes

1 I have elsewhere suggested that the *experience* of an unbridgeable gap between the self and the other may be the essence of the generation of the affect of envy (Bacal and Newman, 1990). The sequence of fear about the inability to bridge a gap—associated with the affect of shame—preceding the experience of the unbridgeable gap that is associated with envy accords with Lansky and Morrison's contention that envy is always "downstream" from shame.

2 The *American Heritage Dictionary* defines narcissism as the excessive love or admiration of oneself.

3 Kohut's view of a primary defect in the self and the situation that determines it—the disruption of archaic states of selfobject relatedness—is remarkably analogous to Balint's conceptualization of the basic fault as resulting from disruption of states of primary love. In other words, Kohut's retention of the theory of primary narcissism was inconsistent with his theory of self psychology.

4 Balint (1959) also coined the terms *ocnophilia* and *philobatism* to denote more-or-less normal characterological types that express more organized reactions to the disturbance of the primary object-relationship. The ocnophil clings to his object as a vital support without whom he experiences intense anxiety. The philobat tends to shun objects, which he experiences as either indifferent, unreliable, or even dangerous and prefers the "friendly expanses" between them, which the ocnophil regards as "horrid empty spaces." Both, however, are seeking, although by very different routes, to recapture the early harmonious relationship with their environment (see Bacal and Newman, 1990, p. 127).

5 Today, we might reformulate—or add to—this the self-psychological view that the child attempts to provide not only "love" but also selfobject responsiveness for the caretaker. It is also important to consider to what extent these provisions entail false self accommodation (Winnicott, 1960) to the requirements of the other, which not only may compromise the sense of self but also may fail to achieve the aim of reducing painful experiences.

References

Bacal, H.A. (1985). Optimal responsiveness and the therapeutic process. In A. Goldberg (Ed.), *Progress in self psychology* (Vol. 1, 1995, pp. 202–226). Hillsdale, NJ: The Analytic Press.

Bacal, H.A. (Ed.) (in press). *Optimal responsiveness*. Norwood, NJ: Aronson.

Bacal, H.A., & Newman, K.M. (1990). *Theories of object relations*. New York, NY: Columbia University Press.

Balint, M. (1937). Early developmental states of the ego: Primary object-love. In *Primary love and psycho-analytic technique* (1965). London: Tavistock.

Balint, M. (1959). *Thrills and regressions*. London: Tavistock.

Balint, M. (1968). *The basic fault*. London: Tavistock.

Kohut, H. (1971). *The analysis of the self*. New York, NY: International Universities Press.

Kohut, H. (1977). *The restoration of the self*. New York, NY: International Universities Press.

Stolorow, R.D. (1987). *Psychoanalytic treatment*. Hillsdale, NJ: The Analytic Press.

Stolorow, R.D., Brandchaft, B., & Atwood, G. (1983). Intersubjectivity in psychoanalytic treatment, with special reference to archaic states. *Bulletin of the Menninger Clinic*, 47, 117–128.

Winnicott, D.W. (1958). The capacity to be alone. In *The maturational processes and the facilitating environment* (pp. 29–36). London: Hogarth Press.

Winnicott, D.W. (1960). Ego distortion in terms of true and false self. In *The maturational processes and the facilitating environment* (pp. 142–153). London: Hogarth Press.

8 Is Empathic Attunement Always the Optimal Response?

Kohut has identified empathy as not only the fundamental psychological data gathering agent (Kohut, 1959) but also as one of the most potent therapeutic experiences (Kohut, 1981). Self psychologists ran with the latter. Empathic attunement as a response came to be regarded as always constituting optimal therapeutic responsiveness. In the author's groundbreaking paper, "Optimal responsiveness and the therapeutic process" (Bacal, 1985), he asserted that, while empathic attunement provides the therapist with awareness of the patient's subjective states, responsiveness that could be therapeutic comprised not only interpretive explication, but also a wide array of other responses. This chapter underscores how responses other than empathy, too, may provide experience specific to therapeutic need. It examines when and why other forms of response may be more beneficial for certain patients in specific therapeutic contexts.

Defining Empathy and Its Role

Empathy in psychotherapy encompasses both cognitive and affective elements, with its hallmark being the direct apprehension of another's subjectivity. As a subjective experience, it represents the therapist's sense of "knowing" the patient's immediate state or feelings. However, this understanding must be distinguished from empathic *responsiveness*, the offering of such understanding.

The Primacy of Empathic Attunement

Kohut's emphasis on sustained empathic immersion revolutionized psychoanalytic practice by prioritizing the patient's subjective experience over theoretical interpretations. It also provided a crucial counterbalance to authoritarian therapeutic attitudes. Clinical experience consistently shows that patients often find the therapist's empathically reflective responsiveness to be profoundly therapeutic, but not always.

DOI: 10.4324/9781003570806-9

Limitations of Empathy as Therapeutic Response: Clinical Examples

Case 1: Ms. Q—When Empathic Reflection Becomes Problematic

Ms. Q was expressing deep despair about various life experiences. While the therapist initially provided empathic understanding and compassionate reflection, the patient became increasingly withdrawn. Eventually, she revealed that the therapist's careful tracking of her affects made her experience the therapist as "down there" with her—reminiscent of her mother's similar stance. She needed someone to maintain a different perspective while understanding her unhappiness, stating, "I think I need someone to be up there a bit more, while I am down here."

Case 2: Christine—The Power of Challenge

Margaret Black's patient Christine (see Black, 1987) demonstrated how invalidation of a patient's subjective experience can sometimes be more effective than empathic reflection. Despite consistent empathic responses and helpful interpretations, Christine's self-disparaging patterns persisted. When Black finally departed from her usual approach and stated firmly but with slight amusement, "You don't really believe that!" it led to a breakthrough. This intervention effectively challenged the patient's articulated sense of self while acknowledging her growing strength.

Case 3: Mr. D—The Limits of Pure Empathy

Mr. D's case illustrates when empathic attunement alone proves insufficient. Despite seven years of analysis with an eminent self psychologist who maintained a consistently empathic stance, Mr. D's life became increasingly chaotic. He experienced his analyst as intelligent and dedicated but found the purely empathic approach frustrating and inadequate. His desperate need for guidance and regulation from a parental figure went unmet, highlighting how strict adherence to an empathic mode of responsiveness may deprive the patient of the specific responsiveness that he needs.

Case 4: Kohut's "Complete Idiot" Intervention

In a notable departure from typical self-psychological technique, Kohut confronted a patient who was bragging about reckless driving by calling him "a complete idiot." This confrontational response proved therapeutic precisely because it demonstrated caring and involvement, providing the patient with a needed experience of paternal concern that pure empathic reflection could not offer.

The Role of Spontaneity in Optimal Response

The Psychiatry Resident Case

A particularly illustrative example involves a psychiatry resident suffering from self-esteem vulnerability. Her analyst's spontaneous suggestion that she apply for a position at the local mental hospital—where he taught—proved to be one of the most valuable therapeutic moments in her long analysis. The spontaneous nature of the suggestion carried more weight than careful interpretation would have, as it conveyed genuine confidence in her abilities.

Kohut's Physical Contact Example

Another significant case involves Kohut allowing a suicidal patient to hold his fingers. While he privately interpreted this as representing "the toothless gums of a very young child clamping down on an empty nipple," he offered no interpretation to the patient. Instead, the physical gesture itself provided what the patient needed at that critical moment—a tangible connection to life and hope.

Optimal Responsiveness: A Broader Framework

Rather than equating optimal therapeutic response solely with empathy as response (empathic reflection), we should conceptualize optimal responsiveness as any therapeutic action that facilitates the patient's self-cohesion, strengthening, and growth. This may include:

- Empathic reflection
- Interpretive interventions
- Quiet acceptance
- Direct confrontation
- Spontaneous authentic responses

The key lies not in adhering to any single response mode but in providing what each particular patient can use therapeutically at any given moment.

Conclusion

While empathic attunement remains a fundamental tool for apprehending a patient's subjectivity, responsiveness must be informed by what the patient specifically needs, therapeutically. Conveying emotional or cognitive understanding of the patient's subjectivity may not always be experienced as therapeutic. The clinical examples presented demonstrate how various forms of therapeutic engagement—from direct confrontation to spontaneous gestures—can prove more effective than empathic reflection in certain situations. The therapist's repertoire must extend beyond empathic reflection to include varied forms of engagement, all guided by careful attention to what facilitates each patient's therapeutic experience.

References

Bacal, H.A. (1985). Optimal responsiveness and the therapeutic process. In A. Goldberg (Ed.), *Progress in self psychology* (Vol. 1, pp. 202–227). New York: Guilford.

Black, M. (1987). The analyst's stance: Transferential implications of technical orientation. *The Annual of Psychoanalysis*, 15, 127–171.

Kohut, H. (1959). Introspection, empathy, and psychoanalysis: An examination of the relationship between mode of observation and theory. *Journal of the American Psychoanalytic Association*, 7, 459–483.

Kohut, H. (1981). On empathy. In P. Ornstein (Ed.), *The search for the self: Selected writings of Heinz Kohut 1950 to 1978* (Vol. 4, pp. 525–535). Madison, CT: International Universities Press.

9 The Use of Theory in Psychoanalytic Practice[1]

Psychoanalytic theories often provide a useful framework for understanding patients, yet they may fail to capture the unique dynamics within therapeutic relationships. With few exceptions, our psychoanalytic theories are rooted in Freud's structured view of mental processes and aim for universal laws in mental health and treatment.

Responses to the rigidity of mainstream theory have primarily included eclecticism (selecting whichever theory appears to be relevant to a patient's issues) and integration (merging different theoretical perspectives). Specificity theory entails a process-oriented approach, which prioritizes the unique, evolving dynamics within each therapeutic interaction. It posits that while structure theories remain useful, their application is optimally effective when they relevantly come into play within the emergent process of the particular patient and the particular therapist.

The Limitations of Structure Theory

Our use of theory of one sort or another in psychoanalytic practice is indispensable and inevitable, yet its usage poses discernible problems that are not infrequently shoved under the couch. Theory can be a helpful partner in our work; but it can also lead us astray, or get in our way. Although we do not openly acknowledge it, we tend to look to our preferred theories, consciously or unconsciously, to inform our understanding and to advise our responses to our patients. These theories are the ones that we have come to feel comfortable working with, the ones that we come to regard as truth. And if we have been trained as psychoanalysts, they will tend to reflect the beliefs of the analytic institutes where we have been trained, or the analytic societies or groups with which we are affiliated.

When Freud first led us from the chaos of psychological ignorance into the order of psychoanalytic theory, he understood emotional suffering, and even certain physical impairments, as arising from mental determinants. Over his lifetime Freud developed a nomothetic theory of human development, and of psychological illness, health, and cure. That is, Freud's theories involved the formulation of general or universal laws that were premised upon an ordered

DOI: 10.4324/9781003570806-10

and structured view of mental life, upon which definitive techniques of psychoanalytic treatment were based. Many analysts have continued to follow Freud's dicta. Freud's critics—a number of them ultimately hailed as psychoanalytic pioneers—have since elaborated many other theories and different ways of applying them. While these theories differ in their conceptualizations and modes of practice, each is premised on assumptions of order, continuity, and universality in human development. It is an open secret—yet one also largely unacknowledged—that our formally articulated theories simply do not always—and sometimes never—account for what happens in treatment, either when it is successful or when it fails, from either the patient's or the therapist's vantage point. Yet, we continue to use these theories as the basis for both apprehending *the* psychological truths about our patients and as guides for our interventions.

Responses to the Constraints of Formal Theory

Some recent contemporary responses to the constraints of formal theory have been to embrace the value of spontaneity and improvisation (Ringstrom, 2001; Kindler, 2010) or to place special value upon something other than interpretation (Stern, Sander, Nahum, Harrison, Lyons-Ruth, Morgan, Bruschweilerstern, and Tronick, 1998; but see Nahum, 2005). As valuable as this may be in certain instances, we cannot avoid using "theories" or "models" of one sort or another; they comprise a significant part of who we are, and will inevitably influence our responses to our patients. So, how is the clinician to "choose" wisely?

Another response to multiple formal theories of psychotherapy has been an "eclectic" or pluralistic approach, that is, to utilize a model, or theory—or combinations of these—with regard to their apparent applicability to a particular patient's problems (see Connors, 2010). And yet a third approach has been an "integrative" approach, that is, to view all theories as "true" but simply reflecting differing dimensions of human experience or reflecting differing points on a continuum of human experience. At first glance, this would seem to be a reasonable way to proceed, either the eclectic or integrative approaches. Our response to Connors's paper, whose theme is the utility of cognitive behavioral therapy within psychodynamic psychotherapy, is titled "Who can do what, therapeutically, with whom, in what way?" (Bacal and Carlton, 2010). Trying to match model to patient from amongst the plethora of possibilities is not a simple, straightforward task. Consider the remarkable multiplicity of perspectives and approaches that reside within the rubric of psychotherapy, each of them privileging different aspects of the person in defining illness, treatment, and cure. A psychotherapist practicing in this 21st century is confronted with a daunting array of major schools of psychotherapy within which multiple theories abound, each with its own view of therapeutic action that is mediated through its corresponding prescribed—and proscribed—responses. Within the world of psychodynamic therapies, the schools of psychotherapy and psychoanalysis also vary in their focus on the past or present of the patient, the intrapsychic world of wishes, dreams, and fantasies of the patient, or the interpersonal world of today's relationships with others inside or outside of the consulting room. Integrationists and eclectics attempt to honor the claim of each model for ubiquitous therapeutic relevance by trying to find commonalities amongst them and diverse application for them. Yet here, too, we run into difficulty if we proceed on the assumption that it is possible to achieve theoretic "reliability" (note, for example, the difficulty we had in doing this during our outcome research at the Tavistock Clinic, in which our theoretical differences were minimal—see chapter 1, Bacal, 2011).

Findings in contemporary ancillary fields—of infant research (Sander, 2002; Lyons-Ruth, 2000; Stern, Sander, Nahum, Harrison, Lyons-Ruth, Morgan, Bruschweilerstern, and Tronick, 1998; Beebe and Lachmann, 2002), neurobiology (Edelman, 1987, 1988, 1989), physics (Cilliers, 1998), mathematics (Prigogine, 1996), and epistemological philosophy (Gadamer, 1975) turn our attention to an equally compelling aspect of all biological life—the unorganized, discontinuous, unpredictable, and unique in the development and functioning of the human mind (see also Spruiell, 1993; Trop, Burke, and Trop, 2002). Contemporary theories in each of these disciplines recognize stable organizations and patterns, but give equal weight to their possible instability over time, and to their openness to change in sudden, unpredictable ways. These systems, or process, theories recognize that substantial change may result from seemingly small perturbations, and that stability may be maintained even in the face of massive stressors in the direction of change. Many traditional structure theories include elements of process, yet such hybrids or compromises are also premised upon assumptions of order, continuity, predictability, and universality in human development. If we do continue to recognize the usefulness of employing the concepts of multiple structure theories, what is the optimal way of utilizing them?

It occurred to me, at first somewhat whimsically, that any alternative way of proceeding would somehow have to include the tenets of established postulates, meet the requirements of those who place value on integration or eclecticism, and perhaps in some way even intrigue those empiricists who would incline toward turning their back on theory-making altogether. A dubiously possible achievement. But what if we think about this in a different way? The application of a process theory of specificity does not require the integration of variegated theory, or model for eclecticism. The concepts that comprise the diverse theoretical perspectives of psychotherapy and psychoanalysis will continue to be variously useful, but as aspects of specific emerging process: Prescriptive application of structure theory yields to its specifically emerging relevance within the process of a particular therapeutic dyad (or other therapeutic constellation).

A theory of this kind is playfully depicted in the parody about a local rabbi whose response was petitioned by two peasants to settle a dispute between them. The first man approached the rabbi with the complaint that his neighbor was repeatedly coming into his yard to milk his goat, which not only disturbed him, but also affected the goat, altering the nature of its milk. The rabbi listened carefully to the peasant and told him, "My good man, I understand; you are quite right." A short while later, the neighbor came in and explained at length to the rabbi why the goat was truly his, and that he was simply exercising his claim to it. The rabbi listened very carefully and then told him, "My good man, I understand; you are quite right in your claim." After the man left, the rabbi's assistant, who had been listening to both claimants and to the rabbi's responses to each of them, turned to the rabbi in total amazement and asked, "How can you think both of them to be right?!" To which the rabbi replied, "You know, you're right, too."

While this situation overtly deals with disputation around ownership and who gets whose goat—and one might be tempted to mine it for caricatures that reflect our various therapeutic approaches and formal theories, and our relationships with each other about them—we offer it not only as a transparently exaggerated apologue to poke fun at attempts to reconcile diversity. We also offer it to seriously suggest that one can have a theory that could honor the validity of even widely divergent perspectives, within process—a theory that therapists as well as rabbis could use wisely. If we look more closely at this little story, we can discern that the rabbi was conveying that he not only apprehended the subjectivity of each of the protagonists—as well as that of his assistant—he conveyed that he felt that each of their theories about the situation could be right.

The apparent silliness of our rabbi's responses can be taken as a metaphoric invitation to consider that a theory that places process and uniqueness at the center of our attention may in fact allow us both to utilize the tenets of established postulates, meet the requirements of those who place value on integration or eclecticism, and possibly even interest those who are skeptical of theory-making altogether. Such a theory would take a perspective on the therapeutic endeavor that is different from a structure paradigm whose tenets determine truth, *a priori*, and concomitantly prescribe responses. A theory that accords uniqueness priority could enhance the possibilities for therapeutic effect. While retaining the potential utility of the multiplicity of formal perspectives, our theory would pre-eminently approach the particularity of each clinical situation without peremptory prescription or proscription.[2] Specificity theory gives substance to the view that every theory of psychotherapy and its methodology is potentially as "right" as it is "wrong"; but that its usefulness depends upon its relevance to the uniqueness of the process in which the particular individuals are participating.

While we think of a structure theory, in contrast to specificity theory, as prescribing a particular response, we need to recognize that any particular orientation, including specificity theory, will influence the dyad in a particular way. Once a theory formulates its view of therapeutic action, the analyst will be attuned to "this" and less "that." With specificity theory, we attempt to discern what is the anticipated or desired or needed response; yet specificity theory is unique in then saying that we continue to examine whether the response was helpful and to alter our responsiveness as best we can. Specific responses that are deemed therapeutic are always in process, and the "process of treatment" is thereby affected in a particular way that will yield a different tilt in the therapy than one that has a more singular notion of therapeutic action.

In other words, if structure theories are understood within the overarching perspective of the specificity of process, a syncretic use of theory emerges. Structure theories are not discarded by specificity theory. Structure theories are useful in at least two ways: they provide a particular structure to consider, and they may serve as a probe to expand our observational field. At the same time, they may occlude aspects of the observational field and impose a structure that is not applicable specifically to a particular patient/therapist pair.

In disputing the psychoanalytic dictum that therapeutic effect is consequent upon only one mode of therapeutic action—verbal explication—I conceptualized a way of working that I called *optimal responsiveness*, which also implied that in any specific instance or context, responses based upon any of our formal theories may or may not be therapeutically applicable to a particular patient (Bacal, 1985, 1998). As the therapist works in this way with her patient, the treatment is affected in a particular way that will yield a different tilt to it. More concepts, theories, and models can thereby be utilized more relevantly, in contrast to the presumptive application of a more singular notion of effective therapeutic action. The concept, *optimal responsiveness*, in effect questioned the validity of a universality of mindset that is intrinsic to all traditional psychoanalytic theory. In other words, it implied an underlying theory of therapeutic specificity.

In contrast to prescribed therapeutic methodology arising from the application of a structure theory, whose tenets direct the therapist to apply prescribed responses in order to achieve therapeutic effect, therapeutic possibility informed by specificity theory emerges within process as the capacity of that dyad to actualize what could be specifically therapeutic for that patient. Therapeutic action, thus informed, will inevitably be imbued with one or another "theory" or "model," but it will come into play in a different way.

From the Universality of Structure to the Specificity of Process—A Different Order of Theory

Concurrent with her elaboration of the neurobiological underpinnings of specificity theory (see Chapter 4, Bacal, 2011), Lucyann Carlton drew attention to a quality of process that is inherent in specificity theory in contrast to a quality of structure that characterizes traditional psychoanalytic theories (Carlton, personal communication, 2004; Carlton, 2009). She pointed out that all theories of psychotherapy are premised upon a theory of mind, its development, health, illness, and cure, and that while the various schools of psychotherapy offer numerous and contrasting views of mind, a fundamental distinction among theories can be drawn from their definitional essence of the nature of the mind either as structure or as process, or system.[3] Carlton has described how defining the nature of the mind as structure or process has important implications for how our theories affect our practice. When the mind is understood as structure, it is objectively knowable and develops and functions in predictable ways primarily according to inherent design. The metaphorical use of the word "structure" (whether as a steam engine, computer, or multi-story building) to define the mind invokes similarities to building or fixing an object with a blueprint for the desired product, and with agreed-upon techniques for its successful completion. Within the world of psychoanalysis, the mind, from this perspective, is conceived of as a type of object with a discernible inside and outside and with a defined organization that is separate from the analyst: for example, Freud's structural model of a mind comprising an id, ego, and super-ego that is formed as the child passes through specified stages of psychosexual development, and motivated by the force of two innate drives. Its study assumes that the analyst can learn about the mind of another through cause-and-effect, linear reasoning. Structure theories are the type of theory with which we are most familiar as psychoanalysts and psychotherapists, such as classical psychoanalytic theory, ego-psychology, object relations, Kleinian, Lacanian theory, or self psychology. This type of theory offers universally applicable concepts for understanding the patient, and prescriptive and proscriptive guidelines for responding therapeutically. In contrast, a theory of therapy that privileges process defines the mind as process that is always in process, and that interaction between minds is unique, unpredictable, and non-replicable. This view of mind derives from the neurobiologic research of Gerald Edelman about the anatomy and function of the brain, which we will consider in Chapter 4 (see Bacal, 2011).

From the perspective of specificity theory, there are neither guidelines for technique nor textbooks for understanding a patient. Established psychoanalytic theories, their structured concepts and the therapeutic approaches they prescribe, are generalities that may or may not illuminate the particularity of process for each dyad.

Carlton's conceptualization of process significantly advances our understanding of specificity theory as a different order of theory—a theory that operates at a level of abstraction that leads us to consider that whatever "specificities" emerge, they are all specific to who the participants are in their particular process. Thus, we may talk of a myriad of qualities that contribute to the specificity of fit, or of linkage, in variegated ways: origin, culture, outlook, humor, values, development, therapeutic quest, motivation etc. In other words, we are speaking about a process, or systems, theory in which specificity is its central attribute (Carlton, 2009).

Notes

1 Reprinted from *The Power of Specificity in Psychotherapy: When Therapy Works—And When It Doesn't*, by Howard Bacal, 2011.

2 Lewis (2009) has questioned whether "the present focus on the particularity of each patient/analyst dyad might be just as extreme, in its own way, as any psychoanalytic theory that seeks to universalize human psychodynamics. It is my hope that human sameness and the uniqueness of our own subjectivities can exist side by side." Our overall response to this challenge is, in effect, offered at various points within this book, where we address its spuriousness as a polemic. In particular, the answer to

Lewis's question is twofold: the higher order theory, with regard to therapeutic possibility, is that of the particularity of process of the dyad, which does not preclude application, at a lower level, of structure theory as it may relevantly emerge in process. Second, the recognition of the uniqueness of the individual and of dyadic process requires the application of a universal human capacity (and perhaps that of some animals) for empathy (see Schwaber, 2010, p. 166)—which itself is variable and dyadically specific—not the invocation of a theory that is regarded as universally relevant.

3 See Bacal (2011, footnote 5, chapter 1).

References

Bacal, H. (1985). Optimal responsiveness and the therapeutic process. In H. Bacal (Ed.), *Optimal responsiveness How therapists heal their patients* (pp. 3–34). Northvale, NJ: Jason Aronson.

Bacal, H. (1998). *Optimal responsiveness: How therapists heal their patients*. Northvale, NJ: Jason Aronson.

Bacal, H. (2011). *The power of specificity in psychotherapy: When therapy works—and when it doesn't*. Lanham, MD: Jason Aronson.

Bacal, H., & Carlton, L. (2010). Who can do what, therapeutically, with whom, in what way? *Journal of Psychotherapeutic Integration*, 20 (1), 46–50.

Beebe, B., & Lachmann, F. (2002). *Infant research and adult treatment: Co-constructing interactions*. Hillsdale, NJ: The Analytic Press.

Carlton, L. (2009). Making sense of self and systems in psychoanalysis: Summation essay for the 30th Annual International Conference on the Psychology of the Self. *International Journal of Psychoanalysis and Self Psychology*, 4, 313–329.

Cilliers, P. (1998). *Complexity and postmodernism*. New York, NY: Routledge.

Connors, M. (2010). Symptom-focused dynamic psychotherapy. *Journal of Psychotherapeutic Integration*, 20 (1), 37–45.

Edelman, G. (1987). *Neural Darwinism: The theory of neuronal group selection*. New York, NY: Basic Books.

Edelman, G. (1988). *Topobiology: An introduction to molecular embryology*. New York, NY: Basic Books.

Edelman, G. (1989). *The remembered present: A biological theory of consciousness*. New York, NY: Basic Books.

Gadamer, H-G. (1975). *Truth and method* (2nd rev. ed.). New York, NY: Continuum.

Kindler, A. (2010). Spontaneity and improvisation in psychoanalysis. *Psychoanalytic Inquiry*, 30 (3), 222–235.

Lewis, J. (2009). IAPSP website communication. November 14. https://iapsp.org/

Lyons-Ruth, K. (2000). "I sense that you sense that I sense...": Sander's recognition process and the specificity of relational moves in the psychotherapeutic setting. *Infant Mental Health Journal*, 21 (1–2), 85–98.

Nahum, J. (2005). The "Something More" than interpretation revisited: Sloppiness and co-creativity in the psychoanalytic encounter. *Journal of the American Psychoanalytic Association*, 53, 693–729.

Prigogine, I. (1996). *The end of certainty*. New York, NY: Free Press.

Ringstrom, P. (2001). Cultivating the improvisational in psychoanalytic treatment. *Psychoanalytic Dialogues*, 11, 727–754.

Sander, L. (2002). Thinking differently: Principles of process in living systems and the specificity of being known. *Psychoanalytic Dialogues*, 12 (1), 11–42.

Schwaber, E. A. (2010). Reflections on Heinz Kohut's last presentation, "On empathy," 1981: Its impact on my own pathway. *International Journal of Psychoanalytic Self Psychology*, 5 (2), 160–176.

Spruiell, V. (1993). Deterministic chaos and the sciences of complexity: Psychoanalysis in the midst of a general scientific revolution. *Journal of the American Psychoanalytic Association*, 41, 3–44.

Stern, D., Sander, L., Nahum, J., Harrison, A., Lyons-Ruth, K., Morgan, A., Bruschweilerstern, N., & Tronick, E. (1998). Non-interpretive mechanisms in psychoanalytic therapy: The "Something More" than interpretation. *International Journal of Psycho-Analysis*, 79, 903–921.

Trop, G., Burke, M., & Trop, J. (2002). Thinking dynamically in psychoanalytic theory and practice: A review of intersubjectivity theory. *Progress in Self Psychology*, 18, 129–147.

10 Specificity Theory

A Process Theory of Psychoanalytic Treatment

The author summarizes the perspectives of specificity theory and personal and professional experiences that led to its development. Specificity theory is a contemporary process theory of therapy that holds that each analyst–patient dyad constitutes a unique, reciprocal system, challenging us to reconsider how psychoanalytic therapy is optimally practiced and taught. Therapeutic possibility is co-created in the specificity of fit between the patient's particular therapeutic needs and that therapist's capacity to respond to them, both of which will emerge and change within the unique process of each particular dyad. Specificity theory recognizes that what each therapist effectively offers a particular patient may include but will also transcend considerations of formal theory and its prescribed technique. Evolving against the backdrop of the innovative thinking of Sándor Ferenczi and from the author's personal work with Michael Balint, Wilfred Bion, Donald Winnicott, Marion Milner, and Heinz Kohut, its perspectives are corroborated within contemporary neurobiology, pre-eminently in the work of Gerald Edelman, and by infant researchers, such as Louis Sander, Ed Tronick, and Karlen Lyons-Ruth.

Every psychoanalytic theory variously reflects significant aspects of its author's personal and professional history (see Stolorow and Atwood, 1979). How much more so, then, must a theory of therapeutic specificity do so! I was therefore glad to accept Peter Rudnytsky's invitation to accent these aspects of the theory in presenting my book, *The Power of Specificity in Psychotherapy: When Therapy Works—And When It Doesn't* (Bacal and Carlton, 2010), at a recent meeting of the American Psychoanalytic Association. My intent, here, is to summarize both the main aspects of specificity theory and the influences on its development.[1]

This article is based on a presentation to the Discussion Group on the History of Psychoanalysis at the meetings of the American Psychoanalytic Association, June 8, 2011, San Francisco.

The cover art for the book abstractly depicts two of the major perspectives of specificity theory: (1) that *therapeutic illumination emanates from the emergent process of the particular dyad*, and (2) that *it shines most brightly in a darkened place*. Specificity theory does not provide the psychoanalytic practitioner with

DOI: 10.4324/9781003570806-11

do's and don'ts. Rather, it considers therapeutic effect to be centrally a function of the *unpredictable uniqueness of process*, and of the *specificity of dyadic fit*.

Wilfred Bion alluded to the intrinsic uniqueness of unfolding process in psychoanalytic treatment when he wrote, "The only point of importance in any session is the unknown … in any session evolution takes place. Out of the darkness and formlessness something evolves" (1967, p. 273). For Bion, therapeutic effect derives "from the emotional experience with a unique individual and not from generalized theories imperfectly 'remembered.'" Sigmund Freud was, in effect, *discovering* the uniqueness of therapeutic process as he was encouraging his patients to talk to him in ways that neither had ever heard before. However, Freud proceeded to develop a nomothetic, or legislative, theory of human development and of psychological illness, health, and cure. That is, Freud's theory involved the formulation of general or universal laws that were premised upon an ordered and structured view of mental life, upon which definitive techniques of psychoanalytic treatment were based. Analysts since Freud have attended to a wider variety of data than Freud did, and in differing ways, but their theories, with few exceptions, still dictated universally prescriptive and proscriptive therapeutic action.

The first chapter of my book (Bacal, 2011) addresses the need for a new *kind* of theory. Our familiar *structured* psychoanalytic theories have yielded manifold benefits, and continue to do so. But we need a theory of therapy that accounts not only for the organized, stable, predictable, and universal patterns of mental life, and for its unpredictable, non-linear patterning; we need a theory that also *gives substance to the unique and specific development and functioning of the mind in process with other minds*. As Gerald Edelman (2004) has shown, the human mind is continuously formed and transformed through ongoing selective, specific interactions with itself and its environment. Closely related to this is the need for a theory of therapy that promotes the efforts of our brain to forestall closure prematurely. Edelman has demonstrated that when the brain is confronted with novel stimuli, the neuronal connections are actively at work to organize and make sense of the stimuli until a familiar pattern is forged or attained. Our brain is not trying to form a scientifically accurate picture of the world, per se, but one that is familiar and meaningful to the perceiver. With this innate biological pull toward closure, curiosity and attention to the novel and unique are blunted. Specificity theory helps us counter this inherent tendency—one that *can* be reinforced by the application of structured concepts—and to reengage our curiosity to search out other elements that *may* transcend the relevance of these theories for the patient.

As variously analysand, analyst, and supervisor, I have always been especially interested in what determines, or detracts from, therapeutic effect. In earlier papers (1985, 1998a), I drew attention to what seemed to me to be both obvious and curiously unrecognized, at least officially: that there are multiple ways in which therapeutic effect can be mediated, in addition to interpretive explication, and that this diversity is matched only by the particularity of the patient's therapeutic experience. And then I began to realize that within the clinical approach that these observations informed, there lurked a *theory* that was just as obvious, but which was just as unrecognized: that *effective treatment is a function of the unique and specific, reciprocal process between its particular participants.*[2]

My colleague, Lucyann Carlton, who has contributed significantly to the development of specificity theory, and to the book (Bacal, 2011), has pointed out that all theories of psychotherapy are premised upon a theory of mind—its development, health, illness, and cure; and that while the various schools of psychotherapy offer numerous and contrasting *views* of mind, a fundamental distinction among theories can be drawn from their definitional essence of the nature of the mind either as *structure* or as *process*. It is important to delineate this difference in order to convey specificity theory adequately.

Structure Theory and Process Theory

When the mind is understood as *structure*, it is objectively knowable and develops and functions in predictable ways primarily according to inherent design. When the mind is understood as *process*, it is regarded as *always* in *process*, unknowable in advance. We are, in effect, talking about different *orders* of theory.

Structure theories define the mind in ways that invoke similarities to building or fixing an object such as a steam engine, computer, or multi-story building, with a blueprint for the desired product, and with agreed-upon techniques for its successful completion.

Defining the nature of the mind as structure or process has important implications for how our theories affect our practice. Theories that define the mind primarily as structure offer universally applicable concepts for understanding the patient, along with prescriptive, and proscriptive, guidelines based upon them for responding therapeutically. Structure theories are the type of theory with which we are all familiar as psychoanalysts, theories such as classical psychoanalytic theory, ego psychology, object relations theory, self psychology, and so on.

A theory that defines the mind as process does not offer guidelines for technique or textbooks for understanding a patient. Specificity theory is a process theory that privileges interaction between minds as unique, unpredictable process, yet it retains the potential utility of the multiplicity of our structured perspectives. Established psychoanalytic theories, their concepts, and the approaches they prescribe are regarded as generalities that may or may not illuminate therapeutic process for that dyad. If structure theories are understood within the overarching perspective of the specificity of process, a syncretic use of theory emerges. Structure theories are not discarded by specificity theory. Structure theories are useful in at least two ways: they provide a particular structure to consider, and they may serve as a probe to expand our observational field. At the same time, they may occlude aspects of the observational field and impose a structure that is not applicable specifically to a particular patient/therapist pair.

Therapeutic action, thus informed, may be imbued with one or another structured concept, or "model," but these models will come into play in a different way. They will emerge and be understood within the overarching perspective of the *specificity of process of that dyad*. This can help the therapist to keep his or her mind open, both figuratively and literally, to what may usefully emerge in process, to counter the mind's tendency to closure.

Such process centrally entails *mutual selectivity*. This is another way of describing what we have loosely called "fit," which we intuitively, though informally, recognize as crucial for therapeutic effect. This entails, as Louis Sander has described, "a sort of resonance between two systems attuned to each other by corresponding properties," or matching specificities (2002, p. 19).[3]

The primary consequence of adopting a process view of mind rather than a structure view of mind is a *radical shift in epistemology*. This is a formal way of saying that a process view of mind changes both *how* and *what* we, as psychoanalysts, know in working with a patient. When specificity becomes central to our consideration of process, the epistemological shift pre-eminently illuminates *how the who* of the participants in the particularity of their process will influence therapeutic effect. From the *process* perspective of specificity theory, therapeutic effect is co-created—or not—within the unique, unfolding process of each *particular* psychoanalytic dyad. Put in yet another way, it is ultimately the capacities and limitations of *that* therapist and *that* patient to understand and respond to each other in their process that determines therapeutic effectiveness. Our book (Bacal, 2011) includes illustrations of how specificity theory is applied in clinical practice and in the supervisory setting. Examples also illustrate how specificity theory alters our view of psychoanalytic concepts and principles and how this affects therapeutic action.

Partly because of a mischievous streak in my personality, I will briefly describe the psychoanalytic treatment of a young man who was pretty well cured in little over three months by my helping him get out of analysis. This case vignette is actually not in the book. The treatment happened a long while ago, yet as I look back on it, it seems to me to be a nice illustration of certain aspects of specificity theory.

Eric was around 20 years old when he was referred to me, about 40 years ago, by a prominent psychoanalytic colleague. Eric's father, an attorney in the city, had asked my colleague to find Eric a good analyst. He was very concerned about his son's state of mind and the direction his son's life was taking. Eric was hardly studying at all for the courses that would enable his admission to law school, and he seemed constantly irritated and depressed. Instead of applying himself to his schoolwork, he spent all his time dabbling in "ridiculous" business ventures. Eric's father not only knew that Eric could benefit from analysis, he also knew what sort of analysis would best benefit Eric. He himself had completed a ten-year analysis some years ago, in London, with Hanna Segal, a senior Kleinian analyst. He had found this to be enormously valuable, and he knew his son would likewise benefit from the same sort of treatment.

From the referring analyst's point of view, I may have looked like the nearest thing in sight to a Kleinian analyst in San Francisco at that time. I had qualified about six years previously from the Institute of Psychoanalysis in London, where two of my six supervisors were senior Kleinian analysts—Bion for an adult case and Betty Joseph for a child analytic case—and where Hanna Segal, herself, was one of my instructors in Kleinian theory. So, I knew "Klein," but I was not a "Kleinian." I'd been affiliated with the so-called Middle Group of the British Society, which was a peculiar non-group group. The Middle Group, which sometimes called itself the Independent Group, was supposedly poised somewhere between Freudian and Kleinian sensibilities, but mainly comprised a coterie of creative, independent thinkers, several of whom I had trained with, such as Michael Balint, Donald Winnicott, Marion Milner, John D. Sutherland, and Charles Rycroft.

I really liked Eric—a straightforward, congenial, bright, and ambitious young man. Eric and I connected well, and we settled in to a four-times-per-week analysis. I recognized, though, not long after our first few sessions, that the best kind of analysis we could do was to engage the issues that could get him out of analysis as soon as possible and allow him to get on with his life.

Psychoanalytic theory that emerged for me during our process turned out not to be Kleinian (though Klein's concepts did variously inform my work then, and continue to do so now). What emerged as particularly useful in my work with Eric was a concept that had been advanced by Harry Guntrip in the late 60s. What Bernard Brandchaft (2004, 2007) later came to elaborate as "pathological accommodation," Guntrip (1968) had first conceptualized in object relational terms as a dilemma centering around the experience of a conflict wherein the needs of the self were threateningly at variance with those of a significant figure in the person's life. To express one's self was to lose the object. To comply with the other was to lose one's self. Eric was struggling with his father's conviction that becoming a lawyer would unquestionably be right for him. Eric and I came to appreciate that were he to accede to his father's wishes, he faced the dangers of losing his sense of purpose and the invalidation of his core ambitions, but that if he did not accommodate his father's wishes, he would, at the very least, seriously displease him. His depressiveness and irritability reflected this unconscious conflict symptomatically.

My not-so-unconscious attitude, which would seem to have specifically connected with Eric's, as our process unfolded, was that pursuing what was centrally meaningful in Eric's life—going into some kind of business, rather than studying to become an attorney as his father required of him—trumped Eric's dread of losing his father's approval and respect. I must have talked with Eric in ways that implicitly gave expression to this understanding. My interpretations about Eric's conflict around this may well have been therapeutically significant; yet what was, arguably, at least as effective was how Eric and I found ourselves able to *be together*, in effect, to fit together, therapeutically, *around this issue*.

What was emerging, within me, in our process, were precipitates of toxic experiences with my mother that were specifically analogous to those with which Eric struggled in relation to his father. These experiences with my mother had been repeated in my recent analysis, with Michael Balint. In that analysis, I felt little recognition of who I was other than being identified as faulty for not measuring up to his standards of mental health. Because Eric wanted to be who *he* could be rather than what his father regarded as right, he was regarded as unhealthy, and therefore should have an analysis.

I now look back on my objections to these attitudes on the part of my first official analyst, and before that, on the part of my first unofficial one, my mother, as the anlage of specificity theory, in the sense that at some level I recognized that neither dyad was a very good *fit*. Until a later analysis, however, I could not experience my considerable protests against any of this as valid for myself.

Eric was luckier than I had been. Unconsciously, or perhaps dissociatively, I must in some measure have registered the validity of my protests, since I could access this sensibility, with feeling—along with a different attitude, and a different sort of responsiveness to Eric—in the specificity of *our* process. In some measure, Eric and I unconsciously connected to stand firm against an unempathic, omniscient, and tyrannical parent.

Traditionally, this would be conceptualized as a transference/countertransference enactment. I, however, locate my connection with Eric under the rubric of the specificity of dyadic process, which designates something more than what is encompassed by the traditional concept—that is, the scope of therapeutic possibility for a particular dyad. A significant aspect of Eric's therapeutic experience with me, I believe, was that I could listen, with sincere interest, to his "ridiculous" ideas for developing commercially viable projects. I was, in retrospect, also finding myself responding to Eric in a way that Kohut would later conceptualize as that of a mirroring selfobject. However, I knew nothing formally, then (in 1971), about self psychology theory. I actually did not come across Kohut's theories for another five years.

Back, now, to Eric and me. After about three and a half months, Eric and I decided we'd gotten to the point where he could get off the couch and head for the door. As he was leaving my office, he turned toward me, and said, with a wide smile on his face, "It was good doing business with you, Doc."

Returning now, to my own analysis, with Balint. Not only did his proclamations about me not feel good, what he was doing didn't feel quite right. In one session, I found myself imploring him to relate to me in a different way. Rather than hurl interpretations at me from up there, could we be like two children sitting on the floor side by side, leaning against the couch looking at something together and discussing what each of us saw in it? My intent with this metaphor was to elicit the sort of responsiveness that I felt would allow me to have a therapeutic experience—comprising not only a non-judgmental attitude but also a sharing of what might interest us together. I have come to learn that this is particularly important for me. My suggestion to Balint that there might be a better way that this activity called analysis could be carried out with *me* was, in retrospect, also my first implicit attempt to field a theory of therapeutic specificity.

I had a very different, very useful, experience with Balint's supervision of my first "control" case. This supervision was conducted in accordance with the Hungarian method of psychoanalytic supervision, which takes place in the setting of the candidate's analysis. I will return to this shortly.

There was no one I felt I could talk to about my dysphoric analytic experiences. In some desperation, I drafted a "paper," toward the end of that first year of analytic training, which I titled "Is analyzing necessary?"—my second incipiently creative attempt to draw attention to *different* ways of experiencing therapeutic effect. I assessed, probably wisely, though, that if I were to bring this little treatise to the light of day, I might not get much further in my analytic training school! I have since wondered whether such specificity may have been a significant factor in Harry Guntrip's experience in analysis with Fairbairn, and then with Winnicott (Guntrip, 1975). Analogous to Guntrip's later more helpful analytic experience with Winnicott, I found a better fit with Heinz Kohut (also see Bacal, 2006), which I will come to in a moment.

My interest in the specificity of therapeutic process was significantly evoked by the methodology of a psychotherapy outcome research project along with one of its unanticipated findings. This project, in which I participated during the same time period that I was undertaking analytic training in London (in the 60s), was conducted under the leadership of David Malan (see Malan, Bacal, Heath, and Balfour, 1968) at the Tavistock Clinic. It entailed the assessment of the psychological status of a series of untreated "neurotic" patients who had been seen at intake at the Clinic at least two years previously. Our aim was to explore at a follow-up interview the extent to which improvement had occurred without formal treatment.[4] We considered the attainment of true change neither on the basis of relief of symptoms nor on the basis of the usual general categories of healthy social and psychological functioning, but rather on significant amelioration in specific aspects of the patient's life situation that appeared to reflect change in his or her susceptibility to experiences that stressed particular vulnerabilities.

While we often did not agree when it came to formulating the patient's dynamics on the basis of traditional psychoanalytic concepts (even though our theoretical differences were minimal), we had little trouble reaching a consensus on what would constitute improvement for the particular patient. Further outcome research on our study itself (Malan, Bacal, Heath, Balfour, 1975) also indicated the operation of an unpredictable process of specificity. It turned out that those who had improved most on psychodynamic criteria had either experienced significant therapeutic effect from particular experience in their initial consultation[5] or/and were subsequently able to "use" similar, specific "therapeutic" responsiveness from others. While this research illuminated the specificity of outcome for the particular individual, it also suggested that therapeutic process that led to whatever outcome is less dependent upon application of any particular formal theory than it is a function of the specificity of dyadic interaction.

Experience with Supervisors

Experience with certain analytic supervisors also stimulated my thinking about the power of specificity in psychoanalytic practice and supervision. These preeminently included Michael Balint, Wilfred Bion, Donald Winnicott, and Marion Milner.

Michael Balint

Balint supervised my first analytic control case for seven and a half years according to the Hungarian psychoanalytic training system, wherein the training analyst supervised the candidate's first case within the candidate's own analysis, as he shares his experience of his patient in the course of his associations. I found this form of supervision to be immensely valuable, as it enabled me to appreciate, with striking immediacy, how specific aspects of who I was, in context, affected my responses to my patient. I found this experience to be remarkably different from those I had when Balint directed his understanding to me alone, in the analysis. A curious situation, the determinant for which I suggested was a significant lack of fit between how he was responding to me and what I felt I needed, therapeutically. In the context of the supervision, though, there *was* a fit. We *shared* something that really interested both of us. I have also wondered whether another determinant for the difference in what unfolded in these two settings could have been a psychoanalytic version of the familiar phenomenon of the heightened tolerance of the grandparent for his grandchildren over that for his own children. In this context, the grandparent was Balint to his trainee-analysand's patients—that is, to my analysands. My analytic grandfather, in this context, was Sándor Ferenczi, with whom, I suspect, I might have experienced a more therapeutic fit.

Balint Groups

In a related setting, I learned from Balint about the importance of specificity of interaction for pedagogic as well as for therapeutic effect through conducting discussion groups for general practitioners in the psychological aspects of their work. These groups, which Balint originated and were further developed by Michael and his wife Enid, also a psychoanalyst, strikingly illuminated the remarkably variegated ways that patients experience their doctors as therapeutic, and how particular doctors could or could not work effectively with certain patients (M. Balint, 1957, 1969; M. Balint and E. Balint, 1961). These groups, which came to be called "Balint Groups," are a form of applied psychoanalysis (E. Balint, 1967). Their central task comprises the study of the therapeutic effect of the *particular* patient–doctor relationship. As Enid Balint observed, on reviewing Michael Balint's work with a research group of general practitioners:

> [Our aim was] to have a wider look at the ... uncertainties which abound in working with patients; while at the same time not attempting to reduce them to neat patterns, leaving the perspectives as wide as possible in the realization that what one person sees from one angle cannot be seen from another's ... the doctors [came to] realize that their healing powers were strictly limited, but ... on the other hand, observed that very small changes in a person can produce amazingly large effects on the life of an individual. It seems that the unique relationship which occurs in the general practice setting informs us as to what the work is really about.
>
> (E. Balint, Courtenay, Elder, Hull, and Julian, 1993, pp. 98–99)

Wilfred Bion

During a substantial portion of my supervision with Wilfred Bion, he was focusing on perspectives that he was writing about in his paper, "Notes on memory and desire" (1967). In this paper, Bion recommended that the analyst expunge any prior knowledge or conception of the patient he is about to see, except his name and the hour that he is expected to appear for his appointment. Bion famously remarked that if you feel you've seen the patient before, you're treating the wrong patient. I could never quite emulate this approach, but it impressed upon me the value of sustaining a truly not-knowing state of mind, and drew me more deeply into attending to the uniqueness of the patient as this impacted me as the analyst.

Donald Winnicott

Donald Winnicott, as many of us recognize, espoused a clinical approach that richly foreshadowed that of contemporary relational self psychology (Bacal, 1989; Bacal and Newman, 1990). Like Ferenczi, Winnicott also recognized—and conveyed to me—that what may be most important to the patient is not what the analyst interprets but how the analyst behaves. I remember Winnicott telling me, some time in 1967, how impressed he was with a young social worker whom he observed treating a child when on a recent visit to New York. Had I heard of her, he asked? Her name, he told me, was Virginia Axline, and she had written a remarkable book, *Dibs, in Search of Self* (1964), in which she effectively treated a child "without making any interpretations at all!" (Actually, it seems that she did, but this is not what impressed Winnicott about how Axline was therapeutic with her young patient.) Winnicott told me a similar story about Melitta Schmideberg, the physician-psychoanalyst daughter of Melanie Klein, who had taken a job working with psychotic children at a mental hospital north of London shortly after the Klein family emigrated to England in the late 20s. "She knew not a stitch of English at the time," Winnicott told me, "yet her therapeutic effect on those children was amazing" (see Bacal, 2011, p. 47).

I vividly recall the preliminary meeting I had with Winnicott when I was about to begin the analysis of a three-and-a-half-year-old girl under his supervision. The child's behavior had become chaotic and bizarre in the situation of the meager one-room flat in which she lived with her father, her mother, and her two-year-old sister. I asked Winnicott how to begin the treatment (as I had never worked with a child before and had not a clue what to do, especially as the child was refusing to leave the waiting room to accompany me to the consulting room). Without hesitation, Winnicott answered, "If she holds out her hand, take it." I have never forgotten this. It became a metaphor not only for the responsivity that enabled me to be therapeutic for my little patient but for my work with adult patients as well.

Marion Milner

I had similar experience of Marion Milner's daring to think quite differently about what a *particular* patient might need. During her supervision of one of my training cases, she understood my sensitive patient's retreat into the woods as a young adolescent, where he would lie for hours in holes he would dig in the ground, as a way to find himself and to grow, rather than as some kind of schizophrenic or seriously schizoid withdrawal, as previous psychoanalysts and psychiatrists had diagnosed. Milner suggested that I might apprehend his behavior as tantamount to the beginning growth of a delicate young plant that needs careful tending as it begins to sprout new shoots.

This sort of supervision of my patients was, understandably, also stirring up a good deal of conflict in me about how analysis does cure, as my own analytic experience, which was going on at the same time, was quite different. It was to take me about 25 more years before I truly appreciated that being confronted with my evident defects was not going to be optimal for *my* personal development. It was only then that I could begin seriously writing about how I thought psychoanalytic treatment could be therapeutic (Bacal, 1985).

How Does Analysis Cure? Beyond Kohut's Two-Step Paradigm

My second analytic experience, with Heinz Kohut, some years later,[6] went much better than the first one, although I came to differ somewhat with Kohut, in both theory and practice, about "how analysis cures" (see Kohut, 1984). In the early days of my analysis with Kohut, I discovered, as a kind of revelation, really, the therapeutic power, for me, of empathy as *response*, which Kohut, in his writings, actually disavowed, asserting that empathy constituted only a data-gathering instrument. Yet, that was how I experienced Kohut's fairly consistent responsiveness to me. I was not *used* to this, and it took me some time to get over experiencing this as somewhat indulgent.

Kohut described two distinct yet overlapping steps in therapeutic action, which comprised a methodology that was, in effect, quite distinct from his self theory. These two steps were: empathic immersion in the patient's subjective experience, followed by explanation, that is, interpretation, of what the analyst had gleaned thereby. My sense was that Kohut needed to believe—as the "classical" analyst that always, in part, constituted his ego ideal—that the second step, interpretation, was essential to therapeutic cure. Kohut's responsiveness to me, and also something he said, once, indicated to me that he did not actually subscribe to this. Kohut told me that he thought "Ferenczi had the right idea." That meant, quite clearly, in the context of the conversation we were having, that Kohut, like Ferenczi, believed that there was a good deal to be said for responding to a patient in ways the *patient* experienced as therapeutic, even if these ways would not be endorsed by traditional psychoanalysis—and, officially, not by him either. Kohut did offer me many carefully considered interpretations, but what positively affected me was not this understanding, as accurate as it could be—actually his interpretations were much too long—what has stayed with me was the accepting quality of his presence, along with kindness and optimism, which accorded with what *I* needed at the time. I also experienced Kohut's explicit responses, *other* than interpretation and empathy, as therapeutic; one of the most salutary of these was an encouraging arm around the shoulder at an especially dispiriting time when we were facing yet another two-week break.[7]

I am not the only one who benefited from Kohut's inconsistency in adhering to his declared two-step procedure for therapeutic action. There are two published examples of this that are quite striking. Perhaps the most famous one is that of Kohut's patient, Miss F—a case that is often cited as the template for the discovery of self psychology (see Kohut, 1971, pp. 283–290). Miss F was a patient for whom the echoing of her subjectivity was the only response she experienced as therapeutic; anything else provoked catastrophically self-disorganizing rage. Kohut could not help her for some time, as he was wedded to a way of working that prioritized conceptualizing and delivering verbal understanding, that is, interpreting. It was to Kohut's credit that he was ultimately able to shift from this mode to one of simply providing a mirror for her experience, which turned out to be remarkably effective. We note that Kohut's response to Miss F that was useful to her was neither that of interpretation nor empathy.

The other—almost equally well known—example is that of Kohut's offering a patient two fingers to hold at the point when he feared she was becoming seriously suicidal (Kohut, 1981). Kohut tells us that as he did this and the patient took hold of his fingers, he made an interpretation—to himself—"because an analyst always remains an analyst … . It was the toothless gums of a very young child clamping down on an empty nipple" (p. 535). In fact, Kohut did not, in this situation, make an interpretation to the patient, nor was he offering his patient empathy as therapeutic response. But because analysts define themselves as analysts by virtue of their adherence to the belief, or doctrine, that only interpretation can "cure," an interpretation had to figure somewhere in Kohut's response, even if articulated silently. In effect, the action he deemed therapeutic was that of offering his two fingers for his patient to hold onto. Kohut understood via his empathic attunement to this patient that, for her, at this time, her *experience* of being apprehended (her experiencing his empathic attunement to her lifelessness) could not be mediated through his verbal expression of his feeling for her. The patient needed to experience Kohut's extension of himself and then the opportunity to hold on. Offering the two fingers was not an interpretation, but it did, in our view (see Bacal and Carlton, 2010), constitute the practice of psychoanalysis at its best, exemplifying Kohut's ability to understand and move to the patient's therapeutic need.[8] Our view is that it was also self psychology, specifically utilized, at its best. While Kohut's empathic understanding and associated response were informed by the structure of his theory, they were not limited by the constraints that would direct him to interpret the patient's archaic selfobject need rather than to provide it, symbolically, in this particular instance.

I explicitly gave substance to a different version of Kohut's two-step paradigm for therapeutic action—empathic understanding, followed by interpretive explication—when I altered the second step to *optimal responsiveness* (1985, 1998a). Interestingly, the more my work was guided by the expansion of Kohut's second step, explanation, in therapeutic cure to optimal responsiveness, the more I felt challenged to explore the first step, empathic understanding, because this step, in effect, constitutes a process of discovery of what the particularity of response might be that the patient may experience as therapeutic. That is, in recasting Kohut's second step in this way I was, in effect, deepening my understanding of Kohut's first step (empathic attunement) with the recognition of the inherent specificity of the empathic method. I did not alter this first step as articulated: empathically informed understanding. But, with Carlton, I began, through specificity theory, to challenge what is meant by the *process* of understanding (Bacal and Carlton, 2008, 2010).

With the development of a theory of the specificity of process, that is, that *therapeutic effect is specific to the particular analyst–patient pair as it might emerge—or not—in their process*, we now propose that the two steps, understanding and response, not only overlap; they are inextricably linked, one with the other. We must now acknowledge that the measure of psychoanalysis as a therapy is neither "empathy" nor "response," but rather the fullness and complexity of both steps. In other words, the *sine qua non* of psychoanalytic therapy is not empathy culminating in verbal interpretation as the response in the second step, but the entire process that includes understanding the complex mental states of another and discerning responses that may be *therapeutic for that patient*, and *possible for that analyst*, in the uniqueness of their unfolding process.

Notes

1 Chapter 5 in the book describes more fully the influences on my development of specificity theory.
2 My focus is on how specificity theory applies to the dyadic situation of psychoanalytic treatment, and to psychoanalytic training; but its perspectives are also applicable to other settings, such as couples therapy, group psychotherapy, and family therapy.
3 The biologist, Paul Weiss, as quoted by Sander (2002, p. 19), describes the essential principle in establishing and maintaining the connections upon which the coherence of living organization depends as one of "matched specificities—a sort of resonance between two systems attuned to each other by corresponding properties" (p. 162).

4 Our intent was to establish a baseline in order to challenge H.J. Eysenck's (1952) hypothesis that, in psychotherapy, one-third of patients will improve, one-third will get worse, and one-third will remain the same. On the basis of our study of "untreated" patients, Eysenck turned out to be right, on symptomatic criteria, but not on psychodynamic criteria (Malan, Bacal, Heath, and Balfour, 1968).
5 Interestingly, Michael Balint was the consultant who did the intake interview with a patient whom our research team considered to be one of the most severely and chronically disturbed individuals in our cohort. Balint confronted this patient with the way she was wasting her life. He told her that she needed to take definitive steps to change her ways if she wanted a chance to live differently. This patient went on to "use" a particular psychologist relative similarly, though informally. He confronted her in the same way Balint had done; she turned out to have the most successful "outcome" in our series of formally "untreated" patients.
6 I saw Balint between 1961 and 1970, and Kohut between 1976 and 1981.
7 I was seeing Kohut for three sessions every other week, traveling to Chicago from Toronto.
8 How this patient actually experienced what Kohut did we cannot know; and analysts have, since that famous moment, debated whether he could have done just as well by interpreting her need for human contact; or, some have felt, perhaps she would have done even better had Kohut offered her his whole hand rather than just a couple of fingers.

References

Axline, V. (1964). *Dibs in search of self*. New York, NY: Ballantine.

Bacal, H. A. (1985). Optimal responsiveness and the therapeutic process. In *Optimal responsiveness: How therapists heal their patients* (pp. 3–34). Northvale, NJ: Jason Aronson.

Bacal, H. A. (1989). Winnicott and self psychology: Remarkable reflections. In D. Detrick & S. Detrick (Eds.), *Self psychology: Comparison and contrast* (pp. 259–271). Hillsdale, NJ: The Analytic Press.

Bacal, H. A. (1998a). Optimal responsiveness and the specificity of selfobject experience. In *Optimal responsiveness: How therapists heal their patients* (pp. 141–170). Northvale, NJ: Jason Aronson.

Bacal, H. A. (2006). Specificity theory: Conceptualizing a personal and professional quest for therapeutic possibility. *International Journal of Psychoanalytic Self Psychology*, 1, 133–155.

Bacal, H. A. (2011). *The power of specificity in psychotherapy: When therapy works—and when it doesn't*. Lanham, MD: Aronson.

Bacal, H. A., & Carlton, L. (2008). *Specificity theory: Discovering therapeutic efficacy in the specificity of process*. Unpublished manuscript.

Bacal, H. A., & Carlton, L. (2010). Kohut's last words on analytic cure and how we hear them now—a view from specificity theory. *International Journal of Psychoanalytic Self Psychology*, 5, 132–143.

Bacal, H. A., & Newman, K. (1990). *Theories of object relations: Bridges to self psychology*. New York, NY: Columbia University Press.

Balint, E. (1967). Training as an impetus to ego-development. *The Psychoanalytic Forum*, 2, 55–62.

Balint, E., Courtenay, M., Elder, A., Hull, S., & Julian, P. (1993). *The doctor, the patient, and the group*. London: Routledge.

Balint, M. (1957). *The doctor, his patient, and the illness*. London: Pitman Medical.

Balint, M. (1969). The structure of the training-cum-research seminars. *Journal of the Royal College of General Practitioners*, 17, 201–211.

Balint, M., & Balint, E. (1961). *Psychotherapeutic techniques in medicine*. London: Tavistock.

Bion, W. (1967). Notes on memory and desire. *The Psychoanalytic Forum*, 3, 271–280.

Brandchaft, B. (2004). To free the spirit from its cell. In R. Stolorow, G. Atwood, & B. Brandchaft (Eds.), *The intersubjective perspective* (pp. 57–76). Northvale, NJ: Aronson.

Brandchaft, B. (2007). Systems of pathological accommodation and change in analysis. *Psychoanalytic Psychology*, 24, 667–687.

Edelman, G. (2004). *Wider than the sky: The phenomenal gift of consciousness*. New Haven, CT: Yale University Press.

Eysenck, H.J. (1952). The effects of psychotherapy, an evaluation. *Journal of Consulting Psychology*, 16, 319–324.

Guntrip, H. (1968). *Schizoid phenomena, object relations, and the self*. London: Hogarth Press.

Guntrip, H. (1975). My experience of analysis with Fairbairn and Winnicott. *International Review of Psychoanalysis*, 2, 145–156.

Kohut, H. (1971). *The analysis of the self: A systematic approach to the psychoanalytic treatment of narcissistic personality disorders*. New York, NY: International Universities Press.

Kohut, H. (1981). On empathy. In P. Ornstein (Ed.), *The search for the self: Selected writings of Heinz Kohut*. Vol. 4, *1978–1981* (pp. 525–535). Madison, CT: International Universities Press.

Kohut, H. (1984). *How does analysis cure?* (A. Goldberg with P. E. Stepansky, Eds.). Chicago, IL: University of Chicago Press.

Malan, D., Bacal, H., Heath, S., & Balfour, F. (1968). A study of psychodynamic changes in untreated neurotic patients—I. *The British Journal of Psychiatry*, 114, 525–551.

Malan, D., Bacal, H., Heath, S., & Balfour, F. (1975). Psychodynamic changes in untreated neurotic patients—II. *The Archives of General Psychiatry*, 3, 110–126.

Sander, L. (2002). Thinking differently: Principles of process in living systems and the specificity of being known. *Psychoanalytic Dialogues*, 12, 11–42.

Stolorow, R., & Atwood, G. (1979). *Faces in a cloud: Subjectivity in personality theory*. Northvale, NJ: Aronson.

11 The Budapest School's Concept of Supervision

Michael Balint's Legacy to the Development of Psychoanalytic Specificity Theory

Michael Balint made original and important contributions to psychoanalytic theory, therapy, research, and training (see Bacal and Newman, 1990). Balint is perhaps best known, though, for his pioneering work in bringing a psychoanalytic perspective to medical practice (Balint, 1957). What is less well-known is that the "Balint Group," a seminar-based clinical training for general physicians in psychotherapeutic work, was Balint's adaptation of the unique approach to supervision in the Hungarian Psychoanalytic Society, that Balint actually offered in its original form[1] *to his analysands at the Institute of Psychoanalysis in London.*

In this chapter, the author describes his experience of the Budapest model of psychoanalytic supervision with Michael Balint, and its application in "Balint Groups," which he led at the Tavistock Clinic.[2] *He traces the influence of the Budapest model on the development of psychoanalytic supervision, in particular how it has influenced his conceptualizing psychoanalytic treatment and supervision as the specificity of dyadic process. The chapter concludes with an example of the application of specificity theory in his own supervisory work.*[3]

Michael Balint trained with Sándor Ferenczi in Budapest and had already assumed a leading role in Hungarian psychoanalysis when he immigrated to England in 1939 with his wife, Alice, also a psychoanalyst. Balint made original and important contributions to psychoanalytic theory, therapy, research, and training (see Bacal and Newman, 1990). To mention only a few: Balint (1935) proposed a radical, relational revision of Freud's theory of psychosexual stages of development; Michael and Alice Balint (1939) described the psychoanalytic situation as a reciprocal process, in effect anticipating contemporary theories of intersubjectivity by almost half a century; and in 1968, building upon his concept of "primary object love" (1937), Balint (1968) elaborated his idea of "the basic fault," breaking deep new ground in the understanding and treatment of early psychological trauma (see also Balint, 1969b).

Balint is perhaps best known for his pioneering work in bringing a psychoanalytic perspective to medical practice (Balint, 1957). The "Balint Group," a seminar-based clinical training whose aim is to enhance doctors' therapeutic responsiveness to the psychological problems of their patients,

DOI: 10.4324/9781003570806-12

began at the Tavistock Clinic in the early 1950s, and continues to be offered worldwide under the auspices of the International Balint Federation and the American Balint Society.

What is less well-known is that this method of training general physicians for psychotherapeutic work was Balint's application of the unique approach to supervision of the Hungarian Psychoanalytic Society, that Balint offered in its original form to his analysands at the Institute of Psychoanalysis in London.

In this chapter, I describe my experience of the Budapest model in psychoanalytic supervision with Michael Balint, and its application in "Balint Groups," which I led at the Tavistock Clinic, and in which I participated with Michael and Enid Balint in a research project at University College Hospital in London. I then trace the influence of the Budapest model on the development of psychoanalytic supervision, in particular how it has influenced my conceptualizing psychoanalytic treatment and supervision as *the specificity of dyadic process*. The chapter concludes with an example of the application of *specificity theory* in my own supervisory work.

My Experience of the Budapest Model of Supervision

Balint supervised my first analytic control case for seven and a half years according to the Budapest psychoanalytic supervisory method, wherein the candidate's training analyst supervises his first case within the candidate's own analysis as he shares his experience of his patient in the course of his associations. No separate session is set aside for this supervision. When the student, whose analysis is five times a week,[4] spontaneously talks about his experience of working with his "control case," his analyst responds as "supervisor." The London Institute of Psychoanalysis permitted Balint to offer the Budapest School's model of supervision, providing that it was voluntarily undertaken, and that the candidate undertook supervision of an additional case according to the traditional model.

I was eager to begin my first analytic training case in this way; but I conveyed to Balint that I was also feeling curiously ambivalent about starting the work with the patient I had selected—an interesting but apparently "difficult" young woman who, I noted during my associations in an analytic session, was around the same age as my younger sister. My resistance began to fade when Balint interpretively inquired whether I was ready for a little sister. His interpretation derived from my having told him earlier that, when my sister's nurse left when she was one year old, I (four and half, at the time) was heard to ask why she was not taking the baby with her; after all, she had arrived with her! Such observations, traditionally regarded as designating countertransference, constituted the focus of the Budapest supervisory model. This focus constituted the reason why, in this model of supervision, it is the first control case that is done with the candidate's own analyst "so that obstructions that stem from his own personality but are not yet revealed would be able to come to the surface as soon as possible" (Mészáros, 2010, p. 85).

The Hungarian method of supervising, however, transcended a focus on countertransference to encompass a particular form of interaction. It enabled me to appreciate, with striking immediacy, *how specific aspects of who I was in relation to my particular patient as our process unfolded*, affected my responses to her.[5] During another analytic session, I anxiously conveyed to Balint that I was having trouble working with another patient, as she seemed to be uncomfortably like me in some respects. I was startled—but enormously helped—to hear him say, "Every patient is the same as every other, yet completely different." Balint was, in effect, according recognition to the uniqueness of every analysis, which was a major theme of the paper he co-authored with Alice Balint in 1939. In that paper, the Balints also offered what was at that time a radically new view of psychoanalytic practice—that "The analytical situation is the result of an interplay between the patient's transference and the analyst's counter-transference, complicated by the reactions released in each by the other's transference on to him" (Balint and Balint, 1939, p. 227). The same awareness—that psychoanalytic practice is dyadically co-constructed, and specific to its participants—is implicit in the Budapest School's view of what constituted optimal supervisory work: the supervision by the candidate's analyst in the setting of the analytic situation. The model was unique in the psychoanalytic world in its focus on *the unique world of that analyst and that analysand in their emergent process.*

What I experienced as pivotal in the Budapest model in psychoanalytic supervision with Balint, and in the setting of its application in the "Balint Group" (Bacal, 1972, 1975), constituted a significant influence in my development of *specificity theory.*

Specificity Theory

Specificity theory (Bacal, 2006, 2011a, 2011b) is a contemporary psychoanalytic systems theory that regards therapeutic effect as being centrally a function of the therapeutic capacities of each analyst–patient pair as they emerge within a unique reciprocal relational process in the moment and over time.

Therapeutic possibility unfolds within the co-created, unpredictable process of any particular dyad. It is, ultimately, determined by "dyadic fit"—by the capacities and limitations of that therapist and that patient to understand and respond to each other. Specificity theory does not provide the practitioner with dos and don'ts. Rather, through its in-depth focus on process, it illuminates how a therapist may practice as best she or he can with each particular patient.

Structured psychoanalytic theories prescribe and proscribe responses and designate techniques that offer methods and guidelines in order to obtain foreseen results. In contrast, specificity theory holds that focusing on the emergent process of the particular dyad can optimally illuminate how such structured concepts may come more usefully into play. When a therapist fully comprehends and privileges the specificity of human relatedness at every level and at every moment in time, the application of both explicitly formulated concepts, as well as implicitly held "theory," within the clinical situation becomes more apparent, and is enhanced.

Specificity theory also offers a valuable new dimension to the education of the psychoanalytic therapist. Focusing on the specificity of process within supervisory situations—both individually and in groups—which was, in effect, how Balint implicitly worked, without actually conceptualizing it as such—educates the practitioner not only about how to become the clinician he or she can be with a particular patient, but also how she or he may become a better therapist for all of them.[6]

The Specificity of the Budapest Model as Applied to Balint Group Training

Balint Group work encourages its participants to explore in depth how aspects of the particular doctor–patient relationship can affect the patient's illness and its treatment. The title of Balint's groundbreaking book in this area is *The Doctor, His Patient, and the Illness* (1957). The Balint Group approach to consultation in effect gave substance to a systems (see Coburn, 2002, 2014) understanding of "illness" and its treatment that was remarkably ahead of its time. It exemplified the application of a dyadic process approach to supervisory work in a group setting that derived from the Budapest model of supervision. Discussion of patients in the Balint Group emphasizes the exploration of therapeutic possibility between that particular doctor and that particular patient (see also Balint, 1969a; Balint and Norell, 1973). The group leader encourages the sharing and discussion of how particular predilections and issues of individual doctors may emerge to interfere with or to enhance therapeutic effect for that patient.

In a book written with members of a research group 20 years after Michael Balint's death, Enid Balint (Balint, Courtenay, Elder, Hull, and Julian, 1993) summarized developments in the psychological aspects of general practice since Michael first elaborated his ideas. Both the group's way of working and what they discovered about the doctors' capacities for therapeutic work underscore the uniqueness and specificity of supervisory, as well as therapeutic, process.

> [Our aim was] to have a wider look at the … uncertainties which abound in working with patients; while at the same time not attempting to reduce them to neat patterns, leaving the perspectives as wide as possible in the realization that what one person sees from one angle cannot be seen from another's … the doctors [came to] realize that their healing powers were strictly limited, but … on the other hand, observed that very small changes in a person can produce amazingly large effects on the life of an individual. It seems that the unique relationship which occurs in the general practice setting informs us as to what the work is really about.
>
> (pp. 98–99)

The traditional psychoanalytic training model keeps supervision and personal analysis separate. Within the setting of supervision, responses that an experienced supervisor may recommend to his supervisee may be helpful, yet may not address specific personal issues that are significantly affecting the therapy at the time. While personal therapy may enable the student therapist to come to know himself better, help him to "change," it may not enable him to address particular issues that are currently emerging with regard to his control case. In other words, neither the setting of traditional supervision nor personal analysis alone reliably offers the opportunity to address actively relevant dyadic process between the supervisee and her patient. The Budapest model does this directly, by illuminating not only what may be therapeutically optimal, but also therapeutically workable, between the student analyst and her particular patient.

The Budapest model has had a profound, though largely unnoticed, effect upon contemporary perspectives on psychoanalytic supervision, even though it was officially banned by the International Psychoanalytic Association in 1947.

The Evolution of Psychoanalytic Supervision

Supervision has come to be accepted by a number of contemporary analysts as a curious kind of hybrid that variously comprises teaching, training, and, in some ways, treatment. Kindler (1998) observes that a good supervisor contributes in more diverse ways to the effectiveness of the treatment under supervision "[than through his] traditional roles of imparting technique, teaching theory, and formulating the psychodynamic meaning of the patient's communications" (p. 376). Yet, how many psychoanalytic educators even now would agree with Wolf that supervision constitutes a process in which learning depends upon the active participation of both participants in a mutually responsive relationship that entails "not only [sharing and creating] information … but simultaneously and necessarily also [sharing, creating, and participating] in each other's inner experience of themselves and of the other" (Wolf, 1995, pp. 261–262)? "The purpose of so-called supervision," Wolf maintains, "is [not only] to facilitate the emergence of … psychological skills and talents [but also] to strengthen … those personality traits that will enable the student-analyst to perform and to improve his psychoanalytic work" (p. 259). Yet, almost 40 years earlier, Michael Balint asserted that "the acquisition of therapeutic skill does not consist only of learning something new: it inevitably also entails a limited, though considerable, change in the [therapist's] personality" (Balint, 1957, p. 299).

The backstory to how psychoanalysts arrived at contemporary views on supervision comprises a tale of battling perspectives and, at times, confusion about just what supervision is or should be.

For some while, Freud and his early followers informally offered instruction to their analysands who were interested in practicing psychoanalysis. The three-column model (the so-called Eitingon model) for the training of analysts—theoretical courses, personal analysis, patients under supervision—was introduced at the Berlin Psychoanalytic Institute in the early 1920s and was later adopted by most other training centers. Ferenczi, however, felt that separating supervised analytic work from the candidate's analysis would limit the student's "opportunity for continuous development through various methods of teaching" (Fleming and Benedek, 1966, p. 12).

The earliest, and most famous, proponent of "teaching" the student how to practice psychoanalysis was Max Eitingon. Eitingon felt that characteristic inadequacies and learning problems of the beginner required that he be taught the technique of psychoanalysis. Eitingon maintained that it was "necessary to teach the technique of psychoanalysis through another method" (i.e., through a method other than the Budapest model) (Fleming and Benedek, 1966, p. 11). While the Budapest analysts did not forgo the teaching of "psychoanalytic technique," they saw their pedagogic task somewhat differently. They emphasized the effect of the analyst's character on the analytic situation (A. Balint, 1935), particularly when he is a beginner. "[The analyst's] technique and improvements in it," according to Vilma Kovacs, "are ... directly related to the analyst's personality" (Kovacs, 1936, p. 348). Kovacs underscored the importance of Freud's assertion, in 1910, "that the pre-requisite for a successful application of psycho-analytical technique is that the physician should begin his analytical training by being analyzed himself" (quoted in Kovacs, 1936, p. 348). The Budapest analysts advocated that the student continue in analysis while he is treating his patients. They also considered it important that the candidate's training analyst supervise his work, in effect giving substance to the designation, "training analyst." They were asserting that self-understanding was maximally usable when it is perceived as relevant to the patient with whom the student analyst is currently working.

At the "Four Countries Conference" in the 1930s, where European analysts met to present papers and to discuss problems,[7] it was agreed that in psychoanalytic training attention should be focused on two areas—the student's reactions to the patient's transference, and the teaching of analytic technique—and that more attention should be paid to the first of these than had hitherto been the case. To emphasize the difference between the two, the focus on the student-analyst's countertransference was termed "Kontrollanalyse," and the focus on teaching the student how to conduct analysis, i.e., "technique," was called "Analysenkontrolle" (Balint, 1948, p. 165; see also Fleming and Benedek, 1966, p. 14).[8] There was supposedly universal agreement about the nature of the latter and that it did not involve the student's countertransference. Yet, confusingly, the participants at the Four Countries Conferences also agreed that the two tasks of training "could not be divided" (Balint, 1948, p. 165). This seemed to imply that both the supervisor and the student's analyst were expected to address both areas, but it was not made clear just how this recommendation should be implemented.

At one of the conferences, in 1933, Kovacs (1936) reported that, in supervising candidates who were not in analysis—even those who had been in analysis with her but who presently were not—she had difficulty orienting herself adequately to the material in order to carry out her supervisory tasks: "I did not know the candidate's character and his modes of reaction, and so I could not say from what point of view he was judging the various situations he encountered" (p. 352). In Kovacs's experience, "Analysenkontrolle" without "Kontrollanalyse" was superficial and unsatisfactory; that is, she felt that she could not adequately supervise someone who was not simultaneously in analysis with her.

In their 1939 paper "On transference and counter-transference," Alice and Michael Balint described the great variation in so many of the supposedly universal ways that analysts work, which suggested that, despite efforts to adhere to Freud's technical recommendations, analytic technique was far from universally the same. This would imply that, in teaching candidates how to conduct an analysis, we should not ignore an omnipresent variable: who the analyst is. In the same paper, the Balints conveyed that we should pay closer attention to the vicissitudes of the analytic dyad. Their remarkable assertion, that "the analytical situation is the result of an interplay between the patient's transference and the analyst's counter-transference, complicated by the reactions released in each by the other's transference on to him" (p. 227), further underscored the relevancy for analytic training of the Budapest supervisory approach wherein the candidate's work is supervised in the setting of his analysis.

Balint (1948) reports that, while the participants at successive Four Countries Conferences

> [agreed that] analysis of the counter-transference must form an essential part of the training, i.e., [analysis and supervision] cannot be divided, no decision could be reached on the point whether the training analyst or another should begin the supervision with the candidate.
>
> (p. 165)

Eventually it was agreed that further experience was needed before this could be decided. However, without further observation or published discussion, the new London Standing Rules—according to Balint, Ernest Jones's rules—were authoritatively proclaimed: "The analyst undertaking the student's personal analysis does not undertake the supervision of his cases" (Balint, 1948, p. 165).

At that point, the "tripartite" system of psychoanalytic training officially came into being, entailing strict separation of its three modalities: the analysis of the candidate, the treatment of cases under supervision, and theoretical lectures and seminars. In Hungary, however, this did not quite happen. Balint (1948) explicitly stated the view of the Hungarian school that the candidate's clinical training can be best done if the personal analysis and the supervision are carried out by the same person, that is, the candidate's analyst, at least with the first case. In other words, the optimal situation for "supervising" the candidate, according to the analysts in the Budapest Institute, is the one in which the analyst is in the best position to address personal issues of the candidate as they may be affecting his work with his patient.

As far as I know, every psychoanalytic training organization apart from the institute in Budapest complied with Jones's edict. The "training" analyst just analyzed the candidate, and the supervisor just taught him "how to do analysis." Yet, while everyone except the Hungarians seemed to welcome this arrangement, the appearance in the literature of many papers in which analysts continued to debate what constitutes optimal supervision suggests that the controversy that began in the 1930s which supposedly ended with the implementation of the "London Rules" in 1947 had not cooled down all that much. It also implied that the implementation of these rules may not have delivered the educational yield that Jones and his faithful followers assumed it would.

Four main themes have emerged in the psychoanalytic literature about supervision. These themes in effect address and elaborate the same issues debated by the attendees at the Four Countries Conferences in the 1930s. They essentially comprise the following questions: (1) Should the supervisor primarily be "teaching" the supervisee how to conduct a psychoanalysis, explicitly focusing on principles of analytic conduct and, implicitly—and inevitably—emphasizing the relevance of particular analytic theory? (2) Should the focus of supervision primarily be on the supervisee's patient or on the supervisee and his characteristic problems? (3) Should the focus be on process—between the supervisee and his patient, or/and between the supervisor and the supervisee? (4) In what ways and how personally should the supervisor engage the supervisee in addressing "transference-countertransference," or "relational," issues, either between her and her patient or/and between her and the supervisor?

Despite recognition by many analysts that "supervision is more than education and less than treatment" (Solnit, 1970, p. 359), discussion in the psychoanalytic literature about the Budapest supervisory model since Balint's 1948 paper was relatively sparse. (Some examples were Ekstein and Wallerstein, 1958; Fleming and Benedek, 1966; Bacal, 1972, 1975; and, more recently, Bacal, 2011a, 2011b; Gábor, 2014).

A number of contributions to the literature do, however, indicate the influence of the Hungarian analysts' perspectives. In his presentation to the Third Pre-Congress on Psychoanalytic Training, Solnit (1970) reported that "Although there [was] general agreement that the resolution of countertransference was the task of the student's own analysis, most institutes expect the supervisor to take it up tactfully and to deal with its educational implications if that is feasible" (p. 359). Pulver's (1984) view is that the ongoing debate as to whether supervision "should be considered purely an educational experience or whether it should, in addition, be therapeutic" is spurious[9]; he concludes that "the question … can be answered solely from the dynamics of the supervisory situation" (p. 489). Pulver "[disagrees] with Keiser (1969) that [Fleming and Benedek] are much too therapeutic in their approach" (p. 490). He conveys that what may be identified as therapeutic work for the supervisee can be very useful for his analytic work with his patient (see also Bromberg, 2013; Levy and Parnell, 2001). Pulver concurs with Ekstein and Wallerstein that it is the purpose to which the supervisor's responses are put that render them appropriate. For

Pulver, "[Supervision] is a powerful interaction, filled with emotions and made even more complex by the fact that it is an interaction about an interaction" (Pulver, 1984, p. 489). Dewald (1981), anticipating Kantrowitz's findings, draws attention to the importance of the supervisor's "[making] an assessment of the candidate's needs and vulnerabilities ... as a guide for interventions" (p. 80).

Supervision as Process: Its Uniqueness and Specificity

Even earlier, Fleming and Benedek (1966) recognized the usefulness of a systems, or process, perspective in supervision.

> Supervisory work requires an even greater span of system sensitivity than is necessary for analytic treatment ... [The supervisor must be] attuned to the patient and the analyst, the relationship between them and to the progress of the analytic process, [as well as to the relationship between himself and the supervisee].
>
> (p. 56)

In their study of supervision transcripts, the goal of teaching the students about *process* was common to all supervisory activity. Their view is that "[teaching] the student to regard psychoanalysis as a process is the most important and probably the most difficult of the supervisory tasks" (p. 53). I have indeed found that when offering case examples in clinical seminars and at psychoanalytic conferences for the purpose of studying the uniqueness of dyadic process, participants tend to wander away from a focus on process to talk about the psychodynamics of the case based on one theory or another and how the analyst might on that basis intervene effectively.

Fleming and Benedek also in effect imply that the recognition of dyadic process as unique and specific meant that "What the student learns in one supervisory session about his patient and/or about himself, he can apply only in the future to situations which are similar but never identical ... The 'experience' itself can never be repeated" (p. 238) (see also Kindler, 1998).

Kantrowitz (2002b), on the basis of her research, arrives at analogous conclusions (see also Coburn, 1997):

> The interaction of the characteristics of candidate, supervisor, and patient [affects] the candidate's learning and analytic work ... The particular gains candidates derive from working with particular supervisors is a function of the specific needs arising from their stage of training, their previous experience, their character traits and conflicts, and their interaction with the character and conflicts of their patients.
>
> (2002b, p. 966)

The application of specificity theory to supervision gives further substance to this (see Bacal, 2011a, chapter 10). In addition, it directs its participants to address, in the particularity of *their* process, not only what constitutes optimal ways of learning, for that supervisee, with regard to the treatment of that patient, but also what is possible for them to accomplish together. Specificity theory makes the latter explicit in its emphasis on the importance of "fit" in supervision, as well as in treatment.

The Specificity of Fit and the Supervisory Process

We need to give more consideration to the importance of "fit" between particular supervisors and particular supervisees. Aronson (2000) writes trenchantly about his experience with three different supervisors whose quite different responsiveness to him and to his work with his patient resulted in quite different experiences of fit and concomitantly of the usefulness of the supervision. My experience affirms Kantrowitz's (2002b) finding that a good "match" between supervisor and supervisee and the supervisee's patient enhances the supervisee's learning experience. It is useful to be aware of when the fit within the educational dyad, or triad, may be significantly less than optimal.

Kantrowitz's (2002a, 2002b) research indicates that a "felicitous match [between candidate, supervisor, and patient] can aid professional and personal analytic development [and that a] clash of characteristics ... can slow or impede learning and adversely affect analytic work" (2002b, p. 938).[10] My own experience affirms this: I have worked with supervisees with whom the fit or lack thereof made a considerable difference to what we could do together (Bacal, 2011a, chapter 10). Yet Kantrowitz also emphasizes the unpredictability of (triadic) process:

> [The] nature and helpfulness of the match cannot be predicted in advance, for several reasons. One is that what is manifest in each of the participants does not reveal all that potentially may emerge; different people bring out different aspects of each other. Another reason is that interactions among the three participants and their specific characteristics evolve and change over the course of the work.
>
> ... The dynamic interplay of patient and candidate may yield surprises. Patients may evoke conflicts in candidates that were insufficiently analyzed, or that did not emerge in their analyses.
>
> (pp. 964, 960)

A most interesting finding, which recalls Vilma Kovacs' observation of the importance to her of having the candidate in analysis with her during the supervision (Kovacs, 1936).

The Specificity of Process and Parallel Process

I have wondered whether the traditional arrangement of separating the modalities of "training" and "treatment" is in some measure responsible for the phenomenon of parallel process. Why does the student therapist bring to supervision an unconsciously disguised representation of the problem with his patient, yet one that is curiously revealing to the supervisor or, as characteristically happens, to a supervisory group? Could this possibly be because he is unconsciously, though ambivalently and "resistively," seeking help with a specific problem in relation to his patient that feels "personal" and similar, a problem that his therapist may not have responded to, but for which he does not anticipate adequate help either, from the supervisor, in that setting?

From the perspective of specificity theory, recognizing and attending to the possible effect of one system operating on another, how in particular supervisory situations specific issues that remain unaddressed in other systems may play out, can be productive. Sometimes the parallel is "seen" at the outset, sometimes not. In my experience, especially in experiential supervisory groups (and in particular where group therapists discuss their experience in their own groups), this can be a useful teaching tool. The important consideration is whether and, if so how, the particular supervisee and that supervisor, or supervisees, can deal effectively with them.

Specificity theory regards the supervisory situation as a process that is constituted by the emergence of dyadic specificities in at least the two situations—of supervisor and supervisee, and of the supervisee and his patient,[11] each of which may reciprocally affect the other. Other systems—the student analyst and his analyst, the supervisor and the student's analyst—as well as those within the psychoanalytic training institute may, implicitly, sometimes also explicitly, come into play. Ultimately, the dyad comprising supervisor and supervisee, variously affected by these adjacent systems, will discover, within the specificity of their process, what constitutes possibilities for optimal supervisory work for the particular candidate's educational needs. What that student needs, and what he or she can use from that supervisor at that time, and how this matches the supervisor's views and capabilities, will unfold within their unique pedagogic process. Supervisee and supervisor must learn together how they can best learn, work, and—as Aronson (2000) suggests—play together.

Aronson (2000) has offered a Winnicottian perspective on supervision that very much matches mine. He characterizes an optimal supervisory process as a

> playful, creative experience ... [a] "to and fro," in which ... each participant [places] his particular stamp on the material and process, creating an exchange of sorts. In essence, the supervisee develops the capacity to discover—himself, the patient, the process of psychoanalysis—while concurrently allowing himself to be found by the patient, by himself, and by the supervisor.
>
> (p. 125)

Ekstein and Wallerstein (1958) recognize that supervisors have particular predilections and preferences for how they supervise, partly as an expression of their personalities. Some supervisors feel comfortable discussing countertransference issues with their supervisees at a personal level and interacting with them around these issues as they emerge, either in relation to the patient or/and in relation to themselves. Some supervisors do not, however, and prefer to address them in general terms, or only didactically, or not at all, and may refer the student back to her analyst for more personal analysis.

Ekstein and Wallerstein express the hope that supervisors "could make choices ... which derive from the specific problems and needs of the learner rather than from their personal preferences and their personal security as teachers" (1958, p. 261). While I resonate with their "hope," I think that the way we could most usefully approach this challenge is by training supervisors to recognize the possibilities and limitations of the particular dyad of that supervisor with that supervisee as they emerge in process, just as we recognize these with regard to the specificity of the process between the trainee-analyst and her patient.

Specificity theory does not pre-empt how supervision "should" be done, or "can" be done, nor what kind of analyst that student should become. Rather, the supervisor and supervisee will optimally "teach" each other by becoming aware of what the supervisee's learning needs are at that time, in relation to that patient, as they become specifically evident, either in the process between her and her patient or/and between her and the supervisor. Intrinsic to specificity theory is its emphasis on uniqueness, unpredictability, and the specificity of process. While the supervisor will inevitably—and *perhaps* usefully—have in mind, consciously or unconsciously, what it means to work in the "right" way as a psychoanalyst, specificity theory allows that neither the supervisor nor the supervisee knows in advance the optimal ways for the supervisor to respond to that student, or what he or she should learn. They can, however, discover this—and how effectively this can be carried out within that supervisory dyad—by attending to the specificity of their unfolding process. In effect, any or all of the four themes described above may variously emerge as *specifically* relevant in any particular supervision.

While the Budapest model of supervision is not formally recognized in any of the four analytic institutes where I supervise candidates, it had not been explicitly interdicted, either, until recently. I offer this kind of supervision informally in two settings, if the fit is right: with my trainee analysands, within their analytic sessions; and with supervisees, in the supervisory situation. With regard to the former setting, I am responsive to my analysand's requests for help with their control cases. My analysand's work with her patient is one of the most important activities in her life. It is a part of who she is, of her personal as well as of her professional development. In addition, my awareness that our shared outside system—our psychoanalytic institute—regards our psychoanalytic work as central to his or her development as an analyst also inclines me to believe that it would be remiss of me not to respond as helpfully as I can to a request for assistance in the treatment of her patient. The alternatives of "just listening," or interpreting associations about her patient only as they may personally relate to her, or suggesting she take the problem she is having with her patient to her supervisor, fall just as short as the traditional recommendation of the supervisor that the supervisee take her "countertransference" problem up with her analyst.

Ekstein and Wallerstein (1958) emphasize the importance of adhering to the educational purpose of supervision: "leading [the student] toward greater skill in his work with his patients" (p. 254). They express concern that, if training and treatment are carried out in the same setting, the educational purpose of supervision could become subverted. Yet they simultaneously recognize that

> supervision—that is, the supervisory process—[is] not simply ... the transmission of knowledge and skills, but rather ... a complex process that goes on between the supervisor and his student. This process is a helping process in which the student is being helped to discover his problems as a psychotherapist, to resolve them with the help of the supervisor ... This process includes affective problems, interpersonal conflicts, problems in being helped, as well as in helping, and is truly itself a helping process.
>
> (p. 251)

Ekstein and Wallerstein's view of the supervisory process so substantially endorses the Budapest model, one might question whether their concern has more to do with its non-adherence to established tradition than about its not effectively adhering to the educational purpose of supervision. Recently, Bromberg (2013, p. 12) describes how he struggled during the process of discovering that, in order to help his supervisee treat her patient effectively, he had to expand his role as supervisor to that of therapist. Perhaps this role expansion might not have entailed such a struggle for Bromberg had he been familiar with the Budapest model of supervision.

The point, it seems to me, that Ekstein and Wallerstein effectively make, and Bromberg's example vividly depicts, is that the path along which any particular supervisory dyad must travel in order to achieve its educational purpose is variegated and unpredictable. Specificity theory underscores both Ekstein and Wallerstein's, and Fleming and Benedek's, view of supervision as process, but adds that the nature and effectiveness of such a process will be specific for that supervisory dyad.

My way of working with supervisees has significantly changed under the influence of specificity theory. Apprehending the nature of the potential and limitations that my supervisee and I encounter and co-create as a particular supervisory couple enables us to discover more clearly what *we* can, and cannot, do together in our process. In particular, when my supervisee and I find ourselves mutually receptive to talking about emotional issues—sometimes even quite personal ones—that arise between her and her patient, or/and between her and me, we may even be able to exceed the expectations for learning ordinarily inherent within traditional supervision and, in this way, potentially enhance the treatment of the patient.

I will conclude with an example of how one of my supervisees and I worked together within the traditional framework of supervision. Our work reflects not only the systems perspective of Fleming and Benedek; it advances the concept of the Budapest model of supervision. In this example, the supervisor's process of listening to himself after responding in a particular way to his supervisee, and then sharing this with her, led to interactions with this supervisee that in turn led to a significant educational experience—for both of them.[12]

Illustration

Dr. P. is an advanced analytic candidate at the Institute of Contemporary Psychoanalysis in Los Angeles, whose third control case I was supervising. Dr. P. was in analysis with a colleague, and conveyed how important that work continued to be for her. Yet she valued the opportunity to present her analytic work with the "free-associative" openness that characterized the Budapest supervisory model.

I would emphasize that, in my experience as a supervisor, the way Dr. P. and I worked together does not ubiquitously happen, even with candidates at this Institute. I have found myself working with supervisees in ways that range from the formal presentation by the student of her account of the analytic hour as she has recorded it to what an observer would find similar in tone and ambience, and to some extent in content, to an analytic session.

Specificities resembling the latter emerged as salient in substantial measure for Dr. P. and myself in our process. A specific aspect of fit between Dr. P. and myself that contributed to the productive operation of our particular supervisory process was our ability to co-create an ambience in which we could comfortably discuss personal aspects of who we are that emerged in a process that might be affecting our supervisory work, and their possible effect on the therapeutic process of Dr. P. with her patient. This does not necessarily mean that this way of working is "better" than others. It does mean that this is the way Dr. P. and I worked best together.

As Dr. P. was about to leave after a supervisory session, I found myself telling her about my work with a patient that reflected problems similar to those with which she was struggling with her patient, N. I was at the time aware of a certain internal pressure to share my experience with her.

After Dr. P. left, I reflected on what I had done, and as we began our next supervision session, I shared my thoughts with Dr. P.—that it seemed to be a curious kind of "narcissistic" behavior. I had felt a need to have her hear what *I* had to say, since she had done virtually all the talking in that session. I added that I was also wondering whether this was what Dr. P. needed to do in that session. I told her that, in my view, she was doing excellent analytic work as she struggled with the problems presented by her patient, and that what she may have indeed needed from me during the last supervision session was in fact to listen to her, and to experience my quiet validation. I wondered, too, whether my reaction could also be understood as expressing a measure of competitiveness with Dr. P., a competitiveness that may have been stirred up not only by my need to be heard, but also by my unconsciously resonating, as it were, with competitiveness between Dr. P. and her patient, an acupuncturist who had been seeing a patient of her own "like an analyst," as Dr. P. had put it, several times a week.

Dr. P. expressed gratitude for my candor about both of us. She had been puzzled about my extending the session; she was aware that I probably needed to stop (a light indicated the presence of someone in the waiting room) yet I did not, and was telling her about my patient. In our further discussion, she told me that she really likes when I share anything with her—whether it be case material, theory, personal experience, or my recent trip to Greece (a country that has particular family significance for her)—especially when she sees that I am enthusiastic and animated about it. She conveyed that she finds this most engaging: "So I guess I sort of enjoyed getting the extra time that day, even though I felt slightly guilty knowing your patient was waiting!" She added that all these feelings likely tied in with the complexity of her pleasure-cum-guilt about being a favored sibling. And she did think it likely that these feelings reflected issues with which she and her patient were struggling, about which she would like to learn more. She also felt there were other aspects of our process that were relevant to her work with this patient.

Dr. P. was aware that she "had done all the talking" in the last supervision session—in effect, she had alluded to it with a small amount of guilt during the session itself—yet she was also aware that, since she hadn't seen me for several weeks, there was a whole lot to tell me in a short time, in order to catch me up. She allowed that she did tend to talk a good deal in her supervisions, as this helped her to clarify for herself what was happening in the analytic work with her patient. In other words, this was a cardinal way in which Dr. P. learned. She was also aware that she could be "dominant", and, as a result of discussing our experiences and thoughts about this, she had begun to consider that, in taking up so much of the talking time in her supervisions, she might, at times, have been interfering with her learning experience. She told me, "You did indeed pick up on something I have been unaware of. That [part of] it has been a blind spot." Dr. P. conveyed that she did find value in my ideas and perspectives—which was evident to me in many discussions we had had—yet at this time, with this patient, she was especially grateful for her experience of me as an attentive and perceptive listener. With regard to my acknowledged "countertransference" reaction—which I believe is more accurately regarded as *a disruption that was specific to our process* [13] (see also Bacal, 2011a, p. 104)—she wondered whether her tendency to be "dominating" in her interactions might have triggered an experience in me that reflected problems with which I had struggled with my mother, which she had read about in a published paper (Bacal, 2006). I told Dr. P. that my mother did listen to me, but that her reaction of "superior knowingness" that I had written about was not how I experienced Dr. P. Rather, I thought my reaction to Dr. P.'s monopolizing the talking time in that session likely reflected a residue of my feeling eclipsed, long ago, by the liveliness of a similarly bright younger sister.

Interestingly, in our supervisory process, disruptively matching specificities of connection were emerging across our dyads: Dr. P. with her patient and me with Dr. P. Dr. P. responded by telling me that, in her interaction with important others, including her analyst, she greatly valued knowing about the other person.

As we were talking in this way, Dr. P. told me that she was now thinking about further experience with her patient, N. She did recall that N was indeed doing a kind of "analysis" with one of her acupuncture patients, but had not been consciously aware that this may have evoked some competitiveness within her in relation to N. She had felt more like N was doing this as a way to feel close to her, even merge with her. Yet, Dr. P. recognized that this also appeared to be suffused with conflict.

While N had felt seduced by her mother's attention, she struggled to free herself from her mother's need for her to serve as an accommodating archaic selfobject. I commented that N had apparently been making progress in respect of this conflict. During a recent European vacation with her parents, on which N's sister was not invited, she had been able to leave for a week and enjoy a holiday bicycling in Rome, on her own, about which Dr. P. jokingly remarked to me that this was more than she would attempt! Dr. P. was initially surprised, though, when N "cut me out completely" when N returned from her vacation. Dr. P. sensed that N might be suffering from a guilt-laden depressiveness that was also likely overdetermined. She understood this as N's guilt about feeling that Dr. P. was more important to her than her mother. Dr. P. also interpreted that N may have been enjoying her time away not just from her parents, but from *her*, too, while she was bicycling and tango dancing her way through Rome. She understood this as N's "not wanting to have to worry about my missing her and having difficulty with the separation, like her mother does." N quite agreed with these interpretations.

I shared with Dr. P. my recollection of how her awareness of struggling with her own guilt (which she had spontaneously shared with me earlier on), about her experience of being preferred by her parents in certain ways over her own sister, has also been helpful to Dr. P. in resonating with analogous issues in the relationship with this patient. I further shared with Dr. P. that I had also wondered whether my "enactment" at the end of our supervision session last week was derived in part from some mutually dissociated awareness (see Donnel Stern, 2004) from feelings variously operating within Dr. P. and myself about being cut out and cutting out with regard to more than one sister-related dyad. Dr. P.'s response was that our discussion about this felt "very useful and apt", and that the themes of competitiveness (both "sibling" and "Oedipal") that were highlighted by my sharing of my reaction (to her earlier monopolization of the talking time) were valuable and useful, "since I may tend to deny and minimize due to guilt about various triumphs in my family (my mother/sister/siblings). It's also really interesting to hear about your mother/sister stuff and how that may have interfaced with my stuff in the process."

Our discussion of these experiences was illuminating and valuable for me as well as for Dr. P. Its usefulness for the treatment of Dr. P.'s patient became especially apparent when Dr. P. and I looked closely at the particularities of our own process. I also learned more about how Dr. P. learned, and how—and why—I, and Dr. P., might at times find ourselves interfering with her learning.

My account of this work with Dr. P. illustrates how supervision informed by specificity theory may enhance its effectiveness through focusing attention on the emergent process of that supervisor–supervisee dyad and on that analyst–analysand dyad, and how these systems may reciprocally affect one another.

The focus on the specificity of process between Dr. P. and her patient and between Dr. P. and myself also illuminates how understanding of what is traditionally regarded as separate occurrences of transference and countertransference or aspects of a mysterious "parallel process" can be enhanced by apprehending them as reflections of the specificity of interfacing processes.

The value of maintaining both personal therapy and supervised work as pillars for the training of psychoanalytic therapists continues to be widely recognized. Yet, the nature of the variegated, and particular, learning needs of each student in treating that patient optimally may emerge in either setting, and the extent to which they may—or may not—be effectively responded to, in either setting, will be discovered within the specificity of the unfolding process of its particular participants. Perhaps analytic training institutes may yet undertake a serious study of the Budapest model of supervision, which has not been officially practiced since 1970, when Michael Balint was offering it at the Institute of Psychoanalysis in London.

Notes

1 This model, which evolved under the strong personal influence of Sándor Ferenczi, would appear to have been practiced as such by Hungarian analysts until World War II. According to Szőnyi Gábor (personal communication), it continued as an option within the Hungarian Psychoanalytic Society when it reintegrated with the International Psychoanalytical Association in 1975. Since then, the Budapest model underwent various transformations (see Gábor, 2014). Currently, the Hungarian regulation allows the first supervision with the personal analyst, but does not further specify the setting.

2 The research was published as the book *Six Minutes for the Patient: Interactions in General Practice Consultation* (Balint and Norell, 1973).

3 For a comprehensive account of specificity theory and its application in psychoanalytic treatment and supervision, see Bacal (2011a).

4 Required at the Institute of Psychoanalysis in London.

5 Not everyone who worked with Balint in this kind of supervision found it so useful. Some years after completing my analytic training, I learned from a fellow student who had also undertaken supervision with Balint in this way that he found it noxious—an interesting reflection of the specificity of pedagogic and personal experience.

6 For further elaboration, see Bacal (2011a, chapter 10).

7 Attendees at the "four countries conferences" (Austria, Hungary, Czechoslovakia, and Italy) also included analysts from other European countries, such as Holland and Germany.

8 Fleming and Benedek (1966, p. 14) clarify that the word "control" has a stricter and more limiting connotation in English than in German. In German, the word "Kontrolle" translates as "*supervision* in the first place and *checking* in the second."

9 More recently, Rosbrow (1997) described the teach–treat split as a false dichotomy based on the spurious premise that only interpretive work is legitimate.

10 In a supervision course Kantrowitz gave recently, what emerged to affirm her research was discovering that the most important variable for supervisory work was the *match* among supervisee, patient, and supervisor (Kantrowitz, personal communication).

11 The Budapest model, at least as Balint carried it out with me, focused on process between the supervisee and his patient. It did not address process occurring between the candidate and his training analyst.

12 From what I gather in reading Mészáros's descriptions of how Ferenczi worked (Mészáros, 2010, 2014), I think that the application of specificity theory to the supervisory process must very much reflect Ferenczi's way of applying the Budapest model of supervision.

13 Because specificity theory holds that psychoanalytic treatment reflects the operation of a *unique reciprocal process for each analyst–patient couple*—in effect, a system that may be complexly affected by other systems, both adjacent and distant—we would refer to what happened between Dr. P. and myself as an example of *disruption that is specific to a particular relational process* rather than only speaking in terms of transference and countertransference, terms we regard as too narrow, circumscribed, and linear to account for such complexity (see also Bacal, 2011a, chapter 8, "How specificity theory alters our view of psychoanalytic concepts and principles and how this affects therapeutic action").

References

Aronson, S. (2000). Analytic supervision: All work and no play? *Contemporary Psychoanalysis*, 36, 121–132.

Bacal, H.A. (1972). Balint groups: Training or treatment? *International Journal of Psychiatry in Medicine*, 3, 373–377.

Bacal, H.A. (1975). The treatment aspect of Balint training. *Journal of the Balint Society*, 4, 10–13.

Bacal, H.A. (2006). Specificity theory: Conceptualizing a personal and professional quest for therapeutic possibility. *International Journal of Psychoanalytic Self Psychology*, 1 (2), 133–155.

Bacal, H.A. (2011a). *The power of specificity in psychotherapy: When therapy works—and when it doesn't*. Lanham, MD: Jason Aronson.

Bacal, H.A. (2011b). Specificity theory: The evolution of a process theory of psychoanalytic treatment. *American Imago*, 68, 267–283.

Bacal, H.A., & Newman, K.M. (1990). *Theories of object relations: Bridges to self psychology*. New York, NY: Columbia University Press.

Balint, A. (1935). Communication reported by Glover, E., 1935, Four Countries Conference. *Bulletin of the International Psychoanalytic Association*, 16, 505–509.

Balint, E., & Norell, J.S. (1973). *Six minutes for the patient: Interactions in general practice consultation*. London: Tavistock.

Balint, E., Courtenay, M., Elder, A., Hull, S., & Julian, P. (1993). *The doctor, the patient, and the group*. London: Routledge.

Balint, M. (1935). Critical notes on the pre-genital organization of the libido. In *Primary love and psycho-analytic technique* (1965, new and enlarged ed., pp. 37–58). London: Tavistock.

Balint, M. (1937). Early developmental states of the ego: Primary object-love. In *Primary love and psycho-analytic technique* (pp. 74–90). London: Tavistock.

Balint, M. (1948). On the psycho-analytic training system. *International Journal of Psychoanalysis*, 29, 163–173.

Balint, M. (1957). *The doctor, his patient, and the illness* (2nd ed.). London: Tavistock.

Balint, M. (1968). *The basic fault*. London: Tavistock.

Balint, M. (1969a). The structure of the training-cum-research-seminars. *Journal of the Royal College of General Practitioners*, 17, 201–211.

Balint, M. (1969b). Trauma and object relationship. *International Journal of Psychoanalysis*, 50, 429–435.

Balint, M., & Balint, A. (1939). On transference and counter-transference. *International Journal of Psychoanalysis*, 20, 223–230.

Bromberg, P. (2013). Hidden in plain sight: Thoughts on imagination and the lived unconscious. *Psychoanalytic Dialogues*, 23, 1–14.

Coburn, W.J. (1997). The vision in supervision: Transference-countertransference dynamics and disclosure in the supervision relationship. *Bulletin of the Menninger Clinic*, 61, 482–494.

Coburn, W.J. (2002). A world of systems: The role of systemic patterns of experience in the therapeutic process. *Psychoanalytic Inquiry*, 5, 655–677.

Coburn, W.J. (2014). *Psychoanalytic complexity: Clinical attitudes for therapeutic change*. New York, NY: Routledge.

Dewald, P. (1981). Aspects of the supervisory process. *Annual of Psychoanaysis*, 9, 75–89.

Ekstein, R., & Wallerstein, R. (1958). *The teaching and learning of psychotherapy*. New York, NY: International Universities Press.

Fleming, J., & Benedek, T. (1966). *Psychoanalytic supervision*. New York, NY: Grune & Stratton.

Gábor, S. (2014). The vicissitudes of the Budapest model of supervision: Can we learn from it today? *Psychoanalytic Inquiry*, 34 (6), 606–618.

Kantrowitz, J. (2002a). The external observer and the lens of the patient-analyst match. *International Journal of Psychoanalysis*, 83, 339–350.

Kantrowitz, J. (2002b). The triadic match: The interactive effect of supervisor, candidate, and patient. *Journal of the American Psychoanalytic Association*, 50, 939–996.

Kindler, A. (1998). Optimal responsiveness and psychoanalytic supervision. In H.A. Bacal (Ed.), *Optimal responsiveness: How therapists heal their patients* (pp. 357–382). Northvale, NJ: Jason Aronson.

Kovacs, V. (1936). Training- and control-analysis. *International Journal of Psychoanalysis*, 1, 346–354.

Levy, J., & Parnell, Y. (2001). The benefits and hazards of working through the supervisee's countertransference in psychoanalytic supervision. *Journal of Clinical Psychoanalysis*, 10 (1), 91–116.

Mészáros, J. (2010). Sándor Ferenczi and the Budapest School of psychoanalysis. *Psychoanalytic Perspectives*, 7 (1), 69–89.

Mészáros, J. (2014). *Ferenczi and Beyond: Exile of the Budapest School and solidarity in the psychoanalytic movement during the Nazi years*. London: Karnac Books.

Pulver, S. (1984). Psychoanalytic supervision: A method of clinical teaching: By Joan Fleming and Therese F. Benedek. Republished in *Classics in psychoanalysis, monograph* 1. New York, NY: International Universities Press.

Rosbrow, T. (1997). From parallel process to developmental process: A developmental plan/formulation approach to supervision. In A. Goldberg (Ed.), *Conversations in self psychology, progress in self psychology* (Vol. 13, pp. 149–164). Hillsdale, NJ: Analytic Press.

Solnit, A. (1970). Learning from psychoanalytic supervision. *International Journal of Psychoanalysis*, 51, 359–362.

Stern, D. (2004). The eye sees itself: Dissociation, enactment, and the achievement of conflict. *Contemporary Psychoanalysis*, 40, 197–237.

Wolf, E. (1995). How to supervise without doing harm: Comments on psychoanalytic supervision. *Psychoanalytic Inquiry*, 15, 252–267.

12 Discovering Optimal Responsiveness within the Salience of Emergent Process

The author traces the evolution of the concept, optimal responsiveness, and delineates its current meaning in the context of dyadic process. He describes and illustrates how attending to the specificity of salience within emergent process significantly illuminates responsiveness that may be optimal. In keeping with the theme of the journal's issue, freedom and free will, the author considers how they may apply to optimal responsiveness in psychoanalytic practice.

I initially introduced the term *optimal responsiveness* (Bacal, 1985) as a counter to the concept of *optimal frustration*, which had been regarded as central to therapeutic effect, from classical theory up to and including Kohut's elaboration of it in self psychology (Kohut, 1984).[1] It never made sense to me, neither as analyst nor analysand. While recognizing that effective working through of disruptions is potentially therapeutic, I argued that frustration is not an intrinsic requirement for therapeutic effect (see also Terman, 1998).

I suggested that the concept, optimal responsiveness, not only replace optimal frustration as central to therapeutic effect but that it denote the patient's experience of the analyst as responding optimally to her particular therapeutic needs (Bacal, 1985, 1998c). I also questioned the ubiquitously held view that the only way to achieve therapeutic effect was through verbal interpretation, suggesting rather that it occurred via a wide spectrum of responses on the part of the analyst.

These were somewhat revolutionary views at the time. Few analysts were inclined to express them. Franz Alexander had effectively been run out of "psychoanalytic town" for introducing the concept of the *corrective emotional experience*, which implied that something other than interpretation and insight may be therapeutically effective—an idea which, today, has heavily influenced contemporary views on change (Bacal, 1990).

I received a lot of attention, mostly negative, for my articulation of *optimal responsiveness*, much of it from self-psychology colleagues.[2] I suspected, though, that many of them practiced in accordance with it. Heinz Kohut himself was one of them. Kohut[3] had posited a two-step process for therapeutic effect: sustained empathic immersion in the patient's subjectivity, followed by interpretation of what had been gleaned thereby. He emphasized that

DOI: 10.4324/9781003570806-13

interpretation was a necessary second step. Yet, two of Kohut's most famous clinical examples (Kohut, 1977) vividly illustrate quite different kinds of therapeutic responses. For Miss F., it was only Kohut's offering his understanding echo of her rage-filled protestations that was effective.[4] And, in his final address, in Berkeley (Kohut, 1981), Kohut contended that offering his two fingers to an imminently suicidal patient to hold rather than interpreting what he felt she needed was a response that may have prevented the execution of her suicidality.[5] Yet, earlier in that address Kohut had emphasized that empathy was to be regarded solely as a data-gathering instrument. In 2010, we (Bacal and Carlton, 2010), suggested that this apparent contradiction could be clarified by defining empathy as the analyst's *utilizing her capacity for empathic attunement*, and that in this sense it was, as Kohut asserted, a data-gathering instrument; and that *the offer of empathic attunement*, such as the recognition of the patient's subjectivity wherein Kohut echoed it, for Miss F, is an example of an *empathic response*.

We may usefully note, though, in consonance with our recognition that the patient's therapeutic experience may result from variegated responses on the part of the analyst, that an *empathic response* is not the only one that is optimally responsive (see Bacal, 1998b). These examples of optimal responsiveness, which highlight non-interpretive responsiveness, also illustrate what was already implicit in my 1985 paper (and later explicitly elaborated in *Optimal Responsiveness: How Therapists Heal Their Patients* (Bacal, 1998c): that *optimal responsiveness denotes the patient's experience of the analyst responding to the uniqueness of her therapeutic needs.*

Specificity Theory

Specificity theory (Bacal, 1998b, 2006, 2011a, 2011b, 2017; Bacal and Herzog, 2003) is a *process* theory of psychoanalytic treatment that considers therapeutic possibility as a particularity emergent within the reciprocal relatedness of a dyadic system, along with the complexity of possible influences on it from without (see Coburn, 2014).

My experience of optimal responsiveness to unique therapeutic need was a hug around my shoulder that provided the sense of Kohut's continuing fatherly presence on the eve of a two-week break in our analytic sessions (see Bacal, 2011a). I do not think that interpreting my distress and need for a hug would have been nearly as therapeutic (see Bacal, 2017).

Specificity theory expands our focus on empathic attunement to the patient's and the analyst's subjective states to discern what may be optimally responsive. In "Kohut's last words on analytic cure and how we hear them now," Bacal and Carlton (2010) opined that the analyst's empathic attunement informs her not only about the patient's subjective states as Kohut has described but also what might be his needed therapeutic response. This may become especially apparent, even in such a fluid system, when the analyst also attends to the *specificity of salience within their emergent process.*

Emergence

Bedau and Humphreys (2008) view "emergence" as "[relating] to phenomena that arise from and depend on some more basic phenomena yet are simultaneously autonomous from that "base" (p. 1), and that "emergent properties are 'novel' and 'unpredictable' from knowledge of their lower-level bases ..." (p. 129). In psychoanalytic practice, "basic phenomena" that underlie emergent process significantly include the specificity of reciprocal interaction within the analytic dyad.

Process

The usual understanding of "process" is that it refers to the entire therapeutic enterprise, as in "the psychoanalytic process is complex"; or to a particular facet of treatment, as in "the process of joining the patient"; or to the "process of making the unconscious conscious." The term "process" is used here to refer to the defining essence of therapy and of the mental life of the person as comprised of sustained, ongoing phenomena emerging from and alterable by reciprocal interactions between therapist and patient (Bacal, 2011a, p. 2).

In *Process Metaphysics*, Rescher (1996) describes several philosophical and scientific perspectives on *process*, the inclusion of which here would impractically extend this paper. Process philosophy is concerned with modes of understanding via "interactive relatedness" (p. 35). In this sense, it has points of contact with intersubjective systems theory (see Stolorow, 2006). It also entails a "commitment to the fundamentally processual nature of the real" (Rescher, 1996, p. 8). In other words, "we live in a world where nothing stands still, and that change is of the very essence of reality" (p. 25). How, then, does the analyst discern at any moment what may be optimally responsive to her patient's therapeutic need? While Kohut's response to my therapeutic need may well have been derived through his empathic attunement, I submit that he may also have sensed this by becoming aware of what was *salient* at that moment in our *emergent process*.

Quantum theory, as applied to psychoanalysis (Gargiulo, 2016), implicitly offers intriguing support for this way of gleaning significance. Quantum theory posits that, while there is no understanding that can be exact, *probability* can become apparent within "a mist of infinite possibilities" (Gargiulo, 2016, p. 7), and that "usually it is the highest probability that is observed" (p. 36). We may observe such specificity in psychoanalytic practice by attending to *salience* within the uniqueness of emergent dyadic process in addition to attuning to the patient's and our own subjective states.

It is not only advisable that we not "know" in advance who the patient is, as Bion recommends (Bion, 1967), but that we also do not know how we may optimally be with him or her therapeutically from moment to moment until we may glean this within our emergent process. Undoubtedly, many psychoanalytic therapists intuitively practice in this way simply because it makes good clinical sense (see Lenoff, 2020); in other words, they recognize the value of attending to therapeutic probability in the unpredictable specificity of emergent process.

Specificity theory regards disruptions that may arise within the transference/countertransference constellation as emergent properties in any particular dyadic system (see Bacal, 2011a, pp. 101–107). In "The psychoanalyst's selfobject needs and their frustration—A new view of countertransference," Bacal and Thomson (1996, 1998) described how disruptions arise not only when the patient's selfobject needs are unmet but also when specific selfobject needs of the analyst are not responded to by the patient, affecting the ability of the analyst to respond optimally to the patient.

Clinical Illustration 1—Beth and Dr. C

This example depicts how an analyst and her patient struggled to discover, within the salience of predominantly disruptive emergent process, how they might co-create optimally responsive experience for the patient. The case is narrated by the patient's analyst, Dr. C. Amplifying comments are offered in square brackets by the author.

The course of this analysis had been marked by rapid, extreme, and seemingly discontinuous shifts from positive to negative transference. In the positive transference, my patient, Beth, experienced me as all good and powerful. She called me her "Jesus with skin." At other times, Beth perceived me as a sadistic seductress creating intimate, loving moments to enhance my power to injure her. And at still other times I was experienced as a neglectful therapist, turning away just at the critical moment when she needed comfort or protection. Beth's perception of me could alter rapidly, shifting from feeling safe with me to feeling either abandoned or even abused by me. And I need to add that these shifts would occur with little awareness on my part of any actual precipitant. To me, I might have felt only a slight alteration in my actual physical posture or expression, or warmth in tone or content of my speech.

This analytic tale begins toward the end of the third year of the analysis: There had been a tension between Beth and me perhaps since the earliest days of our work together. This tension had played at the edges of our relationship. We would feel it and flee from it, yet never fully acknowledge it, or name it. [*This appears to indicate a particular ongoing salience in their process which had not yet been explicitly recognized.*] However, in this session, Beth was obviously upset as she entered my office.

Beth lay on the couch in silence. Her frustration and anger were palpable, as was my increasing tension and confusion. In the silence, I mentally reviewed our last session, and I could not recall anything that would now account for her feelings, something that might help me make sense of Beth's accusatory anger. She finally spoke, demanding, "Will you or will you not … hold me?" For me, the relational tension of this moment was crystallized, not by Beth's stark demand to be held, but in the vulnerability of her anguished plea, "I have to get the holding and soothing touch from you. This is too much for me to sit in your presence, the presence of caring. I just actually need the physical touch. I need to be held."

I expect that my body and facial expressions answered her question in the negative before I could even begin to think about her demand. [*Dr. C. has sensed the vulnerability of Beth's anguished plea as salient within their emergent process; and she unconsciously feels herself recoiling from what Beth regards as the specifically therapeutic response to her plea.*] In general, in my personal life, I am not a very touchy-feely person. I readily touch and hold my loved ones in order to comfort, reassure, or convey love. For a time. But I am not comfortable with holding or being held over time. [*The analyst senses her limitation to respond to her patient's specific demand, which she experiences as potentially continuous.*]

In deciding how to respond to Beth, I do not want to simply say "No." Rather than say, "No" or even "I don't know," I hope to stay with her feelings and convey my understanding, an understanding that might provide for her an *experience* of being held by me. "As you feel your love for me and mine for you, the old feelings of the baby not held or caressed come right along with them. Your suffering today from this early deprivation can only be relieved through my physical holding. Does it help when I understand and try to stay connected with the little one, connected through our daily voice mail exchanges?" [*Dr. C has offered an interpretation, which conveys not only her understanding of the relational dynamics in the here-and-now, and their antecedent determinants, in effect, a "transference" interpretation, but also the hope that this understanding would enable her patient to experience what she was seeking. This does not, however, constitute an optimal response for her patient.*]

Beth turns away from me, from my implicit "no." I remain quiet. I can feel the intensity of her suffering, a pain that has been intensifying over the last several months, a pain that does not remit at the end our sessions. I feel, too, her painful confusion that her need of me creates for her. The mature, intelligent, and competent adult craves being caressed and rocked as if she were an infant. I strain with the dilemma, a simultaneous desire to respond to and to retreat from Beth's plea.

Without a formal prescribed response found within most structure theories, I must examine my own capacities and limitations, in process, to respond to my patient's demand and explore the therapeutic implications of my response. Should I satisfy my patient's felt need, which feels uncomfortable for me, or endure my patient's disappointment, anger, and pain as I feel that I cannot provide the desired response, all within the context of how my responses might or might not be therapeutic for my patient. Without a pre-determined theoretical answer or even guideline, I am called upon to analyze and assess my patient's demand upon me *within the unique context and relationship that is always emergent between us.*

Finally, Beth responds. "Your responsiveness makes these feelings more intense, but more manageable, too. I can talk about this forever, say the same thing forever. But it doesn't change the need to be held by you. *I want to feel you. My desire to be held needs to be satiated.* I am crying and crying to be fed, and you offer me words. Your words don't touch me."

This session initiated many more sessions that moved inevitably to her insistent demand to be held and caressed by me. My understanding of her agonized state deepened as I encouraged Beth to share her feelings, and her memories. [*Beth's distressed state continues to emerge as salient within their process, but Dr. C. cannot yet find a way to respond optimally.*]

Beth was born to a mother who had been too overwhelmed and depressed to respond to Beth. Her mother recounts today of Beth as a baby, she had been such a good baby, content for most of the day alone in her playpen. Beth recalls how she ached to be held, even putting her own small arms around herself, pretending that they were her mother's. She remembered many nights of her childhood where she hugged the plaster wall adjacent to her bed. After a while the wall absorbed and held her warmth, and she could pretend that she was cuddled up to her mother.

When Beth was two years of age, her father's anxiety disorder had become so disabling that he was placed on leave from his job. With her mother's return to work, Beth's care was entrusted to her mentally ill father. Her father would lure her into shared delightful moments of intimacy, to startle, frighten, or injure her. One such "model scene" (Lachmann and Lichtenberg, 1992) is captured in her memory of a cold winter night when she was four. Her father awakened her from sleep to invite her to "Come. There is magic outside." He bundled her up in his large parka, enveloping her head to toe. He carried her outside. He whispered to her, "Now for the magic show," as he lifted the arm of the jacket, like a telescope. From within the dark, warm jacket she lifted her gaze and a sparkly starry sky magically appeared. She recalls the sudden thrill and shared excitement, as her father surreptitiously poured a glass of ice water down the sleeve. She fled, sobbing, wet, and cold to the sound of his satisfied laughter. The others in the family chided her for being unable to take a "joke." Her mother not only was unable to be emotionally responsive to her little daughter, but she also did not protect Beth from her father.

However, my understanding and our deepened understanding of her feelings, through these revealed memories, did not ameliorate the intensity and torment of her desire to rest in my arms. We continued to explore her desire and elaborate the possible meanings and genesis of this need and desire. We worked in this way for many months, but with each new understanding or memory, she would return to her concrete need to be held. She became desperate. She began to make plans to leave the analysis to find a therapist who would hold her throughout sessions. I felt a continual strain and was regularly preoccupied with whether and/or how Beth and I would find a way to address her intensely felt need, a need that I could not actually satisfy.

Had this analysis been conducted with a structure theory, such as classical theory, I would have had a theoretical guide, even an answer. Freud provides the following answer to my dilemma: "Analytic treatment should be carried through, as far as possible, under privation ... in a state of abstinence" (1919, p.

162). The analyst must ensure that "the patient is left with unfulfilled wishes in abundance" (1919, p. 164. See also Lindon, 1994).

In other words, Freud prescribed abstinence. Abstinence was the assumptive stance, and any deviation therefrom constituted a "provision." A provision (such as touching, let alone holding my patient) was anything other than interpretive explication, and was proscribed. A provision according to this theory would gratify my patient's unconscious libidinal wishes, depriving her of the opportunity to have them made conscious. Cure in this theory occurs as the unconscious libidinal strivings are made conscious and interpreted. With this new awareness, renunciation of the infantile wishes and replacement with more mature desires and goals becomes possible.

It is not only within classical theory that touching is prohibited. Most traditional psychoanalytic theories proscribe touch, let alone holding, as detrimental to the patient's healing. However, I work from the perspective of specificity theory, a process theory. Any clinician who uses this theory may or may not actually follow the theory's conclusion (indeed, as Freud himself did not always follow the dictates of his own writings on technique), but regardless of how a particular clinician may use the theory, I am concerned here with the operation of the theory itself. Specificity theory does not interdict touching (or any other response) unless it is illegal or officially proscribed by one's professional organization but directs the analyst to engage with the patient to find out whether such a demand would be therapeutic for the patient and possible for the analyst.

My patient demanded, and believed, that her healing required my sustained, loving caress. However, my capacity to offer this response was limited, and fell far short of the holding that my patient craved. For me, holding has no natural or agreed upon stopping point. I imagined that I might begin to feel anxious over time with the physical or emotional containment that holding would require of me, which she would feel and possibly interpret as rejection. If we decided that I would hold her throughout the session, I imagined awkward discussions to determine the when and length of holding. Or would it become a ritual, the expected way that we would be together in session? With extended holding I imagined limbs going numb and itches left unscratched. How would we talk about *not* holding for a session, and what present and historical meanings would attach to such a discussion?

Further, and more significantly, given the nature of our relationship over the course of the analysis, the extended holding presented the danger that she would begin to feel that I was exploiting or abusing her. Two people experience and share intense feelings through physical holding that may be difficult to identify or talk about. Their meanings can be implicit, intense, and rapidly shifting. Who is holding whom, who needs to be held, do I need her to need me to hold her? [*Dr. C. becomes increasingly aware of the complexity of the task to find a way of responding optimally to Beth's painful vulnerability; she also anticipates that substantially inauspicious reactions could reciprocally emerge for both as she attempts to do this.*] Throughout our relationship, Beth experienced me as abusive and exploitive whenever we felt increased intimacy. [*The analyst also fears the conspicuous emergence of retraumatizing experience within their relational process that might cause unmanageable disruption.*] She was not able to explore these beliefs as her subjective experience, but rather as concrete proof of my malevolent intentions.

I was challenged to discern the response or responses that would provide healing experiences for my patient, and that I felt willing and able to provide. She began to experience my refusal as sadistic, that I had from the inception designed our interactions so as to create this intense need of me in order to enjoy my power to deprive. Or, alternatively, when she was experiencing me as less evil, she felt that my refusal was motivated by my own unconscious desire for her: It was I who desperately needed her, who needed her to be dependent on me. She reasoned that if I held her, she would gain health so that she no longer required therapy. I would then lose her, the one whom *I* so desperately needed.

As I continued to offer my patient my understanding and to undergo suffering with her, and to endure her resentment and anger, I came upon a blanket. It was of a size, heft, and texture that would envelope an adult as a parent would as she held a child. One side was made of a smooth satin that offered a rich, sensual tactile experience, and the reverse was made of a synthetic knit that offered a warmth, depth, and yield to the touch approximating the touch of a human body. I thought that it was possible that the blanket,[6] if it were from me, might provide her with the needed experience of holding. [*Dr. C creatively, and thoughtfully, considers the response of offering Beth a tangible substitute for herself.*]

I wondered whether I should provide this concrete, demanded response. Should I have concluded that my difficulty with providing sustained holding imposed a debilitating limitation on therapeutic possibility in our work and help her find another therapist that worked in a different way than I? Or should I continue to try to respond, now, in this way? Would the comfort of the blanket so soothe that the experiences that gave rise to the unremitting pain no longer be available to the analysis, creating a kind of crippling dependency upon me for continual soothing? Or would it provide a response that would enable her to experience a relational world where loved ones respond to her pain without a desire to injure or exploit her. Or could it be experienced as both a healing response and, for a time, a needed level of dependency? These were the main questions I struggled with as I considered the possible therapeutic effect—or not—of this specific response—which I felt I *could* offer Beth.

As I presented the blanket to Beth in session, I asked "How would it feel if I were to give this blanket to you from me?" Beth was quiet, did not answer, and did not engage with me. As the session neared the end, she wordlessly picked up the blanket.

I awakened the next morning to a voice mail: "You are an analyst. So, you can analyze me, but that is for you. I want you to know that the blanket … It is the coolest, smoothest texture. You were with me last night. I held the blanket tight and it brings me comfort. No panic attacks. You thought of the idea, and it is working beautifully."

Beth was able to use the blanket in other ways to regulate our relationship. When she was angry or disappointed with me, she was able to use the blanket to give more full expression to her feelings. The morning after a stormy session, Beth left me this voice mail: "With the blanket, I have improved my soothing mechanisms because I have you. But now I see that it helps because I can also have my way with you. You are not in that blanket, so I am freer to have my way with it. It is safer than actually having you. It is full of life, yet lifeless. I don't trust. I am willing to try, but I know that I need some deep things, and I don't trust letting you close."

And then the blanket had a surprising negative effect. The blanket so perfectly matched her need and desire that it intensified her belief that I knew perfectly her private thoughts, beliefs, and feelings. "It is like you are God and you know me fully." This belief in my omniscience constrained our relationship. Now, if I acted in ways that were injurious to her, she could only believe that I did so with intention, as she knew that I knew perfectly what she wanted or expected. Further, during our sessions, if I inquired how she might feel about something, she became enraged, as she believed I knew how she felt. There was no reason to inquire, as I was all knowing, other than to delight in my power to injure. [*An injurious experience of the analyst's response had become salient within their process.*] Ultimately, the provision of the blanket did enhance Beth's trust in our relationship and did provide her with an experience that seemed to contribute to an expansion of her ability to tolerate feelings and memories, and later to benefit from verbal interpretations.

My experience in this analysis, however, does not support either the offering of a blanket, even this type of special blanket, as a prescribed or even recommended response. Perhaps, I will never use a blanket in this way again. Nor does this analysis support the theory that allowing for parameters (Eissler, 1953) later permitted the *more ameliorative* verbal interpretation. Perhaps, my understanding as demonstrated through the offering of the blanket was essentially transformative for this patient even absent future interpretations. [*The analyst alludes to two aspects of optimal therapeutic experience that her response may have achieved: that it be specific to therapeutic need, and that it may arise as a result of responsiveness that does not constitute verbal interpretation.*]

In one session, months after the blanket had assumed its complex place in our relationship, Beth shared,

> The angry, isolated place that I have been. It has felt like fighting the world, and now I see it is me. It is because of my trauma. My father was an ill man. He was abusive and sexually very twisted, and I was, am, sensitive, sensual, feeling, and I was left in his care full time. Physically, I had no soothing. I could scream. I could cry. Momma was tense and nervous. There was no calm holding. What I know of being comforted, I have learned through you. I now know that a baby has needs. Those needs need to be tended to and there is no shame. It is as simple as a baby needs to be held and comforted.

By carefully attending to shifts in the salience of their process, Dr. C was slowly discovering how Beth might experience her responsiveness as therapeutically optimal, or disruptive. Ultimately, Dr. C, along with Beth, found a creative way of promoting a workable fit that they could manage at a symbolically archaic level. In this way, therapeutic possibility within this dyad moved toward *therapeutic probability* (see Gargiulo, 2016).

Optimal Responsiveness and Therapeutic Fit

The patient's therapeutic experience is ultimately determined by the capacities and limitations of each therapist and patient to respond to each other in specific ways (Bacal, 2011a). A process perspective on psychoanalytic practice implies that when a therapist and patient meet for psychoanalytic treatment, they will have to find out whether their responsiveness to each other in the moment and over time can bring about optimal therapeutic experience for the patient. This implies a good enough fit, a *specificity of fittedness* [7] between that patient and that therapist (see Bacal, 2011a, p. 13). The fit of the treatment dyad has not been accorded the importance it deserves. Although difficult to predict, the probability of "a good fit" between the participants may become crucial for the effectiveness of the treatment (see Kantrowitz, 2002).

Optimal Responsiveness and the Process Use of Psychoanalytic Theory

Privileging a process perspective in psychoanalytic practice significantly influences how we use psychoanalytic theories that posit universal motives, stages of development, and curative interventions. No psychoanalytic theory that purports ubiquitous application can apply to psychoanalytic treatment when it is viewed as *process*. Our familiar structured psychoanalytic theories (such as classical psychoanalytic theory, ego psychology, object relations theories, etc.) guide our responses by indicating *a priori* how we should therapeutically be with our patients. In contrast, responsiveness guided by what emerges as salient within dyadic process promotes more effective use of these concepts. Rather than *reaching* for the tenets of any formal theory or model, positioning oneself receptively to their relevant emergence, or not—as well to the possible emergence of other concepts, models, or perspectives that the analyst as well as the analysand may bring to the therapeutic endeavor—will allow them to come into play most usefully in understanding and responding optimally to the particular patient at that time. The following example is illustrative.

Clinical Illustration 2—Eric and Dr. B

This example depicts how a significant specificity of fit, which became salient within the emergent dyadic process, contributed to an apparent cure in a remarkably brief period.

Eric was around 20 years old when he was referred to me by a prominent psychoanalytic colleague when I was practicing in the Bay Area in the early 1970s. Eric's father, an attorney, had asked my colleague to find Eric a good analyst. He was very concerned about his son's state of mind and the direction his son's life was taking. Eric was hardly studying at all for the courses that would enable his admission to law school, and he seemed constantly irritated and depressed. Instead of applying himself to his schoolwork, he spent all his time dabbling in "ridiculous" business ventures. Eric's father not only knew that Eric could benefit from analysis, he also knew what sort of analysis would best benefit Eric. He himself had completed a ten-year analysis some years before, in London, with Hanna Segal, a senior Kleinian analyst. He had found this to be enormously valuable, and he knew his son would likewise benefit.

From the referring analyst's point of view, I may have seemed like the nearest thing in sight to a Kleinian analyst practicing in the Bay Area at that time. (How times have changed!) I had qualified about six years previously from the Institute of Psychoanalysis in London where two of my six supervisors were senior Kleinian analysts—Bion for an adult case and Betty Joseph for a child analytic case—and where Hanna Segal, herself, was one of my instructors in Kleinian theory. So, I knew "Klein," but I was not a "Kleinian." I'd been affiliated with the so-called Middle Group of the British Psychoanalytic Society, which was a peculiar, "non-group" group. The Middle Group, which sometimes called itself the Independent Group, was poised somewhere between Freudian and Kleinian sensibilities, but mainly comprised a coterie of creative, independent thinkers, several of whom I had trained with, such as Michael Balint, Donald Winnicott, Marion Milner, Jock Sutherland, and Charles Rycroft.

I really liked Eric—a straightforward, congenial, bright, and ambitious young man. Eric and I connected well, and we settled in to four times a week analysis. I recognized, though, not long after a few sessions, that the best kind of analysis we could do was to engage the issues that could get him out of analysis as soon as possible and get on with his life. Psychoanalytic theory that emerged for me during our process turned out not to be Kleinian (though Klein's concepts did variously inform my work, then, and continue to do so). What emerged as particularly useful in my work with Eric was a concept that had been advanced by Guntrip in the late 60s (see Guntrip, 1968). What Brandchaft (2004, 2007) later came to elaborate as "pathological accommodation," Guntrip had first conceptualized in object-relational terms as a dilemma centering around the experience of a conflict, wherein the needs of the self were threateningly at variance with those of a significant figure in the person's life. To express one's self was to lose the object. To comply with the other was to lose one's self.

Eric was struggling with his father's conviction that becoming a lawyer would unquestionably be right for him. Eric and I came to appreciate that were he to accede to his father's wishes, he faced the dangers of losing his sense of purpose and the invalidation of his core ambitions; but that if he did not accommodate his father's wishes, he would at the very least seriously displease him. His depressiveness and irritability reflected this unconscious conflict symptomatically.

My not-so-unconscious attitude, which would seem to have specifically connected with Eric's, as our process unfolded, was that Eric's pursuit of what was centrally meaningful to him—going into some kind of business, rather than studying to become an attorney as his father required of him—potentially trumped Eric's dread of losing his father's approval and respect. I must have talked with Eric in ways that implicitly gave expression to this understanding. My interpretations about Eric's conflict around this may well have been therapeutically significant; yet what was, arguably, at least as effective, was how Eric and I found ourselves able to be together, in effect, to fit together, therapeutically, around this issue.

What was emerging, within me, in our process, were precipitates of toxic experiences as a child with my mother that were specifically analogous to those with which Eric struggled in relation to his father. These experiences with my mother had been repeated in my recent analysis. In that analysis, as I have described elsewhere (Bacal, 2011a, 2017), I felt little recognition of who I was other than being identified as faulty for not measuring up to my analyst's standards of mental health. Because Eric differed from his father about who he was and how he wanted to live his life, he was unhealthy, and therefore on that account, he should have an analysis. Eric was luckier than me. Although I was unsuccessful in protesting the condemnations of my mother and of my first official analyst, unconsciously—or perhaps dissociatively—I must in some measure have registered their invalidity, since I could access this sensibility, and respond usefully to Eric in the specificity of our process. In effect, Eric and I unconsciously connected to stand firm against an omniscient, unempathic, and controlling parent.

Traditionally, my responsiveness to Eric would be conceptualized as transference/counter-transference enactment. However, it can also be regarded as constituting an optimal therapeutic response within the uniqueness of a therapeutic dyad, which became apparent in the salience of emergent process (see Bacal, 2011a, chapter 8). A significant aspect of Eric's therapeutic experience with me, I believe, was that I could listen, with sincere interest, to his "ridiculous" ideas for developing commercially viable projects. I was, in retrospect, also finding myself responding to Eric in a way that Kohut would later conceptualize as that of a mirroring selfobject, although I knew nothing, then (in 1971), about self psychology theory (I did not come across Kohut's theories for another five years). Back now, to Eric and me.

After about three and a half months, Eric and I decided we'd got to the point where he could get off the couch, and head for the door. As he was leaving my office, he turned toward me with a wide smile on his face, and said, "It was good doing business with you, Doc."

How May "Freedom and Free Will" Apply to *Optimal Responsiveness*?

The question as to whether there is free will is philosophically and scientifically unsettled.[8] However, the question is arguably irrelevant to *optimal responsiveness in clinical practice*, which is experientially contextualized and pragmatically predicated. That is, it does not matter on the local level whether the salience of emergent process, which constitutes a primary data source for discerning optimal responsiveness, is pre-determined or not. What matters is whether the analyst can utilize her experience of the specificity of salience within emergent process to discover responsiveness that is therapeutic for the patient.

Another potential constraint on exercising the freedom to be optimally responsive is found in a particular function of the brain. The neuroscientist, Gerald Edelman, has demonstrated that the brain is a meaning-making organ that tends to close down whenever it encounters meaning, for example when the analyst believes he understands something and reaches for familiar constructs to apply them (see Bacal, 2011a, chapter 4). It therefore requires an extra effort, then—both literally and figuratively—to keep one's mind open. The foregoing clinical examples exemplify, in widely differing contexts, how focusing on the specificity of salience within the fluidity of emergent process can free the analyst from the constraint proffered by this aspect of brain function, to expand the probability of offering optimal therapeutic responsiveness.

While freedom to respond optimally is significantly augmented by attending to the salience of emergent process, it is ineluctably affected by specific capacities and limitations of the analytic dyad that emerge as the individuals comprising it interact, unpredictably, within their process. This is also conspicuously evident in both clinical examples.

Notes

1 In *How Does Analysis Cure* (Kohut 1984), Kohut proffered optimal frustration as a central aspect of the curative process. Yet, earlier, shortly after the publication of *The Restoration of the Self* (1977), he recognized, with one of his critics (his son), the problematic nature of the question, "What is optimal?" (Kohut, personal communication, 1977).

2 At an international self-psychology conference in the late 80s, a senior colleague warned that the concept of optimal responsiveness might promote "wild analysis."

3 Kohut, who had won the sobriquet, "Mr. Classical Psychoanalysis," for his faithful adherence to classical theory, remarkably came to reject Freud's drive theory, and developed a psychology of the self (see Kohut, *The Analysis of the Self*, 1971), that placed the self and its development in relation to "selfobjects" at the center of psychoanalytic theory.

4 This example, which depicts a mirroring selfobject response—and presumably a mirroring selfobject experience—has been regarded by some self psychologists as the prototype response that first illustrated the application of self psychology theory.

5 To the consternation of some of his self psychology colleagues, Kohut had dangerously departed from his two-step paradigm in which interpretation was regarded as crucial for therapeutic effect. They were also worried that Kohut's declaration, in his final address (Kohut, 1981), that empathy alone could be experienced as therapeutic, would bring the guillotine down on self psychology as a "supportive therapy," unworthy of being regarded as psychoanalytic.

6 While this patient's use of the proffered blanket shares some characteristics of Winnicott's concept of the transitional object (Winnicott, 1971), it differs significantly in that this blanket was not "found" by the infant.

7 Robert Stolorow has suggested that "specificity-fittedness" is intrinsic to "optimal responsiveness" (personal communication). Interestingly, Louis Sander regards a similar concept—Paul White's "matched specificities"—as central to therapeutic effect (see Bacal, 2011a, p. 118).

8 But see Coburn (2024) who illuminates a way of exercising free will by assuming personal ownership of what emerges within process.

References

Bacal, H. (1985). Optimal responsiveness and the therapeutic process. In H. Bacal (Ed.), *Optimal responsiveness: How therapists heal their patients* (1998, pp. 3–34). Northvale, NJ: Jason Aronson.

Bacal, H. (1990). The elements of a corrective selfobject experience. *Psychoanalytic Inquiry*, 10, 347–372.

Bacal, H. (1998a). Is empathic attunement the only optimal response? In H. Bacal (Ed.), *Optimal responsiveness: How therapists heal their patients* (pp. 289–301). Northvale, NJ: Jason Aronson.

Bacal, H. (1998b). Optimal responsiveness and the specificity of selfobject experience. In H. Bacal (Ed.), *Optimal responsiveness: How therapists heal their patients* (pp. 141–170). Northvale, NJ: Jason Aronson.

Bacal, H. (Ed.) (1998c) *Optimal responsiveness: How therapists heal their patients*. Northvale, NJ: Jason Aronson.

Bacal, H. (2006). Specificity theory: Conceptualizing a personal and professional quest for therapeutic possibility. *International Journal of Psychoanalysis and Self Psychology*, 1, 133–155.

Bacal, H. (2011a). *The power of specificity in psychotherapy: When therapy works—and when it doesn't*. Lanham, MD: Jason Aronson.

Bacal, H.(2011b). Specificity theory: The evolution of a process theory of psychoanalytic treatment. *American Imago*, 68, 267–283.

Bacal, H. (2017). Credo: My psychoanalytic adventure—a quest to conceptualize therapeutic efficacy. *Psychoanalytic Dialogues*, 27, 1–19.

Bacal, H., & Carlton, L. (2010). Kohut's last words on analytic cure and how we hear them now—A view from specificity theory. *International Journal of Psychoanalysis and Self Psychology*, 5, 132–143.

Bacal, H., & Herzog, B. (2003). Specificity theory and optimal responsiveness: An outline. *Psychoanalytic Psychology*, 20 (4), 635–648.

Bacal, H., & Thomson, P. (1996). The psychoanalyst's selfobject needs and the effect of their frustration on the treatment: A new view of countertransference. In A. Goldberg (Ed.), *Basic ideas reconsidered: Progress in self psychology* (pp. 17–35). Hillsdale, NJ: The Analytic Press.

Bacal, H., & Thomson, P. (1998). Optimal responsiveness and the therapist's reaction to the patient's unresponsiveness. In H. Bacal (Ed.), *Optimal responsiveness: How therapists heal their patients* (pp. 249–270). Northvale, NJ: Jason Aronson.

Bedau, M., & Humphreys, P. (Eds.) (2008) *Emergence: Contemporary readings in philosophy and science*. Cambridge, MA: The MIT Press.

Bion, W.R. (1967). Notes on memory and desire. *Psychoanalytic Forum*, 3, 271–280.

Brandchaft, B. (2004). To free the spirit from its cell. In R. Stolorow, G. Atwood, & B. Brandchaft (Eds.), *The intersubjective perspective* (pp. 57–76). Northvale, NJ: Jason Aronson.

Brandchaft, B. (2007). Systems of pathological accommodation and change in analysis. *Psychoanalytic Psychology*, 24, 667–687.

Coburn, W. (2014). *Psychoanalytic complexity*. New York, NY: Routledge.

Coburn, W. (2024). Freedom and self-ownership: An emergence theory of free will. *Psychoanalysis, Self and Context*, 19 (2), 139–156.

Eissler, K. (1953). The effect of the structure of the ego on psychoanalytic technique. *Journal of the American Psychoanalytic Association*, 1, 104–143.

Freud, S. (1919). Lines of advance in psycho-analytic therapy. In *The standard edition of the complete psychological works of Sigmund Freud* (Volume 17, pp. 157–168). London: Hogarth Press.

Gargiulo, G. (2016). *Quantum psychoanalysis*. New York, NY: International Psychoanalytic Books.

Guntrip, H. (1968). *Schizoid phenomena, object relations, and the self*. London: Hogarth Press.

Kantrowitz, J. (2002). The triadic match: The interactive effect of supervisor, candidate, and patient. *Journal of the American Psychoanalytic Association*, 50, 939–996.

Kohut, H. (1971). *The analysis of the self*. New York, NY: International Universities Press.

Kohut, H. (1977). *The restoration of the self*. New York, NY: International Universities Press.

Kohut, H. (1981). On empathy. In P. Ornstein (Ed.), *The search for the self: Selected writings of Heinz Kohut_1950–1978* (p. 529). Madison, CT: International Universities Press.

Kohut, H. (1984). *How does analysis cure?* (A. Goldberg & P. Stepansky, Eds.). Chicago, IL: University of Chicago Press.

Lachmann, F., & Lichtenberg, J. (1992). Model scenes: Implications for psychoanalytic treatment. *JAPA*, 40(1), 117–137.

Lenoff, L. (2020). Therapeutic goals, functional capacity, and the conditions of therapeutic action. *Psychoanalytic Inquiry*, 40, 271–280.

Lindon, J. (1994). Gratification and provision in psychoanalysis: Should we get rid of the rule of abstinence? *Psychoanalytic Dialogues*, 4, 549–582.

Rescher, N. (1996). *Process metaphysics*. New York, NY: State University of New York.

Stolorow, R. (2006). Intersubjective systems theory. In R. Skelton (Ed.), *The Edinburgh international encyclopaedia of psychoanalysis* (p. 250). Edinburgh: Edinburgh University Press.

Terman, D. (1998). Optimal responsiveness and a new view of structuralization. In H. Bacal (Ed.), *Optimal responsiveness: How therapists heal their patients* (pp. 59–74). Northvale, NJ: Jason Aronson.

Winnicott, D.W. (1971). Transitional objects and transitional phenomena. In *Playing and reality* (pp. 1–25). London: Tavistock.

Index

Made in the USA
Las Vegas, NV
17 July 2026

2a48fd0c-70d8-45f8-ad8f-fe5a6b25ca7aR01